HOME-BASED BUSINESS SERIES

How to Start a Home-Based
Day-Care Business

Fifth Edition

Shari Steelsmith

The Globe Pequot Press

GUILFORD, CONNECTICUT

To my husband, Jim Duffin

This book's purpose is to provide accurate and authoritative information on the topics covered. It is sold with the understanding that neither the author nor the publisher is engaged in rendering legal, financial, accounting, or other professional services. Neither The Globe Pequot Press nor the author assumes any liability resulting from action taken based on the information included herein. Mention of a company name does not constitute endorsement.

To buy books in quantity for corporate use or incentives, call **(800) 962–0973, ext. 4551,** or e-mail **premiums@GlobePequot.com.**

Text design by Nancy Freeborn
Cover images © Eric Kamp/Index Stock (top left), © allOver photography/Alamy (playroom), © S.T. Yiap/Alamy (three blocks), and © Eye Wire (date book)

ISSN 1546-6787
ISBN-13: 978-0-7627-4176-2
ISBN-10: 0-7627-4176-7

Manufactured in the United States of America
Fifth Edition/First Printing

Contents

Contents

Preface

For parents, finding good, reliable child care is often an ongoing struggle. Articles and studies appear routinely in the media describing the child-care crisis working parents must confront. The good news for you is that this crisis provides a ready and waiting market for a family child-care business.

If you are interested in learning how to provide a warm, safe, and stimulating environment for children and how to become a child-care professional, all from your own home, then read on. This book will tell you explicitly what a family child-care business is and how to open and operate one from your home.

Thanks to Karen Townsend and Charolyn Concepcion for specialized help with the manuscript, to Emily Pitts for research help, and to all the dedicated family child-care providers, particularly Deborah Eaton, Camille Vandermeulen, and Gay Hendrickson, who contributed to this book.

Help Us Keep This Guide Up to Date

Every effort has been made by the author and editors to make this guide as accurate and useful as possible. However, many things can change after a guide is published—establishments close, phone numbers change, facilities come under new management, etc.

We would love to hear from you concerning your experiences with this guide and how you feel it could be made better and be kept up to date. While we may not be able to respond to all comments and suggestions, we'll take them to heart, and we'll make certain to share them with the author. Please send your comments and suggestions to the following address:

The Globe Pequot Press
Reader Response/Editorial Department
246 Goose Lane
P.O. Box 480
Guilford, CT 06437

Or you may e-mail us at:
editorial@GlobePequot.com

Thanks for your input!

Chapter One

Family Child Care— Is It for Me?

The Benefits of Family Child Care

There are many rewards in family child care. The principal attractions for most providers are threefold:

Being at Home with Your Kids

These are the days of double-income families. It is often economically necessary for families to bring in two salaries. This usually means that the children are placed in child care while Mom and Dad go to work. Running a family child-care business means one parent has the opportunity to be at home with the children.

Increased Income

Staying home is all well and good, but it's nice to have food on the table, heat, and a mortgage company that likes you because you send the check in on time every month. Running a family child-care business is a stable source of income and can often be quite profitable.

Being Your Own Boss

There are many benefits to owning your own business. The flexibility and control that come with being your own boss are high on the list. You can structure your work hours, enrollment, and fees in ways that work best for you.

Hmmm, sounds great, you say. But is this really for *me*?

Is This for Me?

Family child care is a wonderful option for many of us, but not *all* of us. It behooves you to look carefully at your life situation, family needs, career goals, skills, and talents before making your decision. You may love and adore your own two-year-old but be ready to check yourself into a sanitarium at the end of a day with three two-year-olds underfoot.

There are many factors to consider when you are evaluating your own suitability for running a family child-care business. Perhaps the first and most important is asking yourself, *Do I like being with kids?*

It seems an obvious question, but it's a critical one. Almost all of us love our own children very much and want to be with them. But not all of us like being with other people's children. This is not a character failing, but it is an indication that family child care is not for you.

Claire, a provider from Seattle, shared her thoughts on this matter:

> My good friend Lisa thought she might like to start a family child care. She had seen my success with the business, had a three-year-old son, and with a newborn daughter wanted to give up her part-time job and stay home with her kids. She asked me if I'd write her a recommendation for the licensing people. I had reservations right from the start. Lisa is creative and energetic with her kids, but she's not a very patient person. I'd seen her lose her temper in stressful situations involving more than one child. I told her frankly that her strength lay in one-on-one interaction with children and I didn't think she would be happy dealing with three or more kids at once.

You will be happier and the children in your care will be happier if you truly enjoy caring for and guiding young children. Fortunately, most family child-care providers do. If you are the right person to run a family child care, you are probably the "Kool-Aid Mom" in your neighborhood; children are naturally attracted to play at your house. Your own children are sociable and like to have other youngsters around to play with. You do so much substitute-parenting that you've begun to think, "I should get paid for this." By reading this book, you're well on your way.

Kinds of Family Child-Care Providers

There are as many different kinds of providers as there are families. Here are a few common provider profiles.

- *The parent who wants to stay home with her or his own children and still contribute significantly to the family income.* This describes the classic and most common type of provider. Many of us are happiest when we can be with and available to our young children throughout the day. Some of us have special-needs kids who do better with a parent around than a caregiver. Running a family child-care business is often the perfect way to meet the two objectives of being available to one's own children and adding money to the family budget.
- *The child-care professional looking for more control and independence in her or his work.* Many providers start out working for centers, preschools, or even therapeutic day-care centers, which are designed specifically for children with special needs. Perhaps they disagree with the director's philosophy or would like the freedom to experiment with new kinds of activities. Sometimes they just need to earn more money! The bright lights of owning their own business beckon, and before they know it, family child care is their new career.
- *The single parent who finds that family child care is a wonderful way to earn a living while staying home with her or his own children.* When families separate, it is stressful and difficult for all involved. Children are asked to make a lot of adjustments: the loss of one parent; often a new home, school, and community; and almost always, a formerly at-home parent going out to work. Many single parents find it a blessing to be able to stay home and be more available to their children during this time.
- *The husband-and-wife provider team.* In today's economy jobs are less secure and the idea of being in business for oneself is more and more attractive. There are multiple benefits to such arrangements, which are becoming very popular. You can apply for the larger license (for twelve rather than six kids) and thereby increase your income proportionately. Children benefit from having both a female and a male caregiver. When you function as a team, the burdens of the business

are shared. There are obvious hurdles to get over when you work with a family member, perhaps more so when partners live and work together in the same place, but husband-and-wife teams can be very successful and profitable.

It is not surprising to note that family child-care providers are overwhelmingly female: In the United States 98 percent are female and 2 percent male.* However, as the trend toward home businesses continues and the incidence of husband-and-wife provider teams spreads, I would expect the number of men in the field to increase.

How Is a Family Child Care Different from Other Kinds of Care?

There are as many styles of family child-care arrangements as there are families. Each one has its own features unique to the provider who runs it. There are, however, some basic similarities and distinctions that make family child care different from child-care centers, preschools, and a babysitter's home.

Each state defines family child care somewhat differently. In general, a *family child care* is a licensed and registered professional child-care program in the provider's home, where children are cared for less than twenty-four hours a day. It is run by a provider who has some training in child development and early childhood education; this training can be obtained through previous job experience, academic degrees, or continuing adult education and professional seminars. The number of children cared for in the program ranges from one to twelve, depending on the license held. The age mix of the children is determined by the provider. There is usually a daily schedule of activities.

A *child-care (or day-care) center,* meanwhile, is a local business or a chain (such as KinderCare) that cares for children outside the home in a center setting. These centers are also licensed and regulated, and they must meet certain standards set by the state. Children are usually separated by age group, and there can be sixty or more children in one center, depending on the license held. There may or may not be a schedule of daily activities. Child-care centers are usually in operation during normal business hours and employ a

* Statistics from the Center for the Child Care Workforce, Washington, D.C, 2002.

number of people. The director or manager usually has an early childhood development degree or background; many of the staff, however, do not.

A *preschool* is distinguished from both family child care and a child-care center by its focus on education. The director and teachers commonly hold degrees in early childhood education (oftentimes advanced degrees). A formal curriculum based on current educational recommendations and the philosophy of the school is usually in place. In Montessori preschools, for example, the teachers are trained in the Montessori methods and implement them in the school. Many churches and synagogues run child-care and/or preschool programs. They generally include some kind of religious instruction or focus in their curriculum.

A *babysitter,* whether it be your mother, your nephew, or the teenage girl down the street, provides informal care for children. There is no set schedule or curriculum required for this kind of care. A babysitter can provide care on a one-time basis, on an as-needed basis, or on a regular, weekly basis (same hours each day). Caregiving can take place in the parents' home or in the babysitter's home.

Most people are not aware that many states have laws regulating babysitting. For example, in the state of California, you can care for children regularly in your home for pay, without a license, if at least one of the following is true:

1. The children are your relatives.
2. You are watching only one family's children.
3. You are a parent participant in a babysitting co-op. In this situation, you exchange care for a babysitting "credit"— no money changes hands.

Be very careful about caring for children in your home for pay without a license. If you break laws and someone turns you in, you could be fined or even receive a jail sentence.

A *nanny* is an employee of the parent; the parent is responsible for paying the nanny's salary and payroll taxes. She or he usually lives in the home and cares for the children. Nannies can, however, also work part-time and/or live outside the parents' home.

Another type of nanny is an *au pair,* a student from another country who provides caregiving services in exchange for room and board and, usually, a living stipend. A nanny may or may not have training in early childhood education. Some nannies also have house-keeping responsibilities.

Keep in mind that family child care, preschools, and child-care centers are licensed businesses for which parents are not obliged to pay taxes, whereas legally, parents must pay taxes for regular caregivers in their own home.

Family child care, child-care centers, preschools, babysitters, and nannies all serve an important purpose for children and parents. It would be a disservice to say that one is better than the other; quality child care can take place with any of these types of caregivers. It is important, however, to know the differences among them—especially if you intend to enter the stimulating, enjoyable, and profitable field of family child care.

Styles of Family Child Care

Since each home and provider is unique, every family child care is unique. Deborah, a long-time provider, describes her child care:

> My background is in early childhood education. I worked for some time in preschools and then struck out on my own. I first opened a family child care for six children. Being a parent and a child-care professional, I already had many materials. My background in child care convinced me to set up a curriculum of activities. My child care runs very much like a preschool because it fits my philosophy and training.
>
> As my business prospered, my husband and I decided to buy a new house. We had it built with an even larger child care in mind. I now have a special playroom that looks very much like a preschool, with cubbyholes for children's belongings, an art center, a block corner, and an outdoor play area.

Elaine, a newer provider, has a different setup:

> Our house really lent itself naturally to family child care. We have a large rec room with a small bathroom right off it. I have a look-through window from the kitchen so I can watch the children while I'm preparing lunch. The toys are all in the rec room and the children mostly stay there or we play outside in the yard. I'm a great believer in free play, so I don't structure the day much beyond meals, naps, and playtime. I do make sure that all the toys and books are appropriate and learning-oriented. I didn't have money at first to provide high chairs and playpens, so I asked the parents of the two infants enrolled to provide their own. They were happy to do it.

And Laura, a former nurse, operates this way:

> When I left nursing to stay home with my son, I knew many other nurses who worked swing shift or graveyard hours. I set up my family child care to accommodate the needs of these parents. I'm open from two o'clock in the afternoon until midnight. My husband works swing shift and I'm a night owl, so this works well for us.

As you can see by these examples, there is no one standard family child-care setup—or one "right" way to run one. Each of these three women runs her business according to her skills, values, space, and availability. Your family child care will reflect your particular style. And the children will benefit from your background and experience. Now let's start taking stock of your space and begin to think about how *your* business could be structured.

Do You Have the Room?

One of the first things to consider is your physical space. Most providers have some sort of living room/family room area they use for the main playroom.

Is the room big enough for six kids? Twelve kids? Some states determine your allowed enrollment by the amount of space you have. Depending on the size of license you are applying for, you need to make sure you can accommodate all the small bodies and the toys that accompany them. One way to test this is to have six children over for a morning of play, followed by lunch. See how it goes. Are you tripping over each other? Do the children have room to spread out a bit? Are there conflicts over space? Remember that you need enough room for each child to stretch out on mats for a nap; you may choose to use bedrooms in the house for this, but many providers find it simpler to use the playroom as a sleeping area as well.

Another issue is storage. Where will you put the children's changes of clothes, coats, boots, or other items brought from home?

Think about your bathroom—is it easily accessible to the playroom? Children will need to get there quickly and with as little guidance from you as possible. If they have to trek down a hall, around the corner, and up the stairs, you have a problem. Preferably, the bathroom will be right off the playroom. If it isn't, think about how to make it more accessible to the children. Perhaps you could move your couch to another part of the room and clear a more direct path to the bathroom.

Some providers like to use a separate side or back entrance for the children and their parents. While this isn't necessary, some providers find that it helps keep their family and professional lives a bit more separate.

Consider your kitchen. Where will the children eat? Maybe you're incredibly blessed and bought a house with a low breakfast bar. Perhaps your mother had high hopes for a lot of grandchildren and she bought you six child-size chairs for the bar. That's wonderful; you know where the children will eat. But maybe you're just an ordinary homeowner and you have a regular table with adult-size chairs. Don't worry; you can still successfully feed the children. You just need a little flexibility and creativity.

One provider purchased two child-size picnic tables and brings them into her kitchen at lunchtime. The tables, each of which seats six preschoolers comfortably, do double duty as the site of art activities as well. Another provider had a woodworker relative build a few child-size tables for her. Another brought discarded coffee tables into service.

Some adult-size tables work admirably as they are. Some providers use booster seats or other safe ways to bring a child's nose up off the table. You can also invest in a few sturdy child-size tables and chairs from any one of the numerous preschool supply company catalogs (see appendix).

Let's go outside. Front yards are not usually workable for child care, since they are rarely enclosed. Backyards are commonly fenced. Do not despair if your yard is unfenced and unlikely to become fenced; in most states it is legal for you to have children in an unfenced yard. However, you just have to be there 100 percent of the time the children are outside—no running in to answer the phone, turn off the oven timer, or attend to other matters. All the children must be outside with you if this is the case. Needless to say, fencing is highly desirable.

Do you have room for outdoor play equipment? Many providers already have a sandbox, slide, or swing set. We will cover backyard safety requirements more completely later, but now is a good time to cast a critical eye over your trees and plants. Which plants are poisonous? Do you have thorny bushes that could be dangerous? Which hazardous plants are you willing to do without, or to transplant to a safer spot?

The most common outdoor hazard is a swimming pool. If you've got one, then you have very specific regulations to meet. Drowning is high on the list of causes of death in young children, so pool regulations are strict. Limiting access to the pool is crucial. In most states it must be adequately fenced, with no door or window access from the house. Again, we'll go over this more in chapter 2 of this book, which covers safety and licensing. At this point, what you need to do is begin to determine which areas of your home are workable and which areas are likely to need changes.

Now that you've taken a preliminary look at your space, the next step is to take stock of your skills and background.

Take Inventory of Your Skills and Experience

Do you know enough about child development and guidance?

Well, let's see. If you are a parent, your practical experience could fill three books! You may have had a course or two in school on child care and development. You read parenting books and magazines. Perhaps you've had professional child-care experience.

Everyone has some kind of experience or background, but more to the point, we can *always* use more. However much you already know about children, there is more to learn.

New information and research on young children appear all the time. Every child is different; you will have easygoing and challenging children in every group. The more skills and information you have, the better able you will be to care for and guide these children.

There are three principal areas in which you might consider further study: child development ("ages and stages"), curriculum activities, and guidance (discipline). Numerous other areas are also relevant. For example, nutrition and safety are very important, and much training on these topics is also available to you.

Most providers start out with little experience in dealing with other parents. Many providers describe dealing with certain parents as remarkably similar to dealing with their preschoolers. Your style of communicating with parents will either ease the inevitable problems or exacerbate them. Getting extra preparation and training will pay you back a hundredfold. A regional family child-care support/networking group (discussed in chapter 2) will be of invaluable help to you here.

Training is also a form of support for you. Learning about children's ages and stages and acquiring new skills for handling common (and not-so-common) problems will help you be more confident and effective. And it will naturally benefit the children in your care.

The best place to start is exactly where you are. Take stock of what skills and background you already have, then decide where your gaps lie. Here is a list of possible areas in which you may want to seek continuing education. Check off those that you wish to explore further.

____	Infant and child first aid and CPR
____	Age-appropriate expectations for children from infancy to age six
____	Guidance techniques
____	Nutrition
____	Parent-provider relationships
____	Child-abuse awareness
____	Professional development and community resources
____	Business practices

____ Children's health

____ Special needs/children with disabilities

____ Multicultural/antibias awareness

____ Curriculum and activity ideas

    ____ Art

    ____ Science and math

    ____ Cooking

    ____ Movement/dance

    ____ Music

    ____ Language

    ____ Personal safety

    ____ Dramatic play

Take advantage of any training programs available to you. You can check with the following resources:

- Your local child-care resource and referral agency often sponsors training courses and special seminars.
- Your state licensing department can refer you to relevant programs or classes.
- Many community colleges and universities offer early-childhood classes, parent education seminars, and courses in their adult continuing education departments.
- The YWCA/YMCA often offers courses in parenting and child guidance.
- Your regional Family Child Care Association routinely makes classes and training available to you.
- Many magazines offer up-to-date information (see appendix for suggestions).
- Your local library (or bookstore) is a resource full of guidance and activity materials.

Begin now. Looking at course descriptions will help you identify where your gaps as well as your interests are. Taking a class is an excellent way to spend your time while you're waiting for your license. Start reading and studying, and take advantage of training opportunities as they come along.

Continuing to educate yourself and update your knowledge as your business grows and prospers is highly recommended. Not only will it benefit you and the children, but it is a wonderful marketing tool as well. Parents will see that you take the care of their children seriously.

Are You Willing to Run and Maintain a Business?

Family child care is many things: child-centered, nurturing, rewarding. It is also a business—*your* business. As far as the IRS is concerned, you are self-employed. Being your own boss includes running the business in an orderly, professional fashion. This means keeping accurate and organized records; obtaining the necessary licenses to run a business in your state, city, and neighborhood; filing the appropriate business taxes at the right times; and maintaining contracts and agreements with parents.

Believe it or not, this is not all that hard. By reading this book, you will start out with a good amount of information on generating enrollment, filing taxes, keeping records, and much, much more. Chapters 3, 7, and 8 deal with specific business topics. And remember, there have been many providers before you. Their experiences, mistakes, and successes are there for the asking. Talk to experienced providers or take workshops available to you. The important thing to ask yourself now is, Am I willing to operate in a businesslike fashion? If the answer is yes, then reassure yourself that the how-to information awaits you.

Taking Family Members into Account

OK, you've got the space, your background is solid, you're committed to running a business, and you're ready to pick up your phone and find out about getting your license.

But wait. What about those other people who live in your house? Your family is crucial to the success of your family child care. If your spouse and children do not support your business, you will be miserable. A business in the home affects all who live there. Your family must understand how the business will impact their space and their claim on your time and attention.

Your home is the place where you and your family relax, play, and learn. Now it will also be the place where you work for eight, ten, even twelve hours a day. And not only will you work there; you will bring in a collection of lively, noisy, and needy children. It can get pretty crowded.

Most providers report that it takes some adjustment, and often negotiation and compromise, but their partners are usually supportive of the business. Their children are a different matter, however.

When there's a family child care in the house, young children must share their space, their toys, and *their parents,* sometimes before they are even developmentally capable of sharing. Some children adjust easily and like the other children around. Other children are not so easygoing, dislike change, and don't want to share their parents under any circumstances.

Think about how your spouse and children will react to a child-care business in their home. Talk with them about how it will affect each member of the family. On the next two pages are a few helpful guidelines to get a discussion started. Describe as realistically as you can what will happen. Before going any further, you must have agreement in your family about your plan to open a family child care.

If your spouse and children have concerns for which they are not willing to negotiate, then you need to seriously reconsider your plans. Perhaps this isn't the best time to open a family child care—next year might be better, when your two-year-old will be three and more capable of sharing you. Maybe you have a spouse who just isn't comfortable with the idea of "other people" in the house. Perhaps your thirteen-year-old needs your after-school involvement in her life more than the extra money the business would bring in. Everyone's needs are important.

Even with your family's encouragement and support, there will be conflicts and problems. But when there's a basic agreement to have the business, these problems are usually solvable. Chapter 8 will look at a variety of solutions to common problems.

Sample Family Readiness Worksheet

1. Before the family meeting, list each member of your family in the spaces. After each name, write down which concerns he or she will probably have about a child-care business in your home.

   Name   **Concerns**

   Spouse: _____   _____

   Child 1: _____   _____

   Child 2: _____   _____

   Child 3: _____   _____

   Child 4: _____   _____

2. How might you address these concerns? Think about ways you personally could accommodate them and also ways other family members or the family as a whole could resolve them. Jot down a few ideas. Go over your self-generated list of concerns and possible solutions before you hold the family meeting. This will aid you in bringing up possible conflicts during the meeting and in brainstorming solutions to problems.

   Name   **Ideas**

   Spouse: _____   _____

   Child 1: _____   _____

   Child 2: _____   _____

   Child 3: _____   _____

   Child 4: _____   _____

3. Hold the family meeting. Describe your plan for a family child care. Explain how it would work. Ask each family member to share his or her concerns. Describe the benefits for the family and outline sacrifices the family would have to make. A sample worksheet is included in the appendix. A completed family chart might look like the one shown later in this chapter.

4. If the concerns you predicted for each member are not raised, check them out. For example: "Zach, having a family child care would mean that I couldn't drop everything and go to the park with you whenever you want. We would have to plan our trips in advance. Are you willing to plan your special time with me?"

5. Brainstorm solutions or compromises for the predicted problems. Look for win-win solutions.

Problem: _____

Ideas: _____

_____

_____

_____

_____

_____

_____

_____

Problem: _____

Ideas: _____

_____

_____

_____

_____

_____

_____

_____

Problem: _____

Ideas: _____

_____

_____

_____

_____

_____

_____

Sample Family Benefits-Sacrifices Chart

Family Member	Benefits	Sacrifices
Andrea (Mom)	More money for family; able to stay home with Peter; career satisfaction; no more commuting; able to set hours	Less time for family during work hours; some after-hours work; more tired at end of day
John (Dad)	More money for family; knowledge that children will be cared for by parent; no conflicts with Andrea over time off from work	Sharing home with children in care and parents; wear and tear on house and yard; less family time in the evenings when Andrea does paperwork
Zach, age 6	Mom will be home when he gets home from school; more money for hobbies like soccer	Sharing Mom with the other kids; having family room space invaded after school
Peter, age 3	Can stay home with Mom instead of going into child care; his best friend would be in care with Andrea	Having to share Mom, space, and toys with the other kids

Outfitting a Family Child Care on a Budget

You are undoubtedly wondering how much setting up your child care will cost. The answer for most people is, "As little or as much as you can afford." One of the beauties of family child care is that you already have your work space. In terms of furniture, the basics include a high chair, crib or playpen, infant seat/carrier, and child-size chairs or booster seats. Most preschoolers can easily adapt to the furniture you already own. Basic supplies include toys, books, sources of music, and activity supplies (paper, crayons, paint, child-size scissors, glue, etc.). You might also need safety gates, outdoor playground items, or additional storage space (cupboards and shelves).

Start with what you have and slowly add to it. Shop at garage sales, flea markets, and secondhand stores. Tell your relatives and friends that you'll take discarded toys and equipment off their hands. Many regional family child-care groups and Resource and Referral

(R&R) agencies have toy-lending libraries; you can check out items for a specified period. Remember also to patronize your local library for children's and guidance books. Don't be surprised if you're able to skip the major toy retailers altogether.

Do keep some safety information in mind as you buy supplies. All items should be clean, sturdy, and free of any lead-based paint. Safety regulations on some infant furniture, such as cribs, have changed over the years. Older cribs do not meet current standards for the width of space between the bars; the new standard requires that slats be not more than 2⅜ inches apart (a bit less than the width of a soda can) and that any corner post extend less than 1/16 inch above the headboard so the baby's clothing won't catch on it. Another piece of equipment to be wary of is the baby walker. Pediatricians do not recommend its use, due to its involvement in a high number of accidents. Use your common sense when selecting items for your child care, and check with the Consumer Product Safety Commission (see appendix) for information on any other items you have safety questions about.

Ask your children which toys and books they are willing to donate to the business; be careful to explain that these items must be available to the children in care and cannot be monopolized by the original owner.

In the beginning you may wish to ask parents to bring what you are lacking. One provider started out by *asking* the parents of infants to provide their own playpens and high chairs. One year later she was fully equipped. Another provider makes it a *policy* for parents to bring their own playpens. You can do what works for you. But keep in mind that it usually creates problems when children bring their own toys; many feel possessive about special toys and are not willing to share them. Books and videos, however, are by nature things to be shared.

One provider says she began her first family child care with $100. When she moved into a new home and increased her license to twelve children, she spent more:

> ### What It Costs
> Some useful items you might buy for your child care*:
>
> High chair—$75
>
> Booster seat—$20
>
> Pop-up play hut—$65
>
> Sandbox and bags of play-grade sand—$135
>
> Box of building blocks—$20
>
> Big plastic tubs for activity supply storage—$35
>
> ---
>
> *Note: Prices listed were current, average online prices for such items as of this writing.

We earmarked one particular room for child care as our new home was being built. I purchased tables and chairs, mats for napping, outdoor play equipment, and some additional fencing to block the play area off from the rest of the yard.

The Three Most Common Reasons a Family Child Care Doesn't Succeed

Lots of people leap into family child care and leap back out just as fast. There are three common reasons why this happens.

Lack of Clear Policies

Janet, a mother of two preschoolers, decided to begin a family child-care business to care for the children of working parents in her neighborhood. Because she knew these parents fairly well, she didn't see the need to have formal contracts and policies for pickup and drop-off times, vacation times, and fees. Gradually, parents began to take advantage of their friendship with her and abuse the casual pickup time of 6:00 P.M. Janet had set. Soon Janet had children in her home up until 8:00 P.M. without prior notice. These children needed to eat, so Janet fed them dinner. Janet began to feel ill-used but hesitated to say anything: Since there weren't any rules, the parents weren't really breaking any. Her profitability went down because she had no late-fee policy and was forced to feed the children who were staying late.

Frustrated and worn out, she attempted to set some boundaries and establish fees for late pickups. Some parents felt insulted when her rather irritable announcement reached them, and they took their children out of her care. Bad feelings in the neighborhood resulted. Janet decided that family child care just wasn't worth the hassle.

Lack of Support from Partner and/or Children

Lisa, a new provider, had been working for a child-care center in her community for about six months. Displeased with the large number of children in her care, she decided that a family child care would allow her more opportunity for closer supervision and teaching of the children. Her husband, Tony, was dubious about the idea but liked the fact that Lisa would be there when their second-grader, Brian, arrived home from school; he consented to give it a try. Thinking that Brian would like having his mom home more, his parents didn't think to consult him.

Things were very difficult at first. Brian didn't like the children in care anywhere near his room or toys, and he clearly wanted to have his mom all to himself. Second grade was proving difficult for him, and he often came home tense and grumpy. Lisa, busy with six active preschoolers, had little time to talk with him.

Instead of getting better over time, the situation worsened. Returning home from work, Tony found that the clutter of toys and racket of children leaving for the day got on his nerves more than he had anticipated. He disliked having his space disrupted during the time of day he most wanted peace and quiet. Tony and Brian gave Lisa an ultimatum: Either the child care had to go or they would!

Lack of Developmental Information on Children's Different Ages and Stages

Karen had always loved children. She babysat a lot growing up and had two children of her own, ages two and four. Family child care seemed a natural choice for her. Enthusiastic about the idea, she charged ahead, taking in four children in addition to her own two. She planned eventually to upgrade her license to take twelve children.

Soon, however, Karen found that the five two-year-olds and one four-year-old were chaotic at best and frequently unbearable. Since she didn't have a lot of capital to start with, she planned for the children in care to play with her own children's toys, or to bring their own. When there weren't two of one item, she expected the children to share or take turns. It didn't work that way at all. Karen found herself explaining over and over again why the children had to share and policing them when they didn't.

Worse still, many of the two-year-olds didn't separate easily from their parents and spent the first hour in her care crying. Mornings were particularly unpleasant this way. Karen worried that perhaps she was a bad provider if the children hated to come so much.

Feeling desperate and completely bewildered, Karen closed her child care.

These scenarios can all be avoided. With adequate research, you can set clear and fair policies. With enough communication, you can determine if family child care is viable for your family members. With proper training, you can make good decisions about the age mix of children and have realistic expectations of their abilities. The important thing is to think about these issues ahead of time.

Visit a Provider

One of the best ways to decide if family child care is for you is to visit an experienced provider (or two, or three). If you know someone, great, go see her. If not, ask around; a friend or family member will suggest someone. You can also call your local child care resource and referral agency for some names and numbers.

Providers are a busy but friendly lot. Most are quite happy to answer your questions and show you around. Observe the layout of space. How does the provider use the rooms and yard? Which rooms are off-limits? How does she deal with safety hazards, like pools or hot tubs? What things did she need to change to become licensed?

If you can, visit while the children are present. Notice their activity or level of focus. Do they run right up en masse to you because the toys and activities aren't engrossing enough? Or do they gradually notice you and come in smaller groups to greet you?

Ask the provider what her greatest challenges are in running a family child care. What is her background? What problems did she have in her first year?

Visiting providers before you open your business will help you to set up your own network of colleagues. Running a family child care can be isolating. Meeting and sharing with fellow providers will make your job easier and more enjoyable.

You've done a lot of thinking and taking stock in this first chapter. You've looked at what exactly family child care is and what the benefits are for you. You've taken inventory of your home and your skills. You've taken a good hard look at your family and begun to determine how well they would adjust to having a family child care in the home. And you've thought about the business tasks and professionalism necessary for running a home-based business. If you believe family child care is for you, now it's time to move on to chapter 2 and act.

Chapter Two

Starting Out

You've done your soul-searching and you're ready to start. Begin by contacting the National Association for Family Child Care and then move on to the licensing and registration process. Finally, sit down with a pencil and paper to estimate your monthly income and expenses.

Where to Start

The National Association for Family Child Care (NAFCC) is a professional association for home-based child-care providers, headquartered in Salt Lake City, Utah. (See appendix for its address and phone number.)

Call and get information on joining now. Then, when you've received your license, join NAFCC. It is chock-full of helpful information for beginning and experienced providers. A few of the services and resources it offers are:

- A quarterly newsletter, the *National Perspective* (updates on safety, business, and education issues)
- Resource publications (available by mail order)
- National Family Child Care Conference (held annually)
- Information on trends in state and federal legislation, regulations, and funding
- Opportunity for national networking with providers, associations, and other organizations

- Representation in national policy making and advocacy on behalf of children and providers
- National accreditation program for members

Internet Tips

Find important organizations on the Web:

• The National Association for Family Child Care, www.nafcc.org

• The National Association of Child Care Resource & Referral Agencies, www.naccrra.org. This is the umbrella organization to which your local R&R belongs.

When this edition of the book went to press, membership for an individual provider was only $35 (tax deductible as a business expense). For the amount of help, support, and referrals you get, this is a true bargain.

NAFCC is also quite active in advocacy and child-care legislation on the national front. It is a powerful voice for children and for you. Its accreditation program is available to providers who have been in business for eighteen months or more. We will talk more about accreditation in chapter 9.

Joining NAFCC will plug you into the most organized family child-care network in the country. Your membership in NAFCC is also reassuring to parents who are seeking quality child care.

The Next Step: Licensing and/or Registration

Nearly every state requires providers to be either registered with or licensed by the state or county agency that regulates child care. This requirement means that you cannot care for children in your home without being appropriately licensed. If you are caught doing so, you can be fined for each day you operate without a license and can be jailed. To avoid this very unhappy turn of events, be sure to read this section carefully and be extra thorough in your research.

The licensing process generally begins with an orientation session (usually held at regular intervals at a central location in each county), continues with your written application and a visit from a home inspector, and concludes with your compliance with any changes the inspector asks you to make. It is a straightforward process but one in which it is essential to pay attention to every detail.

A Word of Explanation and Caution

This is a very, very important point: *Not all states' requirements are the same.* What is true in Georgia or Colorado is not necessarily true in Minnesota or New York. Each state is free to set its own rules, and each has done so. For example, nearly all states have strict safety rules; however, each of them has different specifications for how these rules are to be implemented. If your cousin, who is a provider in New Hampshire, can fence her pool at a certain height and meet safety regulations, it doesn't mean you can do the same in Florida. If your fire extinguisher meets the safety code in Idaho, it doesn't necessarily meet the code in Arizona. Going through the licensing, registration, or certification process will put specific information into your hands about your state's rules.

> ### What It Costs
> Here's a general approximation of fees*:
>
>   Business license—$35
>
>   Child-care licensing fee—$24
>
>   Fire inspection—$20
>
>   Criminal history check—$45
>
> ---
> *Fees vary widely by state. This is a very general example of typical fees. Check with your department of child care licensing for the specific fees for your area.

Also keep in mind that some states' regulations vary within the state. One provider in California assumed that because her provider friend in a neighboring county could add an extra child to her capacity, so could she. When the inspector made his annual visit, he informed her that the other county had a special pilot project being tested and the extra child allowance did not apply in her county. She was found in violation of her license and fined.

Here's the second most important point: *You are responsible for knowing what the regulations are in your state and locality and for complying with them.* The provider in the California example was fined because it was her responsibility to know what her county allowed. She should have checked it out before accepting an extra child.

This book cannot possibly list every regulation in every state. What it does is cover some areas that most states have in common and give you a general picture of what to expect. The information in this chapter is not intended to be complete for any state or for you to use as a sole resource. Remember: *It is your responsibility to inform yourself of what your state and county require and to comply.* The best way to start this is by going through your state's licensing process and reading all the regulations you are given.

Why Do We Need Licensing and/or Registration?

Quite simply, to ensure that children are properly cared for and safe. We would all agree that this is important. Unfortunately, the honor system doesn't work in this arena; people have vastly differing ideas of what is safe or appropriate for children. So the government makes the rules and enforces them.

Don't be intimidated. Think of the licensing folks as your colleagues, not as some interfering governmental agency out to get you (believe me, they're much more flexible than the IRS). They are in the business of setting a stamp of approval on your business, and that is worth a great deal. Good child care is hard to find these days, and they know it. They want to give you a license just as much as you want one. It is their job to make sure you meet all the requirements, and they will work with you to help you do so.

Going through the licensing process is an education in family child care in and of itself. You will be amazed at the amount of information about children and child care you will glean from the regulations, orientation meetings, and inspections. You will also be grateful for the many hazards and hassles that the licensing process will save you.

Jeri, a provider of eighteen months, had this to say:

> The licensing process helped me avoid many problems. I never dreamed I had so many potentially hazardous items in and around my house. I thought that because my backyard was fenced, I was ahead of the game. I discovered that many of my ornamental plants were poisonous, that the lock on my gate needed to be self-closing, and that two sturdy five-year-olds could easily tip over my old swing set! It wasn't a lot of work to correct these things; I transplanted the plants to my side yard where the children were fenced off from them; I installed a self-closing lock on the gate; and we got rid of the old swing set, left over from when my three kids were little. All the day-care children have been safe as can be in my yard.

The licensing process also plugs you into a network of suppliers and resources that serve the provider community. Most licensing agencies will provide you with information about your local child-care referral agencies, food programs, training opportunities, and provider support groups.

You will get access to this network right from the start. At an orientation meeting for new providers in Riverside County, California, for example, I received a packet of handouts that included the following:

- The state of California's Regulations for Family Child Care Homes
- An application booklet (containing all the necessary forms for applying for a license)
- Brochures for three local food sponsors (for participating in the federal food program, discussed later in this chapter)
- An application to be listed with the local Resource and Referral agency
- A handout of sample provider-parent agreements and policies from the county office of education
- Descriptions of two training programs immediately available in my community
- Information on the local Resource and Referral agency, with a description of services available

Internet Tips

For licensing links and information by state, check out these sites:

- National Resource Center for Health and Safety in Child Care, www.nrc.uchsc.edu .STATES/states.htm. Offers information on each state's licensing regulations.

- National Child Care Information Center, www.nccic.org. This site disseminates information about child care in the United States. Particularly helpful are the profiles of each state's demographics and links for licensing, food-program providers, state Resource and Referral agencies, and more.

The director from the local Resource and Referral agency was also on hand to explain the agency's role in family child care and to answer any questions.

Whom Do I Contact to Get Licensed?

Look in the phone book. Call up the Department of Social Services (or whatever variation on the name your state has adopted) for your county or state. They will usually refer you to an office of community care licensing. Many such offices license and regulate not only family child care but also all kinds of child and adult care: foster care, child-care centers, rest homes, state facilities for the disabled, and so forth.

The appropriate licensing agency will give you information on how and where to apply for a license, based on where you live. Generally, you will be required to attend an orientation meeting before being given the application forms.

If you're having trouble finding the licensing people (in these days of voice mail, it can be difficult to reach a live person instead of a recording), call the National Association for Family Child Care (800) 359–3817; they can direct you to the appropriate office in your state. You can also look in the appendix for the Internet address of the agency governing child care in your state.

What If My State Has No Licensing Requirements?

If your state has only voluntary registration, there is good news and bad news. The good news is that you may not have to pay for a license and delay opening your business until you apply and are approved. The bad news is that your state has not yet recognized child care as a vitally important component in our society. This has repercussions both obvious and not so obvious. If child care is not regulated, then children are not necessarily safe and well cared for. If your neighbor down the street offers day care for half the price you do, with twice the number of children, and lets them sit in front of the TV all day, there's no legal recourse to the inequity or potential safety hazards.

It is in your best interests to follow the guidelines NAFCC has prepared for all providers (accreditation requirements are described in chapter 9). Just because your state hasn't gotten around to caring about the children who live in it doesn't mean that you don't. NAFCC is active in lobbying for regulation in states where licensing is only voluntary. Eventually, they will succeed in requiring licensing. Be prepared for this by meeting NAFCC's recommendations now.

NAFCC has regional representatives who cover all fifty states. Call yours and ask for a referral to the local support group in your area. The members of your support group can also give you advice and guidance for setting up your family child care.

The Basic Components of Licensing

The following information on licensing is not state-specific, but rather a general picture of what you will find when you read your regulations and go to your orientation meeting. It is your responsibility to find out about and comply with all your state's (and community's) specific requirements.

Size of License

You can get two kinds of licenses from the state: small (generally one to six children) or large (seven to twelve children). The maximum number of children cared for is usually referred to as your *capacity*. In both cases, your own children ages ten and under count in your capacity. So if you are the mother of four children under the age of ten and you have a small license, you are allowed to take in only two extra children.

If infants are cared for, your maximum capacity is further reduced. Check with your state for its definition of *infant* and its regulations regarding how many infants are allowed for large and small licenses.

There are additional requirements for having a large license. Most states make stipulations similar to the following:

- You must have evidence of a certain number of units of early childhood education credits (a transcript will do) or one year of experience at a licensed child-care facility, or have been an experienced small family child-care provider for at least one year.
- You must hire an assistant provider who will be present when the seventh child arrives. The assistant provider must generally be fourteen years of age or older. Many states also restrict providers from leaving the children alone with an assistant younger than eighteen years.
- You must have a legal business license and/or conditional use permit. (These kinds of permits and licenses are discussed later in this chapter.)
- After you have your business license, you must obtain an approved fire inspection from your local fire department or city inspector.

One last word on capacity is in order. If your children's friends come play at your house, they are considered part of your capacity if:

- They arrive without a parent present or at home available to them.
- They are age nine or younger.

The BIG Concern: Safety

Let's go on to the issue that's on everyone's mind: safety. You may be worried that expensive alterations will need to be made to your house or yard. This is probably not the case. Most providers find that a lot of minor changes need to be made, but the big ones (fencing a pool, removing a tree) are few and far between.

It helps to remember that all family child-care homes need to be safe for the three age groups that they serve most: infants, toddlers, and preschoolers. What might not be a threat to a preschooler could be very dangerous to an infant—for instance, glass marbles at the base of a flower arrangement. What you'd trust a school-age child with you would shudder to think about within a toddler's reach—for instance, easy access to the toaster oven.

One home inspector recommends that you get on your hands and knees and creep around your house. You'd be surprised at what you might find down there. During her home inspection one prospective provider discovered that she had an uncovered air-conditioning duct below her stairwell, big enough for a child to crawl into. The home inspector was not impressed.

Let's take a tour of *your* home.

Doors. Any door you normally keep locked but will need to use as an exit in case of emergency (typically the front door) needs to have a single-action lock. With this type of lock, only one action is needed to unlock and open the door. For example, if you turn the knob, the door unlocks and opens at the same time.

Although many providers like to keep the doors locked when everyone is inside, most inspectors feel it's more important to keep exit access open in case of fire or other emergency. Although locked doors can "keep bad people out," they can also trap fire victims inside. The state sees more instances of the latter, hence its preference for unlocked doors.

Stairs. Young children (usually designated as under age five) are not allowed to go up and down stairs. If you have a stairwell, you must fence or barricade it.

Fireplaces. Fireplaces should have screens or doors to prevent any child access to them. Woodstoves should be screened or fenced in such a way that no access by children is possible. Open-face heaters should also be screened or placed in a room inaccessible to children. No inspector likes to see the old-fashioned style of bathroom heater with red coils. If you have one, prepare to replace it with something child-safe.

Fire extinguishers. Find out what your state requires. Often the fire extinguisher required is larger than the size one usually has on hand at home. (Many providers recommend the "ABC" type of fire extinguisher that puts out all types of fires—electrical, paper, wood, etc.) Check to make sure that your fire extinguisher is easily accessible. If you usually store it in your garage and your garage is locked while the day-care children are present, you have an access problem. Also, make sure that your smoke detectors are placed appropriately and have working batteries. States vary in how many and what kinds of detectors they require.

If you are applying for a large license (seven to twelve children) or are caring for children who cannot walk, then a fire safety inspection is generally required. Your local fire department or sometimes your city building department can do a fire inspection.

Poisons. Many, many substances are toxic if swallowed, spilled on skin or in eyes, or inhaled. Here are some general categories of items to beware of:

- Cleaning products—detergents, toilet bowl cleaners, disinfectants, furniture polish, and more
- Medicines—prescription drugs or over-the-counter medicines (e.g., aspirin, allergy pills, or salves)
- Other ordinary products found in your bathroom—rubbing alcohol, shampoo, hairspray, or cosmetics
- Poisonous plants inside the home or outdoors
- Lead paint on walls, furniture, or other older items

There are hundreds more substances, commonly kept in homes, that are poisonous. When it comes to children, expect the worst. It is developmentally appropriate for young children to explore anything and everything; that's their job. It's your job to keep hazardous items out of their reach. Medicine looks like candy; many cleaning products are pretty blue liquids; detergents can look like flour or sugar.

> **Internet Tip**
>
> To find your nearest local Poison Control Center, you can call (800) 222–1222 and your call will be automatically routed to your nearest center. This is a service of the American Association of Poison Control Centers. Visit its Web site at www.aapcc.org. You can also find your nearest center via this site and information on poisoning prevention and education.

The point is to identify the harmful substances and *lock them up*. In fact, one experienced home inspector recommends that you take everything out of the bathroom the children will be using except toilet paper and soap. If this isn't possible, get locks for your cupboards and medicine cabinets.

Firearms. We all know that guns and children should be kept apart. There have been too many tragedies in recent years involving children who have gotten access to guns and killed or seriously injured others or themselves. If you have guns or other weapons in your home, they have to be kept locked up in a gun locker, securely away from children's access. Ammunition should be stored separately from firearms and locked up as well. Some states allow you to use trigger locks or remove the firing pins from guns. In no case should they be accessible to children.

One prospective provider at a county orientation meeting I attended expressed surprise at the firearm requirements. Her husband was a police officer and regularly hung his weapon on the back of the bedroom door. "My children are well-trained never to touch it," she stated confidently. The community care licensing official rolled his eyes and assured her that no matter how well her own children were trained, she would never pass a licensing inspection without all firearms being locked up in a state-approved gun locker.

Be very careful to read your state's regulations on guns. Some states even have laws against keeping a loaded gun in the house with your own children.

Utilities. Your home should be adequately heated and ventilated for safety and comfort. No space heaters are permitted. Gas heaters should be properly vented and permanently installed. Your home should also maintain uninterrupted phone, water, sewer, and garbage service.

Garages. There are some pretty dangerous things in garages, which is why the state isn't fond of letting children play in them. Lawn mowers, hot water tanks, freezers, insect sprays—all of these things qualify as hazardous to a small child. If you have remodeled your garage into a regular room, then the children may play there after your home inspection approves it. Don't let children into your garage unless you have specific license to do so from the state.

Bodies of water. This includes (but is not limited to) pools, spas, fish ponds, sunken wading pools, and hot tubs. Generally, the state requires that any body of water be fenced or covered with a cover that will support the weight of an adult. If the pool is fenced, then the pool area must not be directly accessible from a door or window of the house. It's not much use to fence a pool on three sides, just to have a child climb out a bedroom window and fall into the pool. Most states specify what kind of fence, and how high, is acceptable. There are also regulations concerning the gate to a pool.

Various types of accidents are the leading cause of death of children ages one to fourteen, and drowning is high on the list.* There have been instances in which young children drowned in buckets of mop water. You cannot be too careful about safety around water.

Backyard. Your backyard needs to be fenced according to your state's specifications, or you must be with the children every second they are outdoors. This means no running back in the house to get the phone, go to the bathroom, or anything else.

No toxic plants are allowed. Many common shrubs are poisonous—for example, oleander and rhododendrons. Call your local Poison Control Center and ask for a list of poisonous plants. No dangerous plants are allowed, either—for example, cactus or other thorny, spiky plants children could fall into.

Could the children tip over your swing set? All play equipment must be firmly installed and safe for rambunctious youngsters. Consider also the placement of your play equipment. Recently, a child who attends a local preschool fell off the side of a tall slide onto another piece of play equipment. She fell with such impact that one of her teeth was forced up into her sinus cavity. After two hours of maxillofacial surgery and fifty stitches, she is on the mend. Make sure play equipment is placed a safe distance from other pieces.

An unused refrigerator or freezer can be fatal if a child shuts himself or another child inside. It would not take long for the trapped child to suffocate. Any such unused appliances need to be strapped shut (or the door removed) and kept away from children's access.

Pets. Many households have pets. How safe will the children and your pet be together? As one state inspector put it, "Everybody always says, 'My dog loves kids.' It isn't true. Young children are cruel to animals. Your dog does not love kids, he loves you; he merely tolerates kids. Sooner or later he will get fed up with being poked and prodded and will snap at a child."

Most states require you to keep your pets away from the children at all times and to vaccinate your dogs and cats for rabies. In addition, no kitty litter boxes are allowed within children's access. Cat urine and feces are toxic, and kids think the litter box is a sandbox.

*Statistics from the American Academy of Pediatrics, www.aap.org and www.safekids.org.

Sample Problem Checklist

General

__ Do you have any flaking paint in your house? Have you had it tested for lead? Do you have any dishes that have a lead content in their paint glazes?

__ Are your outlets overloaded? Do you have safety plugs in unused electrical outlets?

__ Do you have any oscillating fans accessible to children? These are generally not safe around young children.

__ Are the toys and play materials in your home safe for the age-group they are intended for? In general, it's best to simply not have toys with tiny pieces (e.g., Legos) or pieces that could break off around the children. It's difficult to keep the older ones from playing near the younger ones.

__ Are there locks or sturdy screens on windows in all rooms children have access to?

__ Do all doors have the state-recommended single-action lock?

__ Do you have a fire extinguisher? Is it stored in an accessible place (to you)? Do you know how to use it?

__ Have you fenced or barricaded your stairwell?

__ Do you have an appropriate number of smoke detectors? Are the batteries working?

Living room/family room

__ How stable is your coat rack? Could a child pull it over? Similarly, check your standing lamps.

__ Are knickknacks and other breakables and "throwables" locked up or out of reach of the children?

__ Do you have an exercise bike or treadmill? Such equipment can be dangerous to small limbs. Where can it be moved to?

__ How safe are your houseplants? Do you know if they are poisonous? Consider giving away any you are unsure about. Where would they best be placed so as not to harm the children?

__ Are your bookcases secured to the walls? Could children (or an earthquake) tip them over? If so, bolt them securely to the walls.

__ Do you have cords or ties on any drapes or curtains (or any other sort of tie that could choke a young child)?

__ How safe is your hearth? Consider purchasing a protective cover for the corners and edges.

__ Is your fireplace screened or fenced appropriately?

Kitchen

___ Are your knives and other sharp kitchen tools locked up, inaccessible to children?

___ Do your low cupboard doors have safety locks?

___ Are your "kitchen poisons" (cleaning products and such) locked up?

___ Are appliances (microwaves, toaster ovens, can openers) placed out of reach of children?

___ Where do you keep your plastic bags? Could a child get to them and suffocate?

___ Does your stove have a safety guard over the controls and knobs?

Bathroom

___ Are there ties or cords on your shower curtain? What can you replace them with?

___ Are any bathroom poisons (cleaning products, medicines, cosmetics, shampoos, mouthwash, etc.) accessible to the children? Could they be removed or locked up?

___ Can children lock themselves in your bathroom? Check your door for a single-release lock.

___ Does your toilet have a lid lock?

Outside

___ Are the doors to your garage (inside and outside access) locked and inaccessible to children?

___ Is your pool fenced or covered according to your state's requirements?

___ Is your yard fenced?

___ Have you checked to see if your shrubs and plants are nontoxic?

___ Are there any unsafe plantings (cactus or other thorny plants) that need to be moved?

___ How stable is your play equipment? Does anything need to be moved, repaired, or replaced?

___ Is your dog penned in or locked away from the children?

___ Have your pets been appropriately vaccinated?

___ Have you removed all tools, equipment (lawn mowers, ladders), and unused appliances from your yard?

___ Have you locked any outside appliances (refrigerators, freezers) in use?

___ Does your deck meet state requirements for safety?

Worksheet for Sue, a Prospective Provider

Problems:

After taking a walk through my home, I found so many safety problems, I felt overwhelmed. My children are all school-age, so it had been some years since I'd had to be vigilant about safety. I made up the following list of problems.

Front yard: No fence, busy street, lots of rosebushes

Front room: Round table with only center support (could tip over) and large metal candelabra on it, exercise bike, lots of delicate pottery displayed low

Kitchen: No locks on cabinets or drawers, second oven close to floor, plastic bags stored in lower portion of pantry, cleaning products stored below sink, knives stored in a block on counter

Family room/playroom: Fireplace has only a metal curtain, fireplace tools set out on hearth, sharp edges on hearth, variety of older children's toys and projects set out in room, standing lamp next to couch

Bathroom: All sorts of cleaning products, cosmetics, and toiletries stored on counter, hair dryers and curling irons on counters, lock on door can be operated only from inside

Backyard: Tendency for mud wasps to build nests on side of house, two fence slats coming loose, gate needs minor repair

The list nearly did me in, but I started looking at ways I could address these problems without giving up my dream of a child care in my home. This is how I solved the problems.

For other common pets, such as birds or hamsters, check with your licensing agency. Exotic pets, such as alligators or boa constrictors, are obviously not allowed.

Cribs. Slats must be spaced no more than $2\frac{3}{8}$ inches apart, so a baby's body cannot fit through. There should be no missing or cracked slats. (My mother tells a story of buying a used crib for me when I was a baby. When I was about ten months old, she heard a funny sound coming from my room and found me merrily kicking each slat out of the crib. She soon discovered that the used crib had been through a fire; someone cleaned it up, painted

Solutions:

Front yard: There were so many problems here that I decided we would not use the yard at all. We would play only in the backyard.

Front room: Here again, I had so many problems that I just gated the room off with an extended baby gate and planned to have the children and parents enter through my side door into the kitchen.

Kitchen: I put child locks on every single cupboard and drawer; it took me only about one and a half hours one afternoon. I moved the plastic bags to a high cupboard. I moved the knives to a locked drawer. I decided to use my upper oven instead of my lower one; the controls and knobs are high and not near a counter, so it was unlikely a child could get to them.

Family room/playroom: I installed glass doors on the fireplace and put the hearth tools in the garage. I put a thick, colorful old quilt over the hearth. I moved the standing lamp into the front room. Last, all "older child" toys were banished to the appropriate child's bedroom (off-limits to the child care).

Bathroom: All cleaning products, toiletries, and cosmetics went into locked drawers and cupboards. I bought a shelf to attach to the showerhead so the shampoos could stay up and out of children's reach. I have a very high medicine cabinet, not near the counter, but I put a lock on it anyway. I took the lock off the bathroom door so no child could lock herself in.

Backyard: I repaired the gate and fence. I hired a pest control company to spray for wasps and made out a schedule for maintenance visits during times children were not present.

it, and sold it. Although the crib didn't burn, it was structurally compromised.) The corner posts should not be more than $\frac{1}{16}$ inch high so a baby's clothing cannot catch on them. Don't buy cribs with cutouts in the headboard, which can trap a baby's head.

On the following pages there is a checklist of common problem areas for most prospective providers. As you answer the questions, physically check out these areas in your home.

First aid. Most states require you to have some knowledge of first aid and CPR (cardiopulmonary resuscitation). NAFCC also recommends that providers be up to date in their first-aid training. Classes and seminars on these skills are widely available. When choosing a class or seminar, make sure it covers first aid and CPR for infants and children (techniques for CPR and helping a choking child differ from the methods you would use on adults). Check with your local Research and Referral agency, family child-care support group, or local hospital.

In addition, it's a good idea to have a first-aid reference book around. A good one for adults is the *American College of Emergency Physicians First Aid Manual,* by Michael Web (Dorling Kindersley, 2004). Another first-aid reference, geared specifically to children ages four and up, is *Kids to the Rescue! First Aid Techniques for Kids,* revised edition, by Maribeth and Darwin Boelts (Parenting Press, 2003). This book is fun and educational for children, who love to practice and role-play first aid. Last, make sure that all emergency numbers—Poison Control, physician, hospital, fire, and police—are posted near your phone for quick use.

Sick kids. In the interest of controlling infection, you are obliged by most states to separate a child who seems to be sick from the other children until he or she is diagnosed. If the illness is communicable, then the child must be kept separate from the rest of the group until the infectious stage is over. Most providers (unless they specifically service ill children) send sick children home until they are better.

TB test. Most states require all providers and their assistants (teen and adult) to have a TB (tuberculosis) test. Your family doctor or local health clinic can easily give you this test and a certificate. Your test must turn out negative and have been administered within the past twelve months. Your own children age fourteen or older, who are not acting as assistants, do not have to be tested. You will have to repeat the TB test every three years.

Emergency information. Generally, the state requires you to have on file specific information for each child in the event of an accident, illness, or other emergency. You should have, written down and easily accessible, the following information on each child:

- Full name
- Date of birth
- Phone number and whereabouts of parent (and one or two other responsible adults) during care hours
- Name and phone number of the child's physician
- Authorization form granting you permission to obtain emergency care for the child
- Allergies the child has
- Immunizations the child has received
- Any pertinent medical history on the child (past surgeries or illnesses)

Sample forms showing this information are provided on the following pages.

Disaster plan. A disaster plan helps you, any assistants you have hired, and the children be prepared for emergency circumstances—for example, a fire or earthquake. You need to plan for such an emergency, and practice with the children how they can safely exit the house. You'll need to draw up a floor plan that shows an emergency evacuation plan (a sample plan is included in this chapter). Your licensing agency can guide you through this type of planning.

Criminal record check. It can be a bit daunting to realize that in order to work with young children in the United States, you have to be checked out by the FBI. Relax. You're a safe person, and you want everyone to know it. The purpose of this requirement is to keep children safe from those who would abuse or neglect them. All child-care workers—from preschool teachers to camp counselors—are screened in some way, either by fingerprinting, a background check, or both.

The state isn't interested in your minor traffic violations, only in any *criminal* offenses on your record. Most likely, the only "traffic" violations they would be interested in would

Sample Emergency Evacuation Plan

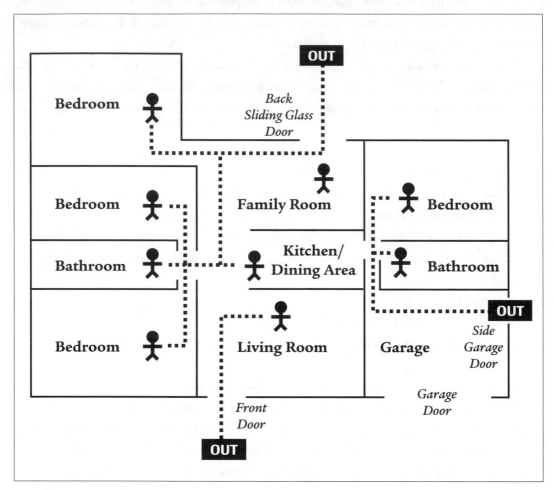

be any driving while under the influence of alcohol, or if you've injured or killed someone with your vehicle.

Licenses are routinely denied for applicants who have committed or attempted murder; done great bodily injury to another; committed voluntary manslaughter; committed rape, child molestation, pornography, or other sex-related crimes; or have had three or more drunk-driving arrests within the past year.

Crimes such as assault and battery and drug-related offenses are evaluated on a case-by-case basis, depending on the state's policy.

Obviously, there are a host of other crimes not mentioned here. If you are in any doubt as to their relevance to your application and license, disclose them. Honesty is critical here. If you lie about *anything,* your license will automatically be denied. It is not unheard of for the state to license a provider who is a recovering alcoholic or a recovering substance abuser; there may simply be restrictions placed upon driving with children. So if in doubt, tell the state about whatever unfortunate incident happened in your past and how your situation is different now.

The criminal record statement must be filed by you and any other adult who lives or spends a significant amount of time in your home. Your spouse, Grandpa who lives upstairs, your nineteen-year-old stepdaughter, your adult assistants, and Uncle Billy who stops by every Tuesday for coffee are all included. Be very careful how you determine "a significant amount of time." A good rule of thumb is to file for anyone to whom you give consistent access to your home (even if their appearances are irregular) during business hours. When your own children turn eighteen, you must file a criminal record statement for each of them within four days. In family child care the majority of abuse cases that occur are committed by a family member of the provider: a spouse, grandparent, or teen.

Remember, you are responsible for the children's safety. If you allow someone to have access to the children and that person molests a child, then you can be prosecuted as an accessory to the crime.

Fingerprinting. Most states require fingerprinting. Usually, once your license application is accepted, the state will direct you to be fingerprinted so that your criminal record statement can be verified before the license is granted. Again, you must have all adults living in the home or spending a significant amount of time there fingerprinted. Your local police department, the motor vehicles department, and some notaries can fingerprint you. The cost is minimal and is tax-deductible as a business expense.

The record of your fingerprints will be added to the federal Child Abuse Index. This means that if you commit any crimes in the future, the information will be available via the Department of Social Services nationwide.

Car safety. Some providers regularly pick up children from school or other child-care programs. If you do transport children in your car, there are some regulations you need to observe. First, and obviously, you have to be licensed to drive the vehicle in which you will be transporting the children. The car must be in safe operating condition. You should be fully insured. You cannot exceed the manufacturer's rated seating capacity for the vehicle; this basically means everyone has to wear a seat belt (no putting two children in one seat belt). Infants and toddlers must be in approved car seats (check your state's specifications for age and weight restrictions).

Although not required by the state, beefing up your car insurance coverage is highly recommended. The risks here are very great.

The topic of safety includes numerous issues, not all of which can be covered in one book. We've gone over some of the major areas in which the state is interested. Read your state's regulations carefully for other, more specific safety requirements.

Nutrition and the USDA Child and Adult Care Food Program

Generally, the state doesn't have a lot to say about food, other than children shall be fed regularly and well. If children bring food into the house, it should be labeled with the child's name and properly stored or refrigerated; it should not be shared with other children. The federal government, however, has quite a bit to say about young children and nutrition.

Providers commonly participate in the U.S. Department of Agriculture Child and Adult Care Food Program (CACFP) established by Congress in 1968. This program was originally limited to child-care centers but became available to family child-care homes in 1975. It exists to improve the health and eating habits of children ages twelve and younger by ensuring they receive nutritious, well-balanced meals while in child care.

What this means for you is you can purchase food from a licensed supplier and be reimbursed for a portion of the expense by the program. Many providers can thus supply all the meals children eat while in care for no, or little, extra charge. Parents like it because they are assured that their children are eating well and they do not have to take the time to prepare food to send with them each day. Face it, the children will eat your food anyway; you might as well be reimbursed for it.

Internet Tips

- Home page for the USDA Child and Adult Care Food Program, www.fns.usda .gov/cnd/Care/CACFP/cacfp faqs.htm
- State agencies who administer the CACFP, www.fns.usda .gov/cnd/Contacts/State Directory.htm
- Information on the CACFP and useful links, www.nal .usda.gov/childcare/Cacfp

Frankly speaking, it is cost-effective and smart to participate in this program. And it is relatively simple. Your local child care Resource and Referral agency can give you the name of your nearest food supplier. Your state can also refer you to suppliers. Call one of them up and make an appointment. A representative will call on you and explain how to use the program, how much money per child and per meal you will be reimbursed for, and how to keep appropriate records for reimbursement and for our old friends, the IRS.

The suppliers also provide other useful services. They offer workshops on nutrition and child development, furnish creative menu and recipe ideas, and oftentimes publish newsletters.

The crucial thing to remember when participating in this program is the importance of accurate record-keeping. You must comply with the program's requirements for records or you will not be reimbursed. In addition, the IRS requires that you report the cash reimbursements as income; however, you may deduct food costs as a legitimate business expense. In the majority of cases, the money you end up spending exceeds the amount you were reimbursed by the program. IRS requirements change from time to time; we will go over them in more detail in chapter 7.

We will talk more about food when we discuss mealtimes in chapter 4.

Discipline

When it comes to guidance, or discipline, the state wants you to keep to the middle of the road. Most states are very specific about a child's personal rights. The following is taken from the state of California's rules and regulations for family child-care homes:

> Each child . . . shall have certain rights which shall not be waived or abridged by the licensee regardless of parental consent or authorization:
> - To be treated with dignity in his/her personal relationship with staff and other persons.

- To receive safe, healthful, and comfortable accommodations, furnishings, and equipment.
- To not be subjected to physical or unusual punishment, humiliation, mental abuse, or punitive interference with daily functions of living, such as eating, sleeping, or toileting.

There you have it, folks. No matter how much your patience is tried, *don't hit the kids.* In chapter 6 we will go over several highly effective discipline techniques that are generally approved of by early childhood educators.

Better Safe than Sorry: Liability Insurance

You either have to have liability insurance to cover possible injury to those in your home or you have to have parents sign a statement stating that they are aware you do not carry it.

Warning: Your homeowner's insurance does not necessarily cover all the possible losses arising from family child care. You need to be protected from liability for bodily injury resulting from accidents on the premises, emergency medical expenses at the time of the accident, damage to someone else's property, and legal costs for defending against any suits.

> ### Internet Tips
> A brief word about another kind of insurance you might be interested in—health insurance. If you need some for yourself, here are two sites that offer small-business-owner policies:
>
> • The National Business Association, www.nationalbusiness.org/nbaweb/General/Ins.htm
>
> • www.ehealthinsurance.com

Many providers carry special liability insurance for family child care as a rider to their existing homeowner's policy. You can find out more about this by contacting NAFCC or an insurance agency that specifically services family child care. Do so before contacting your homeowner's insurance company.

Frankly, it is quite dangerous to operate without insurance. Anyone can sue you at any time over anything, no matter how frivolous. Insurance premiums for family child care are tax-deductible; don't risk your business and livelihood by skimping on this coverage.

Inspections: How Many and When?

An officer or agent of the state will visit and inspect your home prior to licensing. The official will inspect your facility, discuss the record-keeping required for each child, and inform you of any changes needed in your home and yard. The agent will give you an appropriate amount of time to make any needed changes before licensing.

After you are licensed, most states send out an agent once a year, unannounced, to make a spot check of your child care and ascertain that all is in order. In addition, if a complaint is made against you, the state will send an agent out to investigate, again unannounced.

The visits are always made during operating hours, and inspections are confined to only those areas the children have access to. If you are found in violation of any regulations, your license could be suspended or revoked and you could be fined. It all depends on the nature of the offense. If a portion of your fence blew down in the windstorm last week, you'll simply be required to replace it or keep the children inside. If, on the other hand, you're found to be exceeding the number of children you're licensed for, you will almost certainly have your license suspended and/or pay a fine.

City and Business Licenses

The state not only requires you to be appropriately licensed for family child care but also wants you to be appropriately registered for business within your city. If you live within city limits, you need a business license. In addition, you need to be aware of local zoning laws. You may also need a conditional use permit to operate a business from your home.

This is important: *Find out about your zoning laws before you get too far into this.* Some residential areas, especially affluent ones, are intentionally made difficult to run a business in. For example, operating a business from home may be legal but will cost you an arm and a leg to get a conditional use permit. In these cases, it's obvious the city just doesn't want the perceived hassle of home-based businesses and is out to discourage you. If this is true in your area, contact your regional family child-care support group for help and guidance.

If you are a lucky person, you live in an unincorporated area. Generally, city business licenses are not required in these neighborhoods. But the moral of the story is *find out*. Stephanie, a longtime provider, had this to say about business licenses:

> I used to live on the East Coast. The state and city had all sorts of licenses and requirements I had to meet. Then we moved to Salem, Oregon. Intending to set up another family child care, I called the city to find out what licenses I had to get. I said, "I'd like to start a business here in Salem." They essentially said, "So?" Their requirements were minimal compared to my previous state.

Planning to Make a Profit

A profitable business doesn't happen overnight and it generally doesn't happen at all unless you plan carefully. A simple calculation can help you figure out how many children you must take in and what fees you must set in order to be profitable. But first you must make a detailed estimate of your expenses.

Start-Up Expenses

Begin by listing your start-up expenses (see the sample worksheet Figuring Your Start-Up Expenses). By this time you should have a good idea of what you already have and what you need.

Ongoing Expenses

Estimate your ongoing expenses (see the sample worksheet Figuring Your Ongoing Expenses) by figuring out what they will be for one month. For expenses such as training, decide what you will budget for the year and then divide by 12; that will yield a monthly expense for that category.

Safety Cushion
Business advisors recommend having enough extra funds in the bank to support you for about six months. Sometimes it takes a while to get your enrollment up to capacity.

Estimate how much you will spend on child-care food for the month. The CACFP reimburses you per meal, per child.

The reimbursement rates are increased each year on July 1. There are two schedules for reimbursement. Tier I applies to you if you have a low income, live in a low-income area, or service low-income children. If you don't qualify in one of these low-income categories, you will be reimbursed on Tier II (your food supplier will be able to tell you where you qualify). As of this writing, the reimbursement schedules were the following:

TIER I			TIER II		
	Jan.–June	July–Dec.		Jan.–June	July–Dec.
breakfast	1.04	1.06	breakfast	.39	.39
lunch/supper	1.92	1.96	lunch/supper	1.16	1.18
snack	.57	.58	snack	.15	.16
Daily total:	$3.53	$3.60	Daily total:	$1.70	$1.73

Note: If you live in Alaska or Hawaii, your reimbursement rates will be slightly higher. Check with your local food program supplier for current amounts.

Let's say you are classified as Tier I and have six children in your care at any one time. You serve breakfast, lunch, and two snacks a day. If there are twenty-two days of child care in the month, then each child eats twenty-two breakfasts, twenty-two lunches, and forty-four snacks a month. This works out to the following amounts:

Reimbursement for 132 breakfasts (132 x 1.04)	=	$137.28
Reimbursement for 132 lunches (132 x 1.92)	=	$253.44
Reimbursement for 264 snacks (264 x 0.57)	=	$150.48
Total food reimbursement		$541.20

Take your total estimate for food for the month, subtract the amount you are reimbursed, and you then have the amount you will actually spend on food.

Estimating Your Income

You can estimate your income easily. Simply multiply the number of children you plan to have by the monthly fee they will be charged. For example:

Number of full-time children . . . 5
Number of part-time children. . . 2

(Total capacity = 6 full-time children)

Monthly fee for full-time child:	$600.00
Monthly fee for part-time child:	$300.00
5 children x $600.00 per month	$3,000.00
2 children x $300.00 per month	$600.00
CACFP food reimbursement for 6 children in 1 month	$397.20
Total income per month	$3,997.20

Profitability

Now that you've estimated both your expenses and your income, you're ready to determine if your business will be a profitable one.

According to this example, you can expect to earn about $2,400 a month after taxes. Of course, your tax bill may be even less than what is estimated here, depending on how diligent you are about record-keeping in order to claim deductions. We will go over how to prepare for taxes in much more detail in chapter 7.

Keep in mind as you do this exercise that your actual expenses and income will vary from month to month. Your income will vary especially in the summer months, since both you and the children tend to go on vacation. This exercise is useful for helping you zero in on exactly how much money you need to bring in to pay the bills, pay yourself, and remain afloat. It also helps you keep your expenses in line with your budget. Once you open your business, you can do the books each month and get a good picture of your profitability.

Sample Worksheet:
Figuring Your Start-Up Expenses

Start-Up Expenses	
Fees	
Child-care license	$60.00
Business license	(Not applicable in my area)
Other necessary permits	None
Fingerprinting fee	$25.00
Child Abuse Index fee	$25.00
Fire inspection	$75.00
TB test	(Covered by health insurance)
Membership dues	$35.00
Other	None
Equipment	
Fire extinguishers	$85.00
Fencing	None needed
Altering locks	$25.00
Outdoor play equipment	None needed
Furniture (small table and chairs)	$150.00
Other	None
Land Improvements	
Repairs and maintenance	None needed
Supplies	
Toys	$50.00
Books and tapes	$45.00
Activity supplies (art, science, etc.)	$60.00
Other	None
Office Expenses	
Equipment (filing cabinet)	$50.00
Supplies (copies, file folders)	$30.00
Training and Education	
Resource and Referral agency–sponsored classes	$35.00
Other	None
Total Start-Up Costs	$750.00

Note: Figures listed in this sample worksheet are for example purposes only.

Sample Worksheet:
Figuring Your Ongoing Expenses

Ongoing Expenses	Cost per Month
Food (your cost after the food program reimburses you)	$235.00
Car Expenses	
Gas/mileage	$45.00
Additional insurance	$15.00
Liability Insurance	$50.00
Office Expenses	
Postage	$12.00
Membership dues	$10.00
Publications subscriptions	$6.50
Bank charges	$15.00
Laundry and Cleaning Supplies	$15.00
Other Household or Yard Items	$12.00
Repairs and Maintenance	$12.00
Supplies	
Toys, books, and tapes	$15.00
Activity supplies (art, science, etc.)	$15.00
Other	
Training and Education	$30.00
Other	$15.50
Total Monthly Costs	$503.00

Note: Figures listed in this sample worksheet are for example purposes only.

Sample Profitability Worksheet

Gross income per month:	$3,997.20
Expenses per month:	– $503.00
Net income (profit):	$3,494.20
*Set aside for taxes:	– $1,048.26
Take-home pay:	$2,445.94

*You need to set aside a certain percentage of your earnings each month for federal and state taxes. Estimate the taxes on your gross income. Your tax bracket is based on your total family income. Consult your accountant for a reasonable estimate. The provider in this example needs to set aside about 30 percent of her earnings.

It's Not Really as Hard as It Sounds

Licensing and registration can seem like a monster in governmental guise, but thousands of providers sail through the process each year. Know what you're responsible for and be careful to comply. You shouldn't have any undue trouble. Likewise, doing a realistic estimate of your expenses and income will start you off as a careful businessperson and help you get in the valuable habit of watching your cash flow.

In the following chapter we'll look at the next step in preparing to open your family child care: setting up your policies and procedures.

Before moving on, complete the following checklist to be sure you've done what's necessary.

"Have I Done This?" Checklist

Have I . . .

____ Contacted my state for a list of requirements and an application for a license?

____ Applied for a business license? (city business license or conditional use permit)

____ Contacted the NAFCC for information on membership? (See address in appendix.)

____ Contacted my NAFCC regional representative for information on my local providers' support group?

____ Investigated and selected a liability insurance policy for the child care?

____ Taken a safety tour of my home and made a list of changes needed in preparation for an inspection?

____ Checked on my first-aid education status? Do I need additional or refresher training?

____ Gotten a TB test?

____ Prepared a disaster plan (emergency exit) for the house?

____ Filed a criminal record statement for myself and any other adults in the house?

____ Gotten myself and any other adults in the house fingerprinted?

____ Selected one of my local child-care food suppliers?

____ Signed up with my local Resource and Referral agency? (after license is received)

## Chapter Three

Policies and Procedures

One of the three top reasons a family child-care business fails is lack of clear policies and agreements. Some providers get so swept away in the effort and enthusiasm of starting the business that they forget to take some early crucial steps. It is critical that you provide *written* policies and have parents *read and sign* them before you accept a child into your care.

After reading this chapter, you would do well to talk with any provider friends you have, and if you don't have any yet, to call up your local family child-care support group for advice. Advice from experienced providers comes in handy when it comes time to set fees and policies. Ask questions, look at others' policies, and find out about the reasoning behind them.

Other good sources of sample policies and agreements are the National Association for Family Child Care (NAFCC), Redleaf National Institute (see appendix), and your county office of education.

In the following section we'll look at the different types of agreements you'll need and illustrate some samples.

Enrollment Records and Policies

You will need certain kinds of information on each child you care for. A parent or guardian will supply the information, but you need a consistent form for recording and filing it. Each child's file should contain the following information:

Sample Enrollment Record

Name   Audrey Johnson
Address 26245 Belle Vista Court, Boise, ID 84566
Phone   555-2222

Age 3   Date of birth 5/1/03

Mother   Elizabeth Johnson   Father   David Johnson
Cell   Cell
Home Address   Home Address
Phone   Phone
Same as above   Same as above

Workplace   Workplace
Cascade Electric   Ivy & Johnson Assoc.
393 First Street   6785 Muriel Avenue
Boise, ID 84566   Boise, ID 84566
555-6948   555-7890

Doctor
Henry Chan, MD
678 Professional Plaza, #301
Boise, ID 84566
555-8654

Emergency contact person if parent is unavailable:
Sue Johnson (grandmother), 555-7748

List of people other than parents who are authorized to pick the child up:
Sue Johnson, grandmother
Leila Jones, neighbor

Special instructions:
Audrey has ballet lessons Tuesday afternoons; neighbor will pick her up at 3:00 P.M.

Date child entered care: 1-10-06
Date child left care: _____

- Child's full name, address, and phone number
- Both parents' full names, home addresses, workplace addresses, and numbers for home, work, and cell phones
- Child's age and birth date
- Child's doctor's name, phone number, and address
- An adult emergency contact name and phone number (in the event that neither parent can be reached)
- A list of people who are authorized to pick up the child; signatures must be obtained from these individuals too
- Any special provisions needed for the child
- Date child began in care/date child left care
- Medical consent form (see sample form in chapter 2)
- If you do not carry liability insurance, you need a written statement of disclosure to parents, with their signatures
- Some states require you to give parents certain pamphlets and information on child-abuse awareness; if so, you need signed receipts from them in the child's file

Most providers find it wise to start every new child off on probationary terms. Not every child (or parent) will be happy and comfortable with your child care; nor will you be happy with every child. A trial period lets everyone know that a graceful "out" is available. Two weeks is a good trial time for child, parent, and provider. The agreement may be terminated at any time during those two weeks. If all goes well, the agreement becomes a working arrangement and the child is accepted for regular enrollment.

Setting Your Fees

Your income is a crucial part of your business and one of the top reasons why you're opening a family child care. Take your time and do your research as you initially set your fees. Once you've set them, they can be changed, but it is much easier on provider and parents if you stick with these initial fees for a reasonable amount of time. We'll cover appropriate times to raise fees later in this chapter.

Weekly fees for children in family child care range widely. The fees generally depend on the number of hours children are in care, the area where you live, what other providers (both family child care and child-care centers) are charging, the socioeconomic levels of the parents you are servicing, the age of the child, and the unique features of your family child care. Let's look closely at each of these.

- *The hours a child is in your care.* Obviously, if a child is with you part-time, the total fee will be proportionately less than for a full-time child. Do remember, however, that each child needs to bring in income for your business. If you're taking in two children for care after school and you have no corresponding children to fill the morning, you've essentially filled spots for two full-time children at part-time fees. Many providers handle part-timers by charging a flat rate for full-time children and an hourly fee for part-time children. The hourly fee is usually greater than a full-time hourly fee would break down to be.

- *The area you live in.* Cities and urban areas generally have slightly higher fees than suburbs or rural areas. Fees are higher where the cost of living is higher. Call around to various child-care facilities and find out what the fees are. Your local child-care Resource and Referral agency can tell you what the average weekly fee for a full-time child is in your area.

- *What other child care in your area costs.* Your success depends somewhat on what the competition is charging. If Jane Q. Parent can get care for her child at $20 less a week at the local Children's Play-World, she may look less favorably on your establishment, no matter how enriching it is. You don't have to price yourself considerably lower than everyone else, but it is smart to be in the same general range to remain competitive.

- *Socioeconomic levels of parents.* If the parents in your community tend to hold blue-collar jobs, then you'll be charging less than if they hold executive positions. It would be wonderful if we all had enough money to buy good child care at a price that truly reflects the service you provide, but the fact is, some of us do and some of us don't. The moral here is to know your market and get a feel for what families are capable of paying.

- *The age of the child.* Another fact of life: It's more time-consuming to care for an infant than it is to care for a preschooler. The state knows this too; it puts limits on how many infants you may care for at any one time. Your fees should reflect the added work an infant brings you and the limits placed on your capacity. For newborns to two-year-olds, an added fee is applicable.

    Debbie, a veteran provider of family child care, describes her fees for infants.

    I charge $25 extra per week for a full-time infant. Right now I have a little boy, Joshua, age three, and his sister Rosalie, age seven months. The baby takes more constant care so I charge $150 per week for Joshua and $175 per week for Rosalie.

- *The unique features of your child care.* Every provider brings something special to her or his family child care. Your particular skills or the added effort you make may be worth an extra fee to parents. Anne, a provider with a small license, describes her fees.

    I'm a pediatric nurse who has chosen to stay home with my kids for a few years. Because of my medical background, I am uniquely qualified to care for children with special health problems or disabilities. My local R&R and the hospital I used to work at refer parents to me. Right now I have a little boy who is diabetic, a baby with cerebral palsy, and a little girl with a congenital heart condition. The diversity is wonderful for the children, who can see that each and every one of us has special needs and is valuable. And the parents are much more comfortable knowing that I am trained to cope with medical needs and emergencies. My fees for these children are about 20 to 25 percent higher than what a more typical family child care would charge.

    The special extra you provide doesn't have to be as sophisticated as Anne's special training. Perhaps you are willing to pick up children from school. Or maybe you hire a swimming instructor each summer to teach the children swimming and water safety. Your fees can reflect the added services you provide.

One last thing to remember is that parents are responsible for paying for the time they agree to use child care, *whether they bring their child or not*. A suggested policy on absences is covered later in this chapter.

Some providers have a drop-in policy, meaning that if a regular child is absent, another child may take her or his place for the day for a flat fee. If the space is filled, the parent of the regular child is not charged for the day.

Late Fees

Despite their assurances and best intentions, parents will be late picking a child up from time to time. And some will be chronic offenders. Your best defense is a late-fee policy. There are several ways to handle this. Eileen, an experienced provider, describes her policy this way:

> My hours of operation are from 6:00 A.M. to 5:00 P.M. I don't encourage late pickups, but I do give parents fifteen minutes grace. If a parent arrives after 5:15 P.M., a late fee of $5.00 is charged for each fifteen-minute increment. If the parent knows he or she will be late and makes prior arrangements with me, a $3.00 fee per fifteen minutes is assessed.

Other providers give parents three late pickups for free, and then they start charging. You can decide what kind of system works best for you. One last note: Once you establish a late-fee system, adhere to it strictly. If you do not follow through and charge late fees, parents will abuse your policy.

Payment Schedule

Payment schedules vary among family child-care homes. It is best to require payment in advance. Some providers like to receive a check each Monday morning; others will take payment every two weeks; and still others will take a check at the beginning of the month.

It is wise to include a sentence in your fee policy about bounced checks. This will happen occasionally, and if you have already covered bounced checks in the policies the parent reads and signs at the outset, you can deal with the problem in a calm, businesslike manner. Generally, providers allow for one or two bounced checks (assuming the check clears upon resubmission) as long as the parent covers the fee that is assessed to the provider's account. After this, the parent is required to pay the child-care fees in cash and in advance.

Some providers accept cash only as payment. Payment policy is up to you.

Exceptions and Special Situations

Try not to include special situations and exceptions in your regular fee schedule; they can create problems with the other parents. But since life is unpredictable and some people may have legitimate (if unusual) needs, it is quite likely that you will make an exception for someone. Some providers will grant a special discount for two or more siblings in care at once. You might decide to bend your late-fee schedule for emergency situations, or you might even scale back your fee temporarily for someone who has lost a job. In any case, if you decide to make an exception, put it in writing with the parents involved and put limits on the allowance. For example, if you take on three children from one family and decide to give a "group discount," make sure you outline all the provisions to this policy. This agreement becomes an addendum to your basic Parent-Provider Agreement (a full agreement is illustrated at the end of this chapter). The following example shows how your special agreement might be worded.

Sample Addendum to the Parent-Provider Agreement

Jones Family Child Care agrees to accept Tabitha Carr (age three), Jonathan Carr (age five), and Samantha Carr (age eight months) at the reduced rate of:

Jonathan: $135 per week (regularly $150)
Tabitha: $135 per week (regularly $150)
Samantha: $157.50 per week (regularly $175)

If, at any time, fewer than all three children attend, the rate will return to the full fee per week for each child present.

All other standard fee policies, late fees, vacation fees, meal fees, and any other special-occasion fees apply, as stated in the Parent-Provider Agreement.

This special-rate agreement will be in effect until either party gives two weeks' notice.

_____   _____
Provider   Date

_____   _____
Parent   Date

Termination Policy

Since this is your business and livelihood, you need some notice if a child is to be withdrawn from care. The resulting loss of income needs to be planned for. Two weeks is a reasonable amount of notice to require if a parent plans to remove a child from child care. It is also standard to accept two weeks' fee in lieu of notice.

Likewise, you also need to give notice if you plan to stop caring for a child. Except in cases of flagrant misconduct on the part of parent or child, give two weeks' notice.

In cases of severe behavioral disturbance on the part of the child or parent, it is appropriate to terminate promptly. Care is commonly terminated when:

- a child hits, bites, or otherwise consistently hurts the other children.
- a child chronically "acts out" (e.g., swears, throws daily tantrums, or fails to comply with child-care rules) to the point where the child may need therapeutic care.
- a child is genuinely unhappy and unable to adjust to being in child care.
- a parent routinely abuses drop-off and pickup times.
- a parent doesn't pay the provider's bill on time or at all.
- a parent disagrees with the provider's guidance/discipline policy.
- a parent is unable or refuses to comply with ordinary requests for the child's well-being (e.g., a request to send coat and boots with a child on a rainy day, to send diapers, or to bathe the child).

Suspicion of child abuse is another legitimate reason child care is terminated. As a child-care provider, you are mandated by most states to report any observed or reasonable suspicions of child abuse or neglect. If you are unsure about the seriousness of any incident or circumstance, you should phone your local Child Protective Services department. They can advise you on whether or not to make a report and investigate any report you do make. If you report a parent, you most likely will need to terminate care. A parent being reported in this way will be angry or defensive and too disruptive to continue servicing. If you have an unhappy and angry parent who removes a child from your care, it is wise to let your local child-care Resource and Referral (R&R) agency know about it. If they know the facts of the situation, it is less likely that any false accusations of abuse will be credited.

Hours of Operation

It is very important to state your hours of operation clearly. Your business is also your home, and your family has a right to know when the children and parents will be there and when they can expect their home to be their own. Stating these hours up front, establishing and enforcing a late-fee policy, and discouraging special situations will help keep your business from intruding on your family life.

Hours of operation vary widely among providers. You might have a fairly standard morning to early evening schedule, or you might have a nontraditional swing shift or graveyard schedule. In addition, some providers are open a regular five-day workweek; others are open four days a week; and still others are open on weekends.

Whichever portion of the working world you choose to service, it is important to remember that parents need time at the beginning of their "day" to get to work after dropping their children off, and at the other end of the day, they need time to get to your house after work. Some typical hours of operation are 6:00 A.M.–5:30 P.M., 6:45 A.M.–5:15 P.M., 3:00–11:30 P.M., and 7:00 A.M.–6:00 P.M. Any way you look at it, a successful family child care involves a long day.

Many providers find that putting a limit on the number of hours a child spends in care per day is helpful. It may be possible for you to care for a child for twelve hours a day, five days a week, but it is not good for you or the child. No more than ten hours a day (and less is preferable) in care is a good rule of thumb.

Holiday Schedule

It is standard practice in family child care to charge for national holidays that fall during your normal hours of operation. This means that you should be paid for at least the majority of the following holidays:

- Martin Luther King Jr. Day
- Presidents' Day
- Memorial Day
- Independence Day
- Labor Day

- Columbus Day
- Veterans Day
- Thanksgiving (Thursday and Friday)
- Christmas Eve and Christmas Day
- New Year's Eve and New Year's Day

Most providers charge for these holidays when they fall on a regular workday. When one falls on a weekend, it is up to you whether you wish to charge for the holiday or not and take off the preceding Friday or following Monday.

Vacations

When a child goes on vacation, the parent needs to pay you something to "hold his spot." Generally, providers charge half the normal fee for child care for up to two weeks of vacation. It is wise to limit the amount of time you will hold a spot; economically, it's not smart for you to accept a half-fee for more than two weeks when you could fill that spot with a full-fee child. In addition, require parents to give you at least one month's notice of any planned vacation of one week or more. You need to know if your income is going to vary.

When you go on vacation, there is generally no charge to the parent. Some providers even help arrange for alternate care. Plan your vacation well ahead of time, and give all parents at least one month's notice. Many providers find it's helpful to go on vacation at the same time every year so the absence is more predictable for parents.

When the Children (or You) Get Sick

It's part of a child's job to build up his or her immunities by catching every little cold that comes along. But it's part of your job to ensure that a sick child doesn't share an illness. All the state usually says is that any child with a contagious disease must be separated from the rest of the children. Most providers take this policy a few steps further.

Laura, a relatively new provider, shares her policy:

> I ask parents to keep children home during the first two days of a bad cold
> or cough. I also ask parents to let me know if the child has been ill the day

or night before coming to child care, even if she seems OK when she comes in; this way I can keep a good eye on her throughout the day. If a child is contagious, running a fever over 101 degrees, is throwing up, or has any other severe symptoms, I call the parents to take her home.

Remember that all the children deserve your attention. Sick children usually need extra attention and nurturing. If you cannot give such extra attention without shortchanging the other children, then the sick child should be at home, not with you.

Some providers keep a list of babysitters who are willing to care for sick kids and provide these referrals to parents who can't stay home. It's a nice service when you aren't able to take in the sick children. Be sensitive to parents on this issue; almost all of them would prefer to stay home with their sick child, but many do not have such flexibility with their jobs. Be as accommodating as you can without endangering the other children.

If you are to administer medication to a child, the parent must bring it in its original bottle and make sure it is labeled with the child's name and the dosage instructions.

It's not just children who get sick, of course. Adults get sick too. And just as you don't want a sick child spreading chicken pox around, neither do you want to give everyone your own virus. It is smart to have a person lined up who can substitute for you in case of your illness.

Deborah, a longtime provider with a large license, comments on this:

> I have my husband listed on my license so that I can have him substitute for me from time to time. This works well when I'm sick or if I need to be gone for a day to a training session or conference. He isn't a caregiver by profession, but he's a fun change for the children when he substitutes. My teenage assistant knows the daily schedule and will direct the activities for the day. My husband becomes the "responsible adult on the premises" and helps with whatever is needed.

Another option for finding a substitute is to check with your regional family child-care support group. Many such groups are now compiling lists of available substitutes for providers.

In general, providers charge parents for the days their child is absent/sick and *do not* charge for the days the provider must close due to illness and has not provided a substitute.

Medical Consent Forms

Related to sick care is the form you need on hand in order to treat children for illness or emergency. It's basically a statement the parent signs, authorizing you to obtain medical care for the child if the parent is unreachable or if taking the time to find the parent would be a dangerous delay. Sample consent wording can be found in chapter 2.

Meals

Most parents are interested in whether you plan to feed their children and many want to know what you will feed them. Some providers ask parents to bring the children's lunch, and then they serve the snacks. However, feeding six children six different lunches can be quite time-intensive. And it can create food jealousy: "Hey! He's got Twinkies! I want some!"

Most providers supply all meals and snacks and include the expense in the weekly cost of care. Many books have been written on nutrition for young children and on meals for children in child care in particular. Later we will look at some sample menus and food ideas.

Remember that when you provide food for the children, you are eligible for reimbursement from the USDA Child and Adult Care Food Program (CACFP) (see chapter 2). The food suppliers in your area will provide you with the program's requirements for nutritious food and documentation of what you serve and when.

Other Food Policies

When you supply all the meals and snacks for the children, it is advisable not to allow them to bring any candy, gum, chips, cookies, or other snacks to child care. What one child has they all want. You can avoid such upheavals by making a "no non–child-care supplied food" rule.

There are three general exceptions to this rule. First, providers usually require parents to bring formula and baby food for infants. Second, if a child requires a special diet for medical reasons, it is appropriate to ask the parent to supply it rather than have to prepare it yourself. Third, special occasions, like birthdays or Valentine's Day, are often enhanced by having parents bring in outside treats.

Sample Medical Consent Form

Name:	Jonathan Andrew London
Date of birth:	10–1–03
Mother:	Sue London
	Work phone: 555–0936
	Compton Electronics
	5564 86th Avenue East
	Riverton, CT 06253
	Home phone: 555–7623
Father:	Bill London
	Work phone: 555–4746
	Montgomery & Fitzgerald Assoc.
	8562 Maple Street, #250
	Riverton, CT 06253
	Home phone: 555–7623
Physician:	Dr. Elton, 555–8754
Immunizations:	As of 1–1–06, up to date on DTP, Polio, MMR, Hepatitis B, Haemophilus.
Special information:	Had episode with possible hernia when he was twelve months old; allergic to cats.
Authorization:	*Sally Sue Provider* has my permission to obtain emergency medical treatment for my child (including administration of anesthesia if a physician advises surgery) when I cannot be reached or if a delay in my reaching my child would be dangerous for him/her.

_____   _____

Parent or Guardian   Date

Sample Authorization for Another Person to
Consent to Treatment of Child

Dear Parent:

This form may be used in the event that your child requires medical attention and you cannot be contacted. Please have the authorized person try to **CONTACT THE CHILD'S PHYSICIAN FIRST.**

If the physician cannot be reached, or if the physician feels the child should be treated in an Emergency Room, please bring this completed form with the child.

I, _____ , certify that I am the Parent/Legal Guardian of the following children:

_____
Names and dates of birth

As such, I hereby authorize _____ of _____

Address/ Phone number

who is 18 years of age or older, to consent to any normal and/or emergency medical and/or surgical treatment of the above children that the above-named person deems advisable if I cannot reasonably be located through the information set out below when the children are brought in for treatment.

The above authorization will be effective as of _____ , and will expire after six (6) months, or on _____ , whichever occurs first. During this period the Parent or Legal Guardian of the above children will be at the following location(s):

_____

_____

                                                        Car license #

_____

Signature—Mother/Guardian   Signature—Father/Guardian

Witnessed by: _____

Home address of Parent or Guardian: _____

Phone number of Parent or Guardian: _____

Employer: _____ Phone number: _____

Child's Physician: _____ Health Insurance Co.: _____

Phone number: _____ Group number: _____

Twenty-four-hour number: _____

Child's Name	Chronic Illnesses	Allergies	Current Medications	Date of Last Tetanus Immunization	Other

Guidance or Discipline

Let's face it: Most of the time, children do not behave like perfect little angels. It is your job to set limits and keep the children safe. Both child and parent need to know what to expect if a rule is broken. A written policy is helpful here, consisting of a brief statement outlining your guidance philosophy and preferred method of correcting children. For example: "At Sunshine Family Child Care, we have rules to keep all children safe. If a child breaks a rule, we give short time-outs. If breaking rules becomes a persistent problem, we contact the parent and discuss other ways of handling the problem together."

Most providers like to use the time-out method of guidance. Time-out is a technique in which you remove a misbehaving child from the action and require her to sit quietly for a short time. The purpose is to remove the child from whatever stimulus is causing her to act out, give the child the opportunity to calm down, and then let her rejoin the group and try again. A more complete discussion of time-out, as well as other positive guidance methods, is offered in chapter 6.

Helen, a former preschool teacher and a provider with a small license, explains her philosophy:

> I care for two- and three-year-old children. The techniques I use with them are different because their level of understanding is different. With the three-year-olds, I use short periods of time-out (about three minutes) to remove them from the scene of conflict and help them regain control of their bodies and tempers. They know where the time-out spot is (a blue couch in the living room we call the "calm down couch"). When they come back, we talk briefly about what went wrong and what part of their behavior they need to change.
>
> The two-year-olds have a tendency to grab or hit automatically when thwarted and don't always pay attention to orders to stop. If this happens, I gently restrain them to keep them from hurting others or themselves. When they are calmer, I tell them what I want them TO DO. For example, I say, "Touch gently" rather than "Don't hit."

Other Policies You May Wish to Consider

Because each provider has a unique business with its own set of expectations, the policies and rules you set will differ from those of others. Here are some other issues for which you may wish to set a policy.

- *Potty training.* Some providers set rules for how old a child must be before they will assist with potty training (somewhere between twenty and thirty months is considered normal). In addition, it may also be necessary to ask parents to dress the child in easy-to-remove clothing (overalls and jumpsuits are frustrating for a child trying to make it to the bathroom in time). You may also want to require a supply of extra clothes and training pants. In general, the provider and parent must be in agreement as to how potty training will be approached.

    Note: A child is truly "potty-trained" when he or she is capable of using the toilet without an adult's presence or help and accidents are infrequent. Make sure you and the parents are clear about what stage the child is really in.

- *Clothing.* It's hard to believe, but many parents still dress their daughters for child care in fancy dresses and expect them to stay clean all day. Some parents also expect their sons not to get certain clothes dirty. It is sometimes necessary to explain to parents that young children learn by doing and "doing" is often a messy process. Art, cooking, science, and outdoor activities require clothing that is comfortable and washable. Children's learning is more important than their clothing; make sure parents support you on this one.

    Some providers like to require that a change of clothing be kept on hand for every child. Accidents happen from time to time; children will be more comfortable if they are dry and reasonably clean.

- *Parking.* Some providers have special needs with regard to parking in their neighborhood. If you need parents to park in certain spots and avoid others, make it a policy. Your neighbors' goodwill is something to be preserved.

- *Pickups when impaired.* Occasionally, providers find it necessary to state in a policy that no child will be released to a parent who is obviously drunk, on drugs, or otherwise impaired, in the provider's opinion. The child's safety is more important than the parent's "authority."

- *Child-care philosophy.* Some providers find it helpful to include a statement of their child-care philosophy along with their policies. It helps give parents information about your background and approach and reassures them that their children are receiving quality care. It's also a nice touch to list the benefits a multi-age mix offers children in your care (see chapters 4 and 8).

- *Communication.* It is helpful to state in your policies that you would like to know if there are special circumstances in a child's life (divorce, new sibling, other traumas) so that you can give that child the extra attention

Internet Tips

Here are a couple Web sites run by providers who post sample policies (and a lot more):

- A Home Away from Home Family Child Care, www.geocities.com/heartland/hills/2489. Tips for start-up, marketing strategies, sample policies, sample schedules, activities, and more.

- Daycare Provider's Beginner Page, www.oursite.net/daycare. This site's goal is to assist with the start-up phase of family child care. Lots of sample day-care documents, including policies and a sample business plan.

she or he needs. Likewise, it is helpful to invite parents to talk with you about any concerns they have about the care the child is receiving.

You've thought out all your policies and you've made notes to yourself. Now it's time to write them up and create your own Parent-Provider Agreement and Child-Care Policies for parents to read and sign. Keep your policies simple and straightforward. Several examples of agreements and policies that other providers have found useful are illustrated on the following pages.

Strawberry Patch Child-Care Policies

Child-Care Philosophy

For the child:

1. To provide opportunities for being with other children in a setting conducive to the development of wholesome social relationships.

2. To provide appropriate play experiences that contribute to the developmental needs of the child.

3. To provide opportunities for meaningful play that is based on the child's individual needs, interests, handicaps, and abilities, and that will build important foundations for future skills.

For the parents:

1. To provide opportunities to meet with and work with other parents and teachers who have as their common concern the interests and needs of their children.

2. To provide care for the child while the parents pursue their own work or other interests.

3. To provide opportunities to grow in the understanding of child development.

For the community:

1. To help meet the needs of the community for an early childhood education facility.

2. To contribute to the wholesome growth and development of the citizens of the community.

3. To enhance the role of the Strawberry Patch Child Care as an integral part of the community.

4. To provide a setting where people of various religious and ethnic backgrounds can work together.

Schedule/Hours of Operation

1. The first ten days of care are probationary for provider, parent, and child. This agreement may be terminated at any time during that period. Otherwise, two weeks' notice is required if the child is to be permanently removed from this child care.

2. Two weeks' fee will be accepted in lieu of two weeks' notice, and, in fact, will be due with notice of plans to discontinue enrollment. Except in the case of gross misconduct on the part of either parent or child, provider will also tender two weeks' notice prior to cessation of care. Your fee will be due when notice is given.

3. Anytime you pick up your child after 5:30 P.M. without the prior consent of the provider, you will be considered late. A fee of $5.00 for every fifteen minutes, or any part thereof, will be charged for each late pickup. You will be allowed three (3) late pickups (no more than ten [10] minutes each) per month before the late fee is charged. Once you have used up your three late pickups, you will be responsible for adding any and all late fees to your next monthly payment. Please do not ask or expect me to keep track of your late pickup fees; it is embarrassing for both of us. Late pickups that are prearranged will be charged at a rate of $5.00 per half hour, or any part thereof, and will be due with your next monthly payment.

4. Children may be in attendance a maximum of ten (10) hours per day.

5. Please understand: My 6:00 A.M.–5:30 P.M. schedule is only "child-care hours" and does not reflect all of the additional hours necessary to provide quality day care. I am here for you in case of emergency, but I do not want to work "overtime." If I am to do so, it must be worth my while. I, too, have a busy schedule that must be arranged around my providing child-care services.

6. The following is my paid holiday schedule:
   - Martin Luther King Jr. Day
   - Presidents' Day
   - Memorial Day
   - Independence Day
   - Labor Day
   - Columbus Day
   - Veterans Day
   - Thanksgiving Weekend (Thursday/Friday)
   - Christmas Eve Day/Christmas Day
   - New Year's Eve Day/New Year's Day

7. There is no charge for any other time taken off by provider for vacation, sick days, or conferences. In case of emergency or illness, provider will make every attempt to provide substitute care. However, parents should be prepared with own backup.

Fees

1. Although family child care is a form of self-employment, unlike other businesses, there is no room for growth or expansion due to licensing regulations. I do not receive any benefits that most employees take for granted, such as health insurance, paid sick days, vacation days or personal days, worker's compensation, retirement/pension plan, employment insurance, annual raises, and bonuses. My contractual policies reflect this.

2. Fees are due in advance and payable no later than the first day of the week that your child attends. A $5.00 fee will be assessed if your fee is not paid on time, and your child may not be accepted until your fee is paid, except under special circumstances prearranged and agreed to by provider.

3. Checks will be accepted. If, however, two checks are returned by the bank, your fee will be accepted in cash only. You will be responsible for any fees assessed to my account.

Vacation Guidelines

1. Parents are required to notify the Strawberry Patch two full weeks in advance when a child is to be withdrawn to accompany parents on vacation. Parents then will be required to pay one-half the regular week rate, in advance, for the vacation time in order to ensure readmission.

2. I will notify parents four weeks in advance of closure due to family vacation or an educational conference.

Meals

1. Breakfast, lunch, and two snacks are served each day at no additional charge.

2. Should your child arrive later than a mealtime, you will be responsible for feeding him or her. Except for special occasions or illness requiring a special diet, please do

not send any food with your child. This includes but is not limited to gum, candy, chips, cookies, and cereal. Arrangements can be made for special days.

Sick Care

1. If your child is ill to the extent that it interrupts the care of or endangers the health of the other children, it will be necessary for you to make other arrangements for his or her care. Should your child become ill during his or her day here, you will be notified and we will determine the best course of action concerning appropriate care, which may include the child being taken home.

2. I will always respect your need to be at work when it comes to an ill child. I ask, however, that when deciding if your child should be at home, you give consideration to the other children in care and ask yourself how you would feel if your child were here and well and another child were as ill as your child is now.

3. My "bottom line" for not providing care is fever in excess of 101 degrees, vomiting, excessive diarrhea, or any potentially contagious disorder. Further, there are times when a child is not that ill but is terribly uncomfortable and really needs some "one on one" that I cannot provide and be fair to the other children. At those times I will strongly urge you to consider keeping your child at home.

4. Any medication to be given must come in a labeled prescription bottle. Nonprescription medicine, if needed, will also be administered, if provided by parent.

Guidance

1. Some people prefer to use the word *discipline* when discussing helping children learn to accept societal standards of behavior. However, the word *discipline* frequently has a connotation of punishment, which makes it less desirable in our educational setting. That is, the question "How do you discipline your child?" usually translates into, "How do you punish your child?" In the education setting and with a developmental philosophy of early childhood education, the word *guidance* is more accurate.

2. When appropriate, children will be given short periods of "time-out" for guidance.

Potty Training

1. Potty-trained: The child is capable of using the toilet, but it is the adult who is trained to get the child to the bathroom on time. Accidents occur often. It is the first step in the total process.

2. Potty-learned: The child is not only capable of using the toilet but has the developmental ability to express the need to go. Accidents occur, but infrequently.

3. If potty training is begun when your child is ready, the task is easy and quick. If parents undertake the task of potty training when *they* want it to happen, the task is arduous and painful for all concerned. Thirty months of age is a good rule of thumb to start checking for signs of readiness.

4. When we agree that the time is right for your child and until he or she is totally successful in his or her toileting, NO wearing of overalls or clothing with suspenders, snaps, buckles, belts, or zippers. Elastic-waisted pants *only*. Anything else sets your child up for failure. In addition, your child's locker box *must* have two complete changes of clothes and several pairs of thick training pants. If your child does not have immediate success, he or she will be put back into diapers and, after a respite, the process will be attempted again. This does not harm the child in any way; in fact, keeping a child in "grown-up" pants when he or she is not successful is harmful.

Activities

1. Creativity is the basis for all activities at the Strawberry Patch.

2. Creativity integrates physical, mental, social, and emotional growth. Creativity is fostered by a free, flexible, accepting, and open environment and by openly discovering, inventing, and creating. In addition to having the opportunity for self-expression, children are practicing small motor skills, eye-hand coordination, left-to-right progression, and whole-part relationships.

Sample Policy Form

Miscellaneous

1. Any changes in personal address or phone numbers will be given to provider as soon as possible. Names and phone numbers on emergency forms will be kept current.

2. Note that your child will be released to persons other than the parent or legal guardian only if their names appear on your signed emergency form. In case of an emergency, a phone call from you will suffice as long as the person picking up the child shows identification.

3. All possible care is taken to provide a safe and healthy environment; however, children do have accidents. I am certified in pediatric CPR and have Red Cross training. In case of an accident, I will tend to the child and notify the parent. In case of an emergency, I will tend to child, call 911, and notify the parent. Your child will be taken to Grossmont Hospital if that becomes necessary. It is incumbent upon you to check with the hospital emergency room to find out what kinds of forms they require to be on file for treatment in case of parental absence.

4. I am a mandated reporter of suspected child abuse. Your child's welfare will *always* come first. I will consult with you if possible. Please understand that I have few options.

5. Any person picking up your child in an impaired condition (in my estimation, inebriated or on drugs) will be encouraged to allow me to find alternate transportation. I cannot legally withhold a child from a legal guardian, but if I feel a child is in jeopardy, I will not hesitate to contact the police.

6. Open communication is the key to a happy, long-lasting relationship between a child-care provider and her child-care families. Please do not hesitate to contact me about anything that affects the well-being of your child.

DAY-CARE POLICIES AND PROCEDURES

Camille's Day Care

Admission Requirements and Enrollment Procedures

A. Each child must visit my home for a half-hour before placement to help reduce separation fears and to see how the child will fit in.

B. If we agree that the child will be placed, the parents must provide the following:

    1. A completed registration form

    2. A complete record of age-required immunizations

    3. Authorization to receive emergency medical care

    4. Date of last physical exam

    5. Authorization to transport the child in my van

    6. Authorization for field trips, walks, etc.

HOURS OF OPERATION

A. The day care will operate Monday through Thursday from 7:30 A.M. to 5:30 P.M.

B. Day-Care Holiday Schedule

Labor Day	Sept. 3 (Monday)
Thanksgiving	Nov. 22 (Thursday)
Winter break	Dec. 21–Jan. 1
Martin Luther King Jr. Day	Jan. 14 (Monday)
Presidents' Day	Feb. 18 (Monday)
Spring break	April 14–15 (Monday and Tuesday)
Memorial Day	May 26 (Monday)
Summer break	To be announced

I have read and agree to these policies and procedures.

(Please initial) _____ Date _____

C.   You will be charged for all days you agree to have your child attend day care. If your child does not attend, you will be charged the minimum daily rate (see below). There is no charge for days when the day care is closed.

D.   I will give one month's notice if I feel the day-care arrangement needs to be terminated.

E.   I would appreciate at least two weeks' notice if you plan to discontinue day care, but it is not required.

F.   In case of emergency, illness, or other situations that would result in my absence, I have two qualified women who can fill in for me.

PAYMENT PLANS AND FEES

A.   *Fee Schedule Effective September 1–August 31:*

Full day
　　　3 months to 3 years: $190.00 per week, or $38.00 per day
　　　3 to 5 years: $165.00 per week, or $33.00 per day
　　　6 years and up: $140.25 per week, or $28.05 per day
Half-day
　　　Kindergarten: $91.00 per week, or $18.20 per day
　　　6 years and up: $20.00 per day
Transportation from morning preschool to day care: $7.00 per day
Before and after school care: $12.00 per day

B.   There is a late fee after 5:30 P.M. of $3.00 per fifteen minutes.

C.   Charges are based on the time you have arranged to leave your child to the time you actually pick up on the half-hour. For example, if you have arranged to drop off your child at 8:30 A.M., you will be charged from that time even if you drop off later. You will then be charged on the half-hour when you pick up; e.g., if you pick up at 4:15 P.M., you will be charged for 4:30 P.M.

I have read and agree to these policies and procedures.

(Please initial) _____   Date _____

D. You will be charged for the time your child is in another program (preschool, dancing lessons, etc.), since a place is kept open for him or her during that time.

E. This fee covers all meals, diapers, preschool supplies, and field trips.

F. You will be billed on the fifteenth and last day of the month. Your payment is due within a week unless other arrangements have been agreed upon.

G. Rates will be evaluated in June. You will be notified of any changes in July, and any rate changes will be effective on September 1.

TYPICAL DAILY SCHEDULE

A. Mealtimes:
Breakfast—7:30 to 8:30 A.M.   Lunch—11:30 A.M. to noon
Morning snack—9:30 to 10:00 A.M.   Afternoon snack—3:30 to 4:00 P.M.

B. Napping and/or quiet time—1:00 to 3:00 P.M. (Children under eighteen months will be on a demand schedule.)

C. Daily schedule will include:

1. Free-play activities (large variety of toys).

2. Outdoor play (riding toys, swings, climbing toys, slides, teeter-totter, merry-go-round, large sandbox, and grassy area for running and ball play).

3. Small muscle play (Duplos; blocks; waffle blocks; puzzles; beads to string; pegboards; stacking, sorting, and nesting toys; super maze; construction sets; Lincoln Logs; Brio train; mini and micro cars; small dolls; etc.).

4. Preschool activities include painting, coloring, cutting, gluing, Play-Doh, etc. A theme is followed every month, starting with the colors in the fall. The shapes, some numbers, and letters are covered, interspersed with the different seasons' and holidays' arts and crafts.

I have read and agree to these policies and procedures.

(Please initial) _____   Date _____

5. Stories, songs, rhymes, and music.

6. Creative play (dress-up clothes, dolls, dishes, puppets, etc.).

7. Television-watching will be kept to a minimum and will vary depending on the weather, mood of the children, etc. Only PBS, Disney, children's videos, and some cartoons will be watched.

MEALS AND SNACKS

A.   All meals, snacks, and drinks will be provided.

B.   All beverages will be 100 percent fruit juice or 2 percent milk. Bread products will be whole wheat or partially whole wheat. Cheese will be unprocessed. No sugar cereals and sweet drinks will be served. Other sweets and treats will be kept to a minimum.

C.   Meals and snacks will be nutritional and the daily menu will follow the guidelines recommended by the USDA child-care food program.

D.   A weekly menu will be posted.

E.   Birthday and holiday treats will be provided by the day care. Children are not permitted to bring gum, candy, or other treats.

DISCIPLINE POLICY

A.   A "time-out" chair will be used for aggressive, disruptive, or destructive behavior for children two or older. Children less than two will be distracted and guided to other activities.

B.   My house is childproofed and there are very few things that are off-limits to the children. I feel that exploring and "getting into things" are a normal and healthy part of childhood.

_____

I have read and agree to these policies and procedures.

(Please initial) _____   Date _____

C.   A well-organized, well-supervised, and stimulating atmosphere will be provided that should minimize any need for discipline. If a discipline problem should arise involving your child, we will discuss the problem and work out a solution together.

D.   Physical punishment of any type will not be used.

TRANSPORTATION

A.   Your child will be transported only in an automobile in safe operating condition that is covered by insurance and operated by a licensed and safe driver.

B.   Your child will at all times be in a seat belt or other protective device suitable for his or her age and weight.

C.   There will be occasional field trips to the local parks or zoo. There will be at least one adult for every four children. No additional fees or equipment (other than regular outdoor wear) will be required for field trips. You will be notified of any field trips in advance, and I will try to let you know if I will be transporting your child for any other reason.

HEALTH POLICIES AND PROCEDURES

A.   Medical emergencies

1. Immediate first aid will be given.

2. An ambulance will be called and the recommendations of the paramedics followed.

3. Parents will be notified as soon as possible. If you are not available, other family or friends on your registration form will be notified.

4. Parents are responsible for any expenses incurred as a result of emergency room care, ambulance, etc.

_____

I have read and agree to these policies and procedures.

(Please initial) _____ Date _____

Sample Parent-Provider Agreement

5. Hospitals used for emergencies:

NORTHWEST HOSPITAL   STEVENS HOSPITAL
1550 North 155th   21600 76th Avenue West
555–0500   555–0555

B.   First-aid procedures

1. First aid will be in accordance with the Red Cross first-aid class and the Poison Center.

2. Everyone who cares for your child takes an EMERGENCY CARE AND CPR FOR INFANTS AND CHILDREN course each year.

3. A complete first-aid kit, ice packs, and emergency numbers will be kept on the premises.

4. Parents will be notified of all accidents, and a record of injuries will be kept on each child.

C.   Illness

1. If your child becomes ill during the day, you will be notified and are expected to pick up your child as soon as possible.

2. If your child will be missing day care due to illness, please notify me by phone in the morning or the previous evening.

D.   Communicable disease prevention and reporting

1. Your child will be kept isolated from other children as much as possible if your child has a communicable disease. Communicable diseases will be reported to the Department of Health.

2. Each child will be observed daily for illness.

3. Individual bedding, towels, washcloths, glasses, etc., will be used to minimize spreading infections.

E.   Hand-washing, diapering, sanitizing, and laundering policies

1. Day-care provider will wash hands before and after diapering; toileting; eating, handling, and preparing food; and handling contaminated materials.

I have read and agree to these policies and procedures.

(Please initial) _____ Date _____

2. Children will wash after toileting, after handling contaminated materials, and before and after eating.

3. Diapers will be changed regularly and immediately after a bowel movement. Bottoms will be thoroughly cleaned, and cornstarch or petroleum jelly will be used as needed. Other types of preparations must be provided by parents.

4. The diapering area will be sanitized after each use; contaminated utensils and toys will be sanitized.

5. Bedding will be laundered as needed or once a week.

6. Bottles and nipples will be washed in the dishwasher and rinsed again with hot water before filling.

F. Medication management

1. All prescribed medication must be labeled with the child's name and must be accompanied by written permission from the parent to dispense.

2. As-needed medications must be labeled with the child's name and must be accompanied by written permission from the parent to dispense.

G. Health records

1. Immunization records and the date of your child's last physical examination must be kept up to date.

2. Please notify me of any special health problems or concerns regarding your child or family.

RELIGIOUS ACTIVITIES

A. A simple blessing will be said before meals to help settle children.

B. Religious music (e.g., Christmas carols) may be played or sung.

_____

I have read and agree to these policies and procedures.

(Please initial) _____ Date _____

Sample Parent-Provider Agreement

NONDISCRIMINATION POLICY

No child will be discriminated against on the basis of race or religion.

MISCELLANEOUS INFORMATION

A. Parents have free access to all areas of my house and yard that are used by their children.

B. Children are discouraged from bringing their own toys, and the day care is not responsible for any that are broken or lost. Security blankets and/or pacifiers are welcome.

C. No smoking is allowed in the day-care house or yard at any time.

D. Parents are free to call at any time to see how their child is doing. An answering machine will be used at times to avoid interruptions, but I will return your call as soon as possible.

E. Fire drills will be conducted monthly and recorded on the evacuation plan that is posted on the entry bulletin board.

F. As a day-care provider, I am required to report any suspected child abuse or neglect.

G. The schools that serve this area are St. Luke, Crista, Syre, and Sunset. None of these schools is within walking distance for young children. However, there are city and school buses that serve these schools.

H. Parents are encouraged to discuss their child with me at any time, or to call in the evening or on weekends. Good communication is essential to good day care and happy children.

I/We have read and agree to these policies and procedures for the care of my/our child/children.

Parent _____   Date _____

Parent _____   Date _____

Provider _____   Date _____

Now, take a few minutes to fill out this checklist. It will help you see any gaps in your policies and procedures.

"Have I Done This?" Checklist

Have I . . .

____ Made up an enrollment form?

____ Made up a medical consent form?

____ Written up a notice of disclosure for parents? (Only if you are not carrying liability insurance.)

____ Written up my fee and payment schedule, including a late-fee policy?

____ Written up a termination notice to keep in my files for future use?

____ Set and written up my hours of operation and holiday schedule (including vacations)?

____ Written up my meal/food policies?

Chapter Four
Your Daily Schedule

I n planning a daily schedule for your child care, you will need to consider three variables: the age mix of the children, your background and training, and your temperament. We will also discuss devising a daily schedule, including mealtimes, naptime, free play, structured time, special events, and storytime.

Age Mix of the Children

Ages of children can be generally defined as follows: birth through one year = infant; one through two years = toddler; three through five years = preschooler. If you specialize in infants, your daily schedule will differ from that of providers who care for toddlers and preschoolers. Infants take an enormous amount of caregiving time, typically do not interact much with each other, and have limited attention spans. Toddlers are endlessly active, take a great deal of monitoring, have short attention spans, and play more alongside of other children than with them. Toddlers need a lot of intervention from you, since they are not yet capable of sharing. Preschoolers have a good grasp of language, possess an attention span long enough for most activities, adore playing with each other, and need direction more than intervention.

There are well-researched benefits to having children in mixed-age groups:
- Younger children tend to engage in more complex and interactive forms of play.
- A multi-age mix encourages leadership skills and compassion in older children.
- Younger children depend less on adult help or intervention when an older child is nearby.

In addition, family child care is often the best situation for a special-needs child since everyone is already functioning on different levels. Similarly, a very shy older child, or one who functions below age level, can be helped by placement with younger peers.

Since most providers have a mix of ages, this chapter will look at the components of a schedule geared for children ages eighteen months through four years.

Your Background and Training

Perhaps you have just spent two years working as a preschool teacher or have had schooling in early childhood education. If so, then you have a wonderful background with which to begin a toddler and/or preschool curriculum of activities, including art, science, learning games, and more.

Or maybe you're a parent with a well-established routine for feeding and keeping the children occupied—you know it works and you plan to adapt it to child care. Whatever your background, it will influence your choices for how to structure the day.

Your Temperament

All of us have different personalities. Some providers have a strong need for structure. Other providers like to be spontaneous and change activities quickly if the situation seems to warrant it. Children do best with a mixture of both qualities from adults. They need to know what to expect in care and they also need a provider flexible enough to switch gears if an activity is not stimulating or if it gets out of hand. Most providers strike a balance between structure and spontaneity early on.

Devising a Daily Schedule

Your daily schedule will always include mealtimes, naptime, free play, and structured play. Welcoming time and storytime are also commonly included in the day. On the following pages are a few sample daily schedules from experienced providers.

Sample Daily Schedules

Nichols Family Child Care
(Capacity: 6 kids, ages 4–5 years)

Hours of Operation	8:00 A.M. –	5:00 P.M.
Breakfast	8:00 A.M. –	9:00 A.M.
Circle time and welcoming activities	9:00 A.M. –	9:30 A.M.
Preschool project	9:30 A.M. –	10:00 A.M.
Snack time	10:00 A.M. –	10:20 A.M.
Free play	10:20 A.M. –	11:05 A.M.
Outdoor games	11:05 A.M. –	12:00 P.M.
Hand-washing	12:00 P.M. –	12:15 P.M.
Lunch	12:15 P.M. –	1:00 P.M.
Naptime/quiet time	1:00 P.M. –	1:30 P.M.
Storytime	1:30 P.M. –	1:50 P.M.
Structured play	1:50 P.M. –	2:35 P.M.
Afternoon snack	2:35 P.M. –	3:00 P.M.
Free play/outdoor play	3:00 P.M. –	4:00 P.M.
Closing circle time	4:00 P.M. –	4:30 P.M.
Cleanup	4:30 P.M. –	5:00 P.M.

Moore Family Child Care
(Capacity: 12 kids, ages 18 months–6 years)

Hours of Operation	6:00 A.M. –	5:30 P.M.
Arrival/free play	6:00 A.M. –	8:00 A.M.
Breakfast	8:00 A.M. –	8:30 A.M.
Circle time	8:30 A.M. –	9:00 A.M.
Music/math	9:00 A.M. –	9:25 A.M.
Outdoor play	9:25 A.M. –	10:00 A.M.
Morning snack	10:00 A.M. –	10:15 A.M.
Creative art	10:15 A.M. –	10:45 A.M.
Free play	10:45 A.M. –	11:30 A.M.
Language games	11:30 A.M. –	12:00 P.M.
Lunch	12:00 P.M. –	12:30 P.M.
Rest time	12:30 P.M. –	2:30 P.M.
Wake-up/video	2:30 P.M. –	3:15 P.M.
Afternoon snack	3:15 P.M. –	3:30 P.M.
Outdoor play/homework	3:30 P.M. –	4:30 P.M.
Free play/pickup	4:30 P.M. –	5:30 P.M.

```
┌─────────────────────────────────────────────────────────────┐
│                 Bakeman Family Child Care                    │
│              (Capacity: 12 kids, ages 3–5 years)             │
│                                                              │
│    Hours of Operation          7:30 A.M.  –   5:30 P.M.      │
│    Breakfast                   7:30 A.M.  –   8:30 A.M.      │
│    Free play                   8:30 A.M.  –   9:30 A.M.      │
│    Morning snack               9:30 A.M.  –  10:00 A.M.      │
│    Small-muscle play          10:00 A.M.  –  10:30 A.M.      │
│    Preschool activities       10:30 A.M.  –  11:00 A.M.      │
│    Music time                 11:00 A.M.  –  11:30 A.M.      │
│    Lunch                      11:30 A.M.  –  12:00 P.M.      │
│    Free play                  12:00 P.M.  –  12:30 P.M.      │
│    Storytime                  12:30 P.M.  –   1:00 P.M.      │
│    Naptime/quiet time          1:00 P.M.  –   2:00 P.M.      │
│    Outdoor play                2:00 P.M.  –   3:30 P.M.      │
│    Afternoon snack             3:30 P.M.  –   4:00 P.M.      │
│    Creative play               4:00 P.M.  –   4:30 P.M.      │
│    Free play                   4:30 P.M.  –   5:00 P.M.      │
│    Video-watching              5:00 P.M.  –   5:30 P.M.      │
└─────────────────────────────────────────────────────────────┘
```

Mealtimes: An Essential Part of the Day

You'll notice that in each of the sample schedules, providers carefully space food breaks about two to three hours apart. If you let children get hungry, they will get cranky and act out. Regular, predictable mealtimes are essential.

What to Feed the Kids

Your local food-program supplier will give you a plethora of material on suggested foods and menus. Many publish their own cookbooks, which are filled with nutritious, fun, day-care–tested recipes. In addition, there are many books available on child care (including family child care) that have excellent sections on nutrition and suggested recipes. You'll find a list of these resources in the appendix.

Tina, a relatively new provider, has this to say about preparing meals:

My partner and I plan a weekly menu ahead of time. Then we post it for parents to see. We have two children with dietary restrictions, so those parents scrutinize it carefully. Spencer, age four, has PKU and can't have protein. His parents supply his protein substitutes and formula, and we supplement with vegetables and fruit. Amanda, age three, has a milk allergy, so we have to monitor her as well.

I used to pretty much prepare the same kinds of meals each week. Then we bought a cookbook from our food supplier. I spent an hour one day going through it and picking out dishes I could make easily that the kids would like. This has been very successful. The kids like the variety and the fun day-care touches (e.g., peanut butter sandwiches cut out with a heart cookie cutter). And because the cookbook is supplied by the food program, I know the recipes are nutritionally sound.

The food programs can give you up-to-date information on how much kids should eat and from which food groups. It is sometimes surprising to learn how little the portions for young children really are. Familiarize yourself with the recommended amounts of food for children of different ages.

You don't need to prepare elaborate meals for young children. The simpler the meals are to prepare, the better. Children will benefit more from your guidance and presence in their play than they will from having you cook for long periods in the kitchen.

Camille, an experienced provider, talks about simplicity in the kitchen:

I only get a couple kids for breakfast, so I keep it very simple—just oatmeal or another cereal, and fruit and milk. I shop every two weeks and I repeat menus frequently to keep the workload down. My husband drives home by a bakery outlet, so he stops for me once a week to pick up whole-grain bread. It took me a little while to familiarize myself with the food program's guidelines (e.g., no processed cheese, canned soup, SpaghettiOs, frozen pizza) and with the children's tastes (they like milder-tasting things, e.g., albacore tuna), but once I got it all down, I shopped much more quickly. Because the food program covers pretty much all my food expenses, I don't economize heavily.

The following is a short list of tried-and-true, favorite snacks and dishes compiled by family child-care providers. It is by no means complete, but it can give you a bit of a head start when it comes to planning meals or jog you out of the afternoon snack rut of crackers and juice. Sample menus are also included.

Breakfast	*Lunch*	*Snacks*
Cold cereal	Sloppy Joes	Quesadillas (flour tortillas)
Hot cereal with strawberries	Cheese slices	Soft pretzels
Peanut butter toast	Scrambled eggs	Tortilla chips and salsa
Oatmeal	Homemade pizza	Granola bars
Fresh fruit kabobs	Macaroni and cheese	Fruit cocktail
Yogurt	Tuna sandwiches	Dried fruit
Bran muffins	Black beans and rice	Carrot sticks
Hard-boiled eggs with relish	Rice pudding	Celery stuffed with peanut butter
Waffles/pancakes	Grilled cheese sandwiches	Banana bread
	Vegetable soup	Applesauce

On the following pages are sample menus providers use and make available to parents. You'll notice that the sample menu also functions as a record-keeping document for the CACFP (each food supplier has a variation on this form and can supply you with it). The menu also provides information on recommended daily portions of the food groups for young children (also courtesy of the food supplier).

Making Mealtime a Pleasant Experience

Family child care means care in a family setting. This applies to mealtime too. Meals and snacks will be more enjoyable for all concerned if both you and the children sit around a table and make it a group, or "family," experience. One provider takes it a step further:

> I put it in my policy that we will say a short, nondenominational blessing over each meal or snack. I think it helps the kids settle down, appreciate the food, and eat it in a more family-like atmosphere. It also helps emphasize manners.

Sample Menu

Breakfast	Lunch	Snacks
Pancakes Orange juice	Spaghetti (from scratch) Peaches Green beans Milk	Muffin/butter Milk
Eggs Toast Apple juice Milk	Tuna sandwich Carrot sticks Orange slices Milk	Crackers/spread Milk or juice
French toast Pears Milk	Cheese and ham sandwich Celery sticks Apple slices Milk or juice	Banana bread Cream cheese Milk
Waffles Applesauce Milk	Macaroni and cheese Hot dogs (all meat) Fruit salad Milk	Grapes Crackers and cheese Milk or juice
Cereal Banana Muffin Milk	Bean burritos Lettuce and tomato Oranges Milk	Carrot bread Milk or juice
Hot oatmeal Cantaloupe Toast Milk	Omelette Roll/butter Pears Carrots Milk	Raisins Crackers and cheese Milk or juice
English muffins Melted cheese Orange juice Milk	Toasted cheese sandwich Apples Broccoli (cooked) Milk	English muffins Peanut butter Milk or juice

Sample Menu

Date: Record Daily Attendance:			Monday ATT _____
Amount **Ages 1–2**	**Amount** **Age 3–6**		**Food Items**
¼ cup ½ slice ¼ cup ½ cup	½ cup ½ slice ⅓ cup ¾ cup	**Breakfast** Vegetable or fruit or juice Bread/equivalent or cereal Milk	Corn Chex fruit cocktail milk \#
See your food program guide for snack amounts		**A.M. Snack** Choose 1 item from 2 groups: Meat, Bread, Milk, Fruit-Veg	Rice Krispies milk \#
1 oz. ¼ cup Total ½ slice ½ cup	1½ oz. ½ cup Total ½ slice ¾ cup	**Lunch** Meat and/or meat alternative 2 fruits or 2 vegetables or 1 of each Bread/equivalent Milk	tuna sandwich (tuna, whole-wheat bread) broccoli, fruit cocktail, milk \#
See your food program guide for snack amounts		**P.M. Snack** Choose 1 item from 2 groups: Meat, Bread, Milk, Fruit-Veg	cottage cheese fruit cocktail milk \#
1 oz. ¼ cup Total ½ slice ½ cup	1½ oz. ½ cup Total ½ slice ¾ cup	**Dinner** Meat and/or meat alternative 2 fruits or 2 vegetables or 1 of each Bread/equivalent Milk	 \#
See your food program guide for snack amounts		**Evening Snack** Choose 1 item from 2 groups: Meat, Bread, Milk, Fruit-Veg	 \#
Note: Where you see the symbol \#, please enter the number of children claimed at this meal.			

Tuesday ATT _____	Wednesday ATT _____	Thursday ATT _____	Friday ATT _____
Food Items	**Food Items**	**Food Items**	**Food Items**
Cream of Wheat strawberries milk ＃	Rice Chex pears milk ＃	whole-wheat toast with peanut butter and honey ＃	Rice Krispies mandarin oranges milk ＃
rice cakes milk ＃	wheat hearts milk ＃	peanut butter toast milk ＃	soft pretzels milk ＃
Sloppy Joes (Sloppy Joe mix, hamburger, buns, tomato paste) carrots, pears, milk ＃	peanut butter and jelly sand-wiches, green beans, pineapple, slice of cheese, milk ＃	vegetable soup cheese slices saltines, mandarin oranges, milk ＃	scrambled eggs whole-wheat toast cheese, pears, corn, milk ＃
granola bars milk ＃	whole-wheat toast milk ＃	graham crackers raisins ＃	Cheerios milk ＃
  ＃	 ＃	 ＃	 ＃
  ＃	 ＃	 ＃	 ＃

Another provider creates a family atmosphere by having the children help serve the food. Others prefer to set food on the table in serving dishes and allow children to serve themselves, as feasible.

Tips for Mealtime

Many children are fussy eaters. In general, providers agree that it's best not to cater to a picky eater. Don't go looking for a substitute food if a child says he hates peanut butter and won't eat his sandwich. Don't worry; he'll eat at the next meal or snack and, after a while, will learn to like different foods.

Children accept new foods more easily if they look appetizing and are presented in small portions. Again, be patient with children's tastes.

Never force a child to eat something or punish him or her for not cleaning the plate. Try not to withhold a treat or dessert for any reason. Some educators believe using food this way gives it an exaggerated importance.

When it comes to cleanup, one provider has this tip:

> In the interests of reducing work and preventing accidents, I use "sippy" cups (a child-size plastic cup with a snap-on lid and a drinking spout—you can get them from Tupperware) for all the children, no matter what age. The cup is labeled with the child's name, and she uses it all day long.

Mealtime becomes even more fun when children are allowed to help prepare some of the dishes. In chapter 5 we'll look at cooking with children.

Naptime

As a general guideline, all children up to age five either take a nap or "rest" during the day. Obviously, infants nap more frequently and for more of the day. Children vary widely in how well they go down for a nap, how well they sleep (if at all), and how long they sleep.

You will do well to manage these differences by insisting that everyone nap or rest at the same time, every day. There are some children who just won't go to sleep or who wake early. Most providers handle this by telling them they can "just rest their bones" but they must stay on their mats or beds and not talk or play. Other providers care for older children who have given up rest time for good; these children are commonly allowed to stay up and do "quiet-time" activities, like looking at books, while the other children sleep.

Sleep habits in child care are generally influenced strongly by the child's sleep habits at home. If a child is accustomed to waking frequently and crying for Mom, having three glasses of water before bed, or having a parent lie down with him or her, then there will be a period of adjustment—and probably resistance—before the child settles down to your routine.

Having a routine and sticking to it will make naptime refreshing for everyone. Parents will also appreciate picking up a child who is not cranky and overtired at the end of the day.

Free Play

You'll enjoy devising your own mixture of free, or independent, play opportunities. Be sure to include indoor play as well as outdoor play and all the toys that go with them.

Playing Outside and Inside

Brenda, an experienced provider with a large license, talks about what her kids like best:

> For some reason I've always had a lot of boys in care. So I schedule as much free outdoor play as possible. When they are playing outdoors, the children's favorite things to play with are the swings and sandbox. I encourage sandbox play and give them water, scooping utensils, and buckets. They do tend to track in sand, but the learning they get out of it is worth it. I found they lost interest quickly in the expensive ride-on toys I bought. If I had to do it over again, I would have built a bigger sandbox and skipped the Big Wheels.

Outdoor play is doubly useful in that the exercise tires the children before nap/quiet time, they sleep better, and they tend to get along with others better.

Indoor play is no less enjoyable for children. Jan, a newer provider with a small license, lives in a state where the weather is often rainy.

> Because of the weather, we have to stay inside much of the year. My kids' favorite free-play areas are the construction toy area (I have a big Duplo

train they can take apart and put back together) and the doll corner. They also love the book nook, where they can curl up with a favorite book on big pillows.

Tina, another fairly new provider, tells about how she facilitates smooth play during free-play time:

> I make it a rule that no more than three or four kids can play in any one play area at a time. It cuts down on sharing problems and space issues. The kids really do respect the rule.

Toys

Because young children learn through play, toys are natural learning tools. Providers are wise to select toys carefully for high interest and long-term use.

Children do tire of the same toys after a while. One way to deal with this is to rotate the toys available. Bring out the construction toys for a few days, then put those away and bring out the dress-up clothes, followed by a dollhouse, and so on. Watch to see when the children's interest flags and then make the change for the next day. You'll get a feel for how long each toy entertains.

Camille, an experienced provider, offers these tips:

> First, don't use toy boxes. When the toys are all in a jumble, kids are not attracted to them. If they are organized neatly on low shelves, children are much more likely to play with them.
>
> Second, change your main room around every so often. For whatever reason, finding the block area in a different corner of the room makes block play fresh and alluring. An added bonus is that it evens out the wear and tear on your carpet.

Parents often complain that their young children vastly prefer to play with pots and pans in the kitchen, or with big empty boxes, rather than with the beautiful new toys eagerly purchased for them. You can avoid this problem to a certain extent by tuning into children's interests, being aware of their developmental capabilities, and educating yourself on the purpose of play before you buy the toys.

Here are a few criteria to keep in mind as you go about selecting toys for children:

- Make sure the toy is safe for the age you intend it for. Infants should not play with toys that have small pieces or parts that can be swallowed, or with toys that have long strings that could get wrapped around their necks. Toys with sharp edges, that have lead paint on them, or that contain hidden wires are all hazardous to young children. Most toys have a recommended age range printed on the package.
- A toy needs to be challenging to the child without frustrating him or her. For instance, a toddler isn't developmentally ready for a puzzle of more than two or three pieces.
- Try to have a good selection of open-ended toys for children—that is, toys that can be used for more than one type of play. For example, paint, blocks, or dolls can be played with in many ways; a coloring book, though, has one use and one use only. When the toy is open-ended, you give children permission to stretch their imaginations in play.
- Toys should match the children's current interests. Many preschoolers are passionately interested in dinosaurs. One provider purchased a set of small, sturdy plastic dinosaurs and then gave the children a box of items to create an environment for the dinosaurs. The children made roads and houses out of Lincoln Logs, trees and caves from Play-Doh, and then brought out some small Flintstones characters to play with the dinosaurs. The plastic dinosaurs matched their current interest, and obviously the children were quite capable of extending the play.
- The toys you choose need to be well made and hold long-term interest for the children. Open-ended toys—for example, blocks—tend to be best for this.
- Be sensitive to sex-role stereotyping and racial bias in toys. Not every traditional "girl toy" needs to be pink, pretty, and passive. And not every traditional "boy toy" needs to be army green and destructive. You want the children to play with the opposite sex as well as with same-sex friends and you want them to engage in both nurturing play and action play. A good selection of nonstereotyped toys will encourage this. In addition, scrutinize your doll collection and play figures carefully; are they all blond and Caucasian? Children need to see a variety of ethnic backgrounds, even if you service only one type of family.

Toys for Babies

Many toys for babies are created to appeal more to the parents who buy them than to the children who play with them. Babies are far likelier to prefer common household items, which make terrific toys.

Here is a list of items you probably already have on hand, all of which are perfect for babies to play with:

Tennis balls

Shoeboxes

Nesting measuring spoons and cups

Cardboard tubes (paper towel or toilet paper)

Pie tins

Colored sponges

Wooden and plastic spoons

Old purses

Pots and pans with covers

Bells (big enough not to be swallowed)

Drawers or cupboard doors to open and close

And here are some simple toys you can purchase:

Blocks (wooden or soft)

Stuffed animals

Color cone (graduated rings on a post)

Music box

Plastic shapes (circle, square, triangle) that can be dropped into a
    box with same-shape holes

Pail and shovel

Dolls

Jack-in-the-box

Toys for Toddlers

Toddlers are very busy, have short attention spans, and touch everything. They are attracted to many things but don't stay with them for very long.

As with babies, toys don't need to be elaborate or expensive; many popular toddler toys are simple, household items. Toddlers like fairly realistic toys—a vehicle that looks like a bus or a doll that looks like a baby.

Here are some playthings you may already have on hand:

Sand

Water and cups for filling and dumping

Rocks (medium-size) to put into containers and dump out

Empty bandage boxes

Old telephone

Safe kitchen utensils and bowls

Dress-up clothes

Plastic dishes

A big cardboard box

Soap bubbles and wands

And here are some toddler-tested toys you may wish to purchase:

Blocks

Dolls

Puzzles with big pieces

Stuffed animals

Stacking toys

Cars/trains/trucks/buses/airplanes

Duplos (toddler-size construction blocks)

Rubber or soft balls

Housekeeping toys (stove, sink, etc.)

Screw toys

Toys for Preschoolers

Now some serious imagination begins to show itself. Whereas a toddler will play with an airplane by making it fly with some accompanying engine sounds, a preschooler will turn a jumbo crayon into a jet and explain that it has no propeller. Dramatization is also coming on strong, and many preschoolers use toys as props in their dramatic play.

Preschoolers' fine motor skills have increased so that they are much more capable of manipulating smaller objects and construction toys. But they still love playing with big toys. Their play becomes much more cooperative; they are now interested in other children's ideas and suggestions for play rather than protecting a toy from them. They become more interested in how different toys can fit or work together; thus, construction toys and Lincoln Logs are now popular.

Karen shares how she observed this combining behavior in two of her four-year-olds:

> Tyler and Alexa were playing with miniature cars. First they built a track
> for the cars out of flat blocks, and then they hitched up a little toy wagon
> from another set of toys to one car. "It's a trailer!" they told me.

You'll notice that many preschoolers spend more time talking about playing, deciding what to play, and directing who does what than actually playing.

Here are a few items preschoolers like to play with that you might have around the house:

Large appliance boxes (be sure to remove all staples)

Flashlights

Soap bubbles and wands

Baskets

Boards for balancing on

Unopened, discarded junk mail

Dress-up clothes (including pieces of fabric for capes and veils)

Costume jewelry

Sandbox

Suitcases

Empty food containers (oatmeal boxes, milk cartons, etc.)

Blankets, pillows

Here are some toys for preschoolers you might like to purchase:

Rocking horse

Blocks

Dolls and doll clothing

Musical instruments

Puzzles

Wagon

Housekeeping toys

Toy animals

Puppets

Construction toys (Legos, Tinkertoys, Lincoln Logs, etc.)

Dollhouses

Small figures (e.g., families: Mom, Dad, boy and girl children)

Beginning board games (e.g., Candyland, Chutes & Ladders)

A Word about War Toys

Many parents and child-care providers are concerned today over the issue of buying children war toys (guns, tanks, GI Joes) and allowing war play at home or in child care. Symbols of power or strength are very attractive to young children; they will beg for commercial war toys or, if denied them, will make sticks or fingers into weapons and play anyway.

Many children also enjoy playing "superheroes." Again, this stems from wanting to feel powerful. The play, however, often incorporates more constructive themes (rescuing those in distress) than typical war play, which always includes shooting or killing. Most providers allow superhero play but place limits on it (e.g., no weapons).

Some providers ban war toys and war play altogether. Early childhood educator and therapist Susanne Wichert makes this compelling case for disallowing war toys:

- Watching others be aggressive (in cartoons or in books) models aggressive behavior. Children act out what they see.
- Toys that glamorize violence diminish a child's sense of security in the long run. It

is irresponsible to give children a view of death that is temporary when the likelihood that death will touch their lives is great.

- When children engage in war play, they tend to become very excited and escalate out of control. This usually results in hurt or angry children.
- Commercial war toys encourage children to limit their play content to the "script" provided by the toy manufacturer.
- If children are treated with respect and feel comfortable about their rate of growth, they have less need to escape into characters who rule others.*

If you do ban war play, it is critical that you provide ample alternative adventure play for the children. You must intervene when violent play emerges and direct the children to other, more appropriate action play.

Find stories with strong adventure themes. *Where the Wild Things Are* by Maurice Sendak is a good, adventurous, nonviolent story. For younger children, Helen Oxenbury's version of *We're Going on a Bear Hunt* is also a good choice. Children will act out these themes and stories in their play.

Other providers choose to allow some war play but impose strict limits. Betsy, a long-time provider, describes her policy:

> We have a few hard-and-fast rules. (1) No commercial war toys (those bought at toy stores) are allowed here. If children choose to make a sword out of a stick, or use their crackers as "bombs," we do allow that, since it engages their imagination in dramatic play. (2) Absolutely no pointing "guns" or other weapons at people or animals. They can "shoot" at targets or other inanimate objects.

Watch for appropriate dramatic play. Sometimes war play degenerates into just one action (shooting) and the children get into an unending loop of pretend violence. One provider shares how she was able to redirect some inappropriate play:

---

* From *Keeping the Peace: Practicing Cooperation and Conflict Resolution with Preschoolers* by Susanne Wichert (Philadelphia: New Society Publishers, 1989). Now out of print, but check your library for a copy.

Three preschoolers were playing cowboys and bandits. Two children were the cowboys, and they insisted the third be the bandit. Jason, the bandit, got tired of being shot all the time and wanted to be a cowboy. The other two refused to switch, and the situation went downhill from there. I intervened, suggesting that they all be cowboys and go on a dangerous mission. "Now what could the dangerous mission be?" I mused. "We could find a wild beast," offered Mason. "Great," I said, "what will the beast be doing?" "He's got some kids!" announced Jason excitedly. "Yeah, and we have to save them," contributed Eric. All three boys went racing off to enact this scenario.

If you do allow war play, make sure the materials you provide encourage children to expand this play and use their imaginations. More learning results from open-ended dramatic play than it does from manipulating a toy that just does one thing (e.g., shoots a missile or fires a dart or "bullet").

Structured Time

Structured time means you choose the activity or play for the children, plan it, and direct it. Examples of structured time include welcoming time, circle time, curriculum themes and activities, TV time, and special events such as holidays, birthdays, and field trips.

Circle Time and Welcoming Time

Circle time is a classic child-care activity that can be personalized to fit a curriculum theme for the month, used as a welcoming ritual, or adapted to teach specific skills. Children and provider sit in a circle (usually on mats or carpet squares) for different group activities. You can tell stories, sing songs, have sharing time, and more. Welcoming time uses the circle format to formally welcome and recognize each child. For the children, welcoming time is esteem-building, consistent, and a nice way to start off the day's activities. Here's how various providers use circle time and welcoming time.

Karen uses a little song as a welcoming ritual and a self-esteem builder:

Where's Jason? Where, where?
Where's Jason? Where, where?
Where's Jason? Where, where?
There's Jason, there, there. (Whisper this line)
Is he up on the mountain? No, no.
Is he down by the fountain? No, no.
Has he gone out to play? No, no.
I see Jason is here today!
One, two, three! (Child stands up)

Camille shares her use of circle time:

We generally use circle time as a lead-in to the curriculum activity. One feature is always the same. We start out by acknowledging all the children present with our spelling song:

Caitlyn, Caitlyn, is here today,
She's so special in every way.
Now we'll play the spelling game,
By spelling the letters of her name,
C-A-I-T-L-Y-N!

When we spell, I point each letter out on a name placard I have on the wall. It helps them begin to learn about the alphabet.

Tina uses circle time more casually, tuning into the children's moods and interests that day:

Sometimes we do a lot of knock-knock jokes (the three- and four-year-olds love them), sing songs, read books, or have sharing time.

Activity Time

Some providers have a very structured activity time organized into a preschool curriculum and based on a theme. Camille, mentioned earlier, follows the theme schedule, which follows on the next page, every year.

It is often useful to plan out the year this way, because you can repeat the program and reuse the materials year after year, thereby dramatically reducing your preparation time. Camille laminates the materials for the wall with either clear contact or self-laminating paper; the materials adhere to the wall with Fun Tac, a putty that will stick to the wall without damaging the paint.

Felt boards are also a good option for a thematic curriculum. You can buy them in "story sets" (e.g., all the pieces you need to tell the story of the Three Little Pigs) or in curriculum sets (numbers, letters, farm animals, etc.). Children enjoy watching each piece go up on the board as you teach or tell a story. You can reuse the felt pieces year after year. Use Velcro on the backing to help them stick to the board. Camille talks about how the children respond to the felt board:

> The children love the felt-board stories even more than TV, if you can believe that. It takes them one or two stories at the beginning of the year to get used to it, but after that, it's clear sailing.

Many providers plan their activities loosely around the seasons. Laurel, for instance, plans art projects according to what holiday is approaching:

> In the fall we carve pumpkins and make Pilgrim hats. When Christmas nears, we make ornaments for the tree out of shells (children glue in a picture of themselves and sprinkle glitter on it). In the spring we make Easter baskets and color eggs. And then for Mother's Day and Father's Day, we make decorative soaps for the moms and rock turtles for the dads. For each season, we sing songs about that holiday and decorate the room.

Karen, a provider for special-needs children, plans a theme for each month as she goes along:

Sample Seasonal Project Plan

September:	Bugs, insects; "all-about-me" name-tag tree (wall display)
October:	Fall, Halloween; hang pumpkins on the name tree
November:	Farm animals; big leaves on the name tree; field trip to the zoo
December:	Holidays (Dutch Santa Claus—make wooden shoes; Swedish Santa Lucia—make wreaths with paper candles; Hanukkah—play dreidel)
January:	Transportation, occupations; wall displays with children's names
February:	Winter
March:	Dinosaurs
April:	Wild animals, Noah's Ark display on wall
May:	Ocean, water; field trip to aquarium
Summer months:	No set curriculum; outdoor play

I get ideas for the curriculum from activity books, and then I plan activities based on the theme. This month we're learning about sand and the desert. I put up a big cactus cutout on the board, with prickly-pear blooms with each child's name on it. I read different children's books about the desert and what lives there. The hands-on activities are generally cooperative and involve sand.

On the next page is one provider's mix of activities for the week. She has three activity times built into her daily schedule.

You don't have to be as structured as this provider, but having a plan and a schedule is helpful. Feel free to make up plans and change directions, if need be. If the children don't enjoy a game, play something else. If it's raining outside, try another idea.

Chapter 5 offers a wide variety of child-tested activity ideas based on the traditional curriculum areas of language, science, learning games, movement, cooking, music, art, and safety.

Sample Weekly Activity Plan

	Monday	Tuesday	Wednesday	Thursday	Friday
1. Activity Music/math	**Monday** Singing with guitar	**Tuesday** Counting games	**Wednesday** Musical chairs with classical music	**Thursday** Sorting beads	**Friday** Make a band and parade with homemade instruments
2. Activity Messy art	**Monday** Play with Play-Doh	**Tuesday** "Paint" the fence with water and large paint brushes	**Wednesday** Finger painting	**Thursday** Make home-made putty	**Friday** Collages with nature materials
3. Activity Movement games	**Monday** Dance with scarves to music	**Tuesday** Caterpillar game (described in chapter 5)	**Wednesday** Obstacle course outside	**Thursday** Play "Red Light, Green Light"	**Friday** Play tag outside

Your Daily Schedule

TV Time: Should You Allow It?

The debate over whether television-viewing is ultimately a positive or negative experience for young children is about as passionate as the debate over war toys. Research has found that:

- TV is an excellent teacher of action and dynamic processes (such as how a plant grows) but is less effective at conveying feelings and thoughts.
- TV can teach letters, numbers, concepts, and prereading skills.
- TV promotes aggression. Children's programs are typically more violent than adult programs. Weekend morning cartoons depict twenty to twenty-five violent acts per hour. Children model the aggression they see on TV.
- Heavy TV-viewing interferes with educational achievement. Studies show that elementary school-age children who watch a lot of television do worse in school than their counterparts who watch less television. Preschool children who are heavy viewers engage in less imaginative play.
- TV learning is passive, and it is known that children learn best from interaction.
- TV perpetuates stereotypes. Males outnumber females on TV three to one and are pictured in active, independent, problem-solving roles. Females are predominantly portrayed as deferential and passive, and more than 80 percent are portrayed as homemakers (as opposed to the real-life statistic of well over 50 percent of adult women in the workplace).

The evidence here is pretty clear: Heavy and/or indiscriminate viewing is harmful to children. For this reason, many providers do not allow TV-viewing.

Other providers take a more middle-of-the-road approach and allow selected, approved viewing. Laura describes her policy:

> We have a rainy-day policy with regard to TV. If we can't play outdoors in the afternoon, children have a choice of watching *Mr. Rogers' Neighborhood* or engaging in free play. I will occasionally allow *Sesame Street*, but I don't like them to watch more than one show a day.

An alternative to TV is to offer the children a choice of videos. There are many good videos on the market. Deborah, a provider with a large license, talks about how she handles videos:

> We watch one video a week. I like to let the children bring in their favorite. The videos we've watched in the past few months were mostly Disney. The only problem I run into is every child wanting to bring in the same movie. I solve this by talking with the parent ahead of time and thereby avoiding 500 screenings of *The Incredibles*.

Be cautious with how much TV you allow children to watch. Once you form your policy on it, stick to it.

Special Events

Experienced providers find it wise to structure special routines or set rules for handling holidays, birthdays, and field trips. Here are a few tips.

Holidays

Children love holidays and the special celebrations that come with them. But unless you're providing care for all your friends from church, it's best to keep holiday celebrations fairly secular or make an attempt to note most of the major religious holidays.

Camille chooses to celebrate the Christmas season by incorporating Dutch and Swedish "Santa" traditions into the activities; she also teaches the children to play the Hanukkah game of dreidel. For Easter, Tina focuses on the bunny part of the holiday instead of the religious story.

This is not to say that you absolutely cannot include Bible stories or prayer in your child care. But you should be very sensitive to the ethnic and religious traditions of the families you service and structure your holiday celebrations accordingly.

Brenda shares her thoughts on this:

I try to celebrate the holidays that the children observe at home. I have three children who are Mormon, so I always do something for their "Pioneer Day" on July 24. Last time we dressed up as pioneers and pretended to have a wagon train.

This past fall I had a few moms who were very uncomfortable with Halloween. So instead of making jack-o'-lanterns, we had a barn party. I decorated the playroom with hay and a scarecrow, and all the children came in animal or farm costumes. They loved it.

Another provider recommends downplaying major religious holidays, like Christmas or Passover, and playing up the secular ones, like George Washington's Birthday.

We do lots of reading about and looking forward to Presidents' Day. We read beginning biographies about Washington and Lincoln and talk about who the president is now. Then we make George Washington hats (like the one he wore in the painting crossing the Delaware) out of newspaper and Lincoln top hats out of construction paper. We make cherry tarts for a snack. We all have great fun in February.

Birthdays

Young children's birthdays are probably the most exciting day of the year to them. It is very easy, however, for children to become overexcited and overstimulated. Providers find that setting consistent rules on how birthdays are handled helps eliminate any problems. Here are some suggestions.

From Tina:

I ask the parent to bring a low-sugar treat for all the children. Usually it's pink Rice Krispies treats or applesauce cupcakes. We sing "Happy Birthday" before we eat the treats.

Camille's birthday routine is more structured and rigid, due to problems she's had:

I was very bothered by the unequal treatment the children received when the treats and favors were left up to the parents. Some parents would go all out—even do too much—and others would practically ignore their child's birthday. So, to even things out, I established my own birthday routine.

I made a special, reusable paper crown that the birthday child gets to wear at mealtimes. The other children wear reusable party hats. After lunch, instead of a cake (many children don't like cake and I find cupcakes too messy) I make a small pyramid out of frozen ice cream sandwiches, cut in half. I put a few candles on top. Sometimes I give them noisemakers (I get them in bulk) to play with or we play a no-lose version of musical chairs (where there are chairs enough for everybody).

When the child leaves that day, I give him a special, small present from me. He's not allowed to open it until he gets home.

Remember, if there are favors or treats, there should be one for everyone. Children three and younger are not really ready for structured games, while fours and fives do better with party games. You can set whatever birthday routines and rules work best for you.

Field Trips

Getting out of the house occasionally and exploring the world are good for you and the children. There is virtually no end to places that young children will find fascinating. Some common field trip destinations are:

- The zoo
- An indoor children's gym
- A children's museum/science center
- A park or nature preserve with trails for hiking
- An airport
- An aquarium
- A fire station
- Your public library (they often have special storytimes and events)

Karen tells about the time she and her assistants took five four-year-olds to an indoor children's gymnasium:

> I care mostly for children from low-income families. They had never been to such a place. After a few minutes of wide-eyed wonder, they plunged in, sliding, jumping, and climbing on the equipment. They talked about it for days.

Always inform parents ahead of time of an upcoming field trip and get permission to take each child. The logistics of finding additional adult escorts and adequate transportation is usually the hardest part of a field trip. There should be, however, a willing volunteer or two from your group of parents to help out. If there is an entrance fee, you can ask the parents to be responsible for the cost of their child's fee. Give one to two weeks' notice.

In a public place, try to have one adult for every three children. Talk to the children ahead of time about where you are going and what kind of behavior you expect from them. The buddy system, whereby you assign two children to each other and direct them to hold hands at all times, often works well.

Be creative in the places you take the children. Perhaps you have a friend with a pottery wheel in her garage who is willing to demonstrate for the children. Or maybe the neighbor across the street who works at a bakery would arrange for a tour.

Jan, a provider with a small license and a small budget, shares her novel idea for a field trip:

> I live in the area of Seattle called Fremont. There is a huge bridge nearby. At the top of the hill, underneath the northern corner of the bridge, some local artisans have created an enormous troll. Its eye is a headlight from a car, and it is clutching a real Volkswagen bug.
>
> First, we read stories about trolls (*The Three Billy Goats Gruff,* and *The Trouble with Trolls* by Jan Brett). Then I took the children to see the Fremont Troll one day; it was just a short walk from my house. Now it is their favorite field trip destination.

Try also to bring in interesting people occasionally who can talk about their jobs with the children. Some possibilities are:

- A pilot
- An author
- An artist
- A police officer

The list could go on and on. Take care to show women and men in a variety of roles—both traditional and nontraditional. One provider had a teenage friend who played football come in and talk to the children. The hook? The teenager was a girl.

Storytime

Make storytime a regular part of your day. It's just as important as block play or outdoor play. Few things bring adults and children more fun and intimacy than reading a favorite story together.

There are literally thousands of books published each year for young children. Selecting and buying them can be one of the more fun tasks for your business, and one of the most important. How can you choose well?

The appendix lists some top picks for individual children's books as well as some suggested mail-order catalogs that sell books for children and adults. A low-budget way to increase your personal library of children's books is to buy from your school-age child's Scholastic Book Club order (most elementary schools and preschools send order forms home every two months or so). These are special "book club" editions of children's books and are priced much lower than the trade or library editions. Some providers will take advantage of special sales and buy twelve copies of a title at $1.00 apiece; they save these books to wrap up for the children as birthday or Christmas gifts. What follows are some points to keep in mind when selecting and reading books to young children.

Internet Tips

Online resources to help those who read aloud to children:

- Reading Is Fundamental, Inc., www.rif.org/parents
- International Reading Association, www.reading.org
- Parents Choice Foundation, www.parents-choice.org
- American Library Association, www.ala.org/yalsa/booklists

Children get myriad benefits from being read to. A few of them are:

- Learning new ideas and words
- A fun chance to sit together as a group or to sit on a lap with one adult and be cuddled
- Practice at sorting out what is real and what is pretend
- A way to identify with and sort out feelings
- Stimulating imagination
- A chance to participate in a story

In addition, curriculum activities can include stories or even be structured around them. For example, Sherry, a relatively new provider, shares how she uses books in her curriculum:

> We're doing a unit on "Other Lands." I started with France and have read a variety of books that are set in Paris to the children: *The Cows Are Going to Paris* by David Kirby and Allen Woodman; *Flight* (the story of Charles Lindbergh's historic flight to Paris) by Robert Burleigh; *Madeline* by Ludwig Bemelmans; and *Minou* by Mindy Bingham. Some of the books are too text-heavy for the three-year-olds, so I just abbreviate the story as I go along, focusing mostly on the illustrations. It works well. The children are so excited now if they spot a poster of the Eiffel Tower or see it on TV.

There are many ways you can help children learn to love books (which often translates later into a love of reading) and increase their appreciation of how powerful books can be in their lives. The following is a list of general tips for reading to children and some specific information on reading to children at various ages.

- Always read a book yourself first, before reading it to the children. Be on the lookout for stories that show children as competent problem-solvers. Stories that show adults always solving the conflict for children are poor models.
- Willingly read old favorites over and over to children; avoid an endless stream of new books. Familiarity with a certain story will help children incorporate aspects of it into their dramatic play.

- Take the children to a library or bookstore regularly. Let the children see the "source" of books and the wide variety of them available.
- When children ask a question you don't know the answer to, such as "How many miles is it to Paris?" let them help you look up the answer. This will show them that answers can be found in books.
- Provide a wide variety of books (fiction and nonfiction) for free play in a cozy spot. Encourage children to use the book corner. Although most children can't read text yet, they can look at the pictures. If the corner goes unused for a while, change the books and go there yourself to read one of them. If children see you reading, they will want to do so too (a bean bag chair can made the corner more alluring).
- Select books that are not racially or gender biased, and remember that children need to see themselves in stories. Balance your collection of books. A little girl will not identify with an unending parade of boy characters in trucks; nor will a Hispanic child identify with books that show only Caucasian families. Even if you care for just one ethnic group, children live in a richly varied world; it's good for them to see the differences.
- Also be aware of sexist language lurking in the text. "Policeman" really should be "police officer." Words, however, are more easily altered by you than pictures are. Be on the lookout and do your own editing as you read stories.

Pointed Questions

When reading with a baby or toddler, point to objects in the illustration and ask, "What's that?" If the baby isn't verbal yet, you can ask, "Where's the [object]?" See if he or she will point to it.

Books for Babies

Very young babies like looking at pictures of faces, familiar objects (bottles, shoes, hats, spoons), and other babies. They tend to be more attracted to color photographs than to drawings, though as they grow older, they will like both.

Find sturdy board books, cloth books, or plastic books that babies can chew on and not destroy. It's OK to chew on a book when you're a baby—it's just another way to explore what a book is and what it does. (Books for babies are made of nontoxic materials. Be sure to wipe them off as the book gets passed around.)

Reading to a baby should last only as long as his interest does. If his attention span is no longer than forty-five seconds, go on to some other activity. As babies near their first birthday, they will begin to choose to play with books, and by about age fifteen months, they will be helping you turn pages.

Don't be intimidated by books without words. Look at the pictures with the baby, name the objects or action, and see if the child can point to what you name. A sample "dialogue" might go like this: "Look at that. The daddy is feeding the baby. They look cozy, don't they? Let's turn the page. Where's the baby? That's right! There she is." Wordless books are also good choices for preschoolers to "read" with babies. Many four- and five-year-olds enjoy sharing books with their young friends.

Older babies are attracted to simple text with rhymes or a strong rhythm and colorful, familiar illustrations.

Reading with Toddlers

On-the-move toddlers will often settle down surprisingly well for a story. They love reading the same book over and over again, for as long as you have patience. Simple text (not too many words on a page) holds their attention best, and like older babies, they respond eagerly to rhythm, rhyme, and repetition. Nursery rhymes are very popular with this age group. Toddlers also like books about what is familiar in their own lives: going to bed, playing, eating, getting dressed, and so on.

You can still abbreviate text with this age group (although by the time children are age two and a half, you may get strong protests if you skip even a word). One provider talks about how she shortened a book for toddlers:

> My toddlers love *Max's Dragon Shirt* by Rosemary Wells. The text is too long for them to sit through, so we just turn the pages, looking for the dragon shirt in each picture. "Is it there?" I ask at each page. They respond eagerly, looking forward to the pictures that show the dragon shirt. I also ask them, "How does Max feel?" when the illustration is particularly expressive. They love to see him feeling happy and covered with ice cream at the end of the story.

Reading with Preschoolers

Books continue to be of major interest to preschoolers, and happily, their attention span has increased. Books that show aspects of their everyday lives remain popular, but preschoolers are also interested in all sorts of themes and settings they haven't encountered before. They still like to have books read over and over again and become very upset if you skip anything; many children will memorize the text and recite it or "read" it to themselves later.

Many children develop favorite authors. Andrea shares a story about Dr. Seuss:

> I've got some hard-core Dr. Seuss addicts in my care. They know by the look of the book if it's a Dr. Seuss, but they still ask me to make sure it's written by him. I even get questions about where he lives and what kind of doctor he is.

Preschoolers are receptive to all kinds of books—not just storybooks. Try out children's nonfiction: Read books about bugs, trains, or whatever their interests may be. Don't forget beginning biographies ("This book is about a real person") or life-skills books (e.g., personal safety).

A Word about Teaching Young Children to Read

Many providers report parents trying to teach their toddlers and preschoolers to read, or pushing for the provider to do so or support their efforts.

But before they learn to read themselves, children need a solid base of prereading language experiences. Being read to is high on the list. It is more important that preschoolers have active experience playing and interacting with the world and then be given the opportunity to talk about it than to have formal reading training.

Discourage parents who want their toddlers or preschoolers to learn to read. It is not appropriate for this age. Occasionally, an exceptional or gifted four- or five-year-old may develop reading skills. You can encourage and foster these skills in cooperation with the child's parents.

Chapter Five

Fun Activities for Children

The activities you do with children are often among the most rewarding aspects of providing family child care. It is gratifying to watch young children become absorbed in the many learning experiences you can provide. Remember, activities done with infants should have your constant and careful supervision, especially when the older children are assisting.

A good mix of activities includes indoor and outdoor play as well as active and quiet play. When planning activities, allow for both provider-initiated play (organized projects and games) and child-initiated activities (free play). Activities should involve a mix of fine motor skills (drawing, using scissors, playing with puzzles) and gross motor skills (running, jumping, climbing) and should also provide frequent opportunities for process-oriented creative play (art, water and sand play, music).

Providers need to be aware of the children's developmental levels and estimate how much time is appropriate for each planned activity. No child should be forced to participate, but neither should he or she be allowed to wander aimlessly; give the child a choice of what he or she could do while the others participate in the activity.

As you get to know your particular mix of children and become familiar with their levels of development and interests, certain activities will hit you as "right." Some work better with a small group of children, and some are geared to large groups. Trust your instincts as you select activities, and feel free to adapt them to your group's needs.

Language Activities

Babies have an innate capacity for language. They learn through the "conversations" and games the adults in their lives share with them. Most of us naturally make language interesting for babies; we vary the pitch in our voices, use accompanying dramatic facial expressions, repeat words, ask questions, and react enthusiastically when the baby responds. Babies understand far more than they can express (this is generally true of children of all ages) and benefit from the talking and playing you do with them. Language activities for babies are generally simple and fun for both of you. Crying and cooing are the first sounds babies make. As they grow, they begin to babble (also called "jargoning") and then first words begin to appear.

Enormous leaps in language development occur in the toddler and preschool years. During the second year of life, toddlers will make a two-word sentence, give their first and last names, and begin to use plurals. Toddlers' language tends to focus on the here and now, and sentences are rarely longer than two or three words. They describe things ("Big truck!"), make requests ("Milk, now!"), and use language to accompany their play (make engine noises as they push a toy train across the floor).

From here on, language development snowballs. Preschoolers comprehend prepositions, talk about the past ("When I was a little baby . . .") and the future ("My daddy's takin' me to Disneyland in August") as well as the present. They remember and proudly repeat information imparted by adults ("That's a '57 Chevy") and they eagerly listen to and discuss stories and mimic reading.

There is no end to the amount of enriching language experiences you can provide for the children. Activities can range from simply having a group conversation or reading a story to more complicated projects, like making their own books. Here are a few ideas.

Good Books

Two books that provide some excellent activity ideas based on familiar story and picture books:

- *Story Stretchers: Activities to Expand Children's Favorite Books* by Shirley Raines, 1989, Gryphon House

- *Story Stretchers for Infants, Toddlers, and Twos* by Shirley Raines et al., 2002, Gryphon House

Language Activities for Babies

- Babies like to hear you, as well as the other children, talk, sing, or hum. They tend to react to higher-pitched voices more readily—hence their interest in women's and children's speech. Get into the habit of talking to the babies in your care about what you are doing. The sound of your voice will comfort them. As they get older, they will understand more and more of what you are saying. The older children will see and hear you interact this way with the babies and will mimic you.

- You can also sing or hum to the baby. Some well-known songs you might like to try include: "Twinkle, Twinkle, Little Star," "Hush, Little Baby, Don't You Cry," "Rock-a-Bye Baby," "Itsy Bitsy Spider," "I'm a Little Teapot," "This Old Man," and "Three Little Monkeys." Many of these have accompanying finger motions the babies will enjoy.

- The nonsense words in nursery rhymes are fun for babies, and the rhymes and rhythms will help them learn to listen. Babies like to hear these chants and rhymes over and over again. It's often fun for the older children to join in as well. Try "Pease Porridge Hot," "Eeeney, Meeney, Miney, Mo," "Hey, Diddle Diddle," "Hickory, Dickory Dock," "This Little Piggy Went to Market," and "Here's the Church." See the appendix for sources of nursery rhymes and finger plays.

- Even very young babies love books. If they learn that books mean fun time with you and the children, they will look forward to storytime. It will help them learn to listen for rhythm and rhyme, and they will like looking at the pictures.

- Choose sturdy board books or cloth books. For suggested titles, see the appendix. Preschoolers will enjoy "reading" wordless picture books to the babies. For a more complete discussion of reading to babies, see chapter 4.

Language Activities for Toddlers

- Save the lids that come on cans of frozen juices. Wash and dry them. Sit down with the toddlers and have them choose pictures of people from old magazines. Later, on your own, cut and glue these pictures to one side of the juice lids. (This activity is even more fun if you glue snapshots of the children to the lids.)

Then, with the children, put the lids face down on the floor. Take turns picking them up. When a child picks one up, say, "That's the mommy," "That's the baby," or "That's the daddy." Ask the child to point to the eyes, ears, nose, and so on, of each face. Soon the children will be telling you which person they've picked up and will name the features.

- Toddlers also love books. Suggestions for good ones to read to them can be found in the appendix. It is also fun for toddlers to make their own books. Look through old magazines, and ask the children to select pictures. Cut them out, and then have the children mount the pictures on thin cardboard. Punch the pages with a hole-punch and tie them together with string or yarn. You and the children can make up a story to accompany the book. Remember to follow the child's lead. If he wants to read the pages as "banana day, apple day, pear day," then cooperate and honor his choice. When adults edit children's creations too much, the children get the message that what they've done isn't good enough.

- When selecting books for toddlers, look for sturdy books with cardboard pages or those made from cloth. Toddlers tend to be rough with pages and dislike dust jackets. Children this age also enjoy books with rhyming or rhythmic text and very few words. Younger toddlers tend to prefer clear photographs. As they get older and with reading experience, they will love colorful drawings.

- When you read with toddlers, feel free to ignore the written text and just talk about the pictures. Or simply abbreviate the text to fit the attention span of the kids at hand.

- Toddlers love to hear the same story over and over again. One fun thing to do is to tape yourself reading a favorite book. Read slowly, with a great deal of expression. As you make the tape, it's helpful to include reminders like "Turn the page now." Talk about the pictures ("Boy, he sure did get ice cream all over his shirt, didn't he?"). Then let a few toddlers listen to the tape and "read" the book by themselves.

Language Activities for Preschoolers

- Preschoolers wield their language mightily in dramatic play. With some easily obtained props, you can facilitate some rich play environments and watch them go at it. For example, create a mock office for preschoolers to play in. Set up some tables and chairs, and small desks, if you have them. Provide the children with a variety of supplies—paper, pencils, felt-tip markers, discarded junk mail to open, play telephones, and stickers that look like stamps.

Get Floored
Story time with more than two children is better when you're on the floor with the kids. They are much more engaged and pay better attention when you're down on their level.

- Children love to play house too. Many providers already have play kitchens; if you don't, you can easily create one with large boxes. Supply the kitchen with extra plastic dishes; small, rinsed-out milk cartons; plastic fruit; and anything else that is safe to make believe with.

- Provide dolls and cradles (use shoebox beds if you don't have wooden cradles) for added play. One provider showed children how to tie shawls in order to carry babies on their backs, as is done in many other countries. She reports the children (boys and girls) loved this and carried their dolls around with them during play and mealtimes and even tried to nap with them.

- You can also create a space for building forts. It can be as simple as bringing out chairs, blankets, and pillows and letting the children use their imaginations to build a house, pioneer fort, or motor home.

- Books can be used for more than storytime. Choose a favorite story the children know well, such as Maurice Sendak's *Where the Wild Things Are*, Graeme Base's *Jabberwocky*, or Ludwig Bemelmans' *Madeline,* and read it one more time. Then give the children puppets, stuffed animals, or dolls, and have them act out the story.

- Telling stories is a fun way to exercise language and creativity. Have children tell you a story, and write it down for them. If necessary, give them a starter line—for example, "Once upon a time there was a little flower growing on the hill . . ."—and let them finish the story.

- Be sure to write down the story exactly as the child utters it; do not correct grammar or pronunciation. Then read the stories back to the children in a natural voice. Children will enjoy hearing their own words and feel proud of their creation.

Fun Activities for Children

Science Activities

The natural world is an endless source of fascination to young children. Everything is new and fresh to them. They are just learning about cause and effect, and they eagerly experiment with just about anything. Take advantage of this curiosity and foster it with fun science and nature activities.

Science Activities for Babies

- Babies learn about the world through sensation. Helping them exercise their sense of smell can be fun for all involved (older children usually enjoy helping with this activity). Try offering babies a mixture of sweet and pungent smells, such as vanilla extract, cinnamon stick, dill pickle, garlic powder, and mild perfume.

  Hold the object under the baby's nose (but not too close). Gently move it back and forth. Have the older children watch the baby's face and decide if he likes the smell. If so, say, "You like to smell vanilla." If not, say, "You don't like to smell vanilla" and put it away. If a baby dislikes the smell, don't offer it again.

- Babies enjoy the feel of water. One safe way to facilitate this is to fill a large Ziploc freezer bag with water (only about three-quarters full—if you overfill the bag, it could burst open). Cut out simple shapes from sponges and put them in the water. Letting out any air, firmly seal the bag.

  The babies can pat the bag, feel the texture of water through the plastic, and look at the colorful sponge shapes.

- Babies learn a great deal about the world through their sense of touch. The many tactile experiences they have help their brains develop. Invite the older children to help you as you try the following sensory experiences: While you're changing a baby's diaper, give her a sticker or a piece of tape to play with. Say, "It's sticky, isn't it?" Let her play with it until she loses interest.

Science Activities for Toddlers

- Water play is fun and a wonderful sensory experience for toddlers. The pouring, dumping, and measuring they do helps develop eye-hand coordination and fine motor skills.

  Get a plastic dishpan of water and plenty of towels, and find a good place to play, such as a small table, outdoors, or your open dishwasher door (the water will run into the dishwasher instead of onto the floor).

  Give the children various props to use with the water, such as measuring spoons, funnels, yogurt containers, sponges, and plastic soda bottles cut in half (smooth the cut edges or tape them over with duct tape).

  Remember that whenever children are around water, you need to supervise the play very carefully and ensure safety.

- Simple science experiments are fun for older toddlers. The different seasons lend themselves to different activities. In the summertime you can fill two small glass jars evenly with water. Put one in a sunny window or outside in the sun. Put the other in a shady, cool spot. Let the children look at the jars a few hours later and see how they compare. Talk about how water evaporates quickly when it's hot.

- In the wintertime have the children make snowballs. Put the snowballs in two baking dishes. Put one dish in the freezer and place the other dish on a counter. After twenty minutes compare the two dishes. Talk about what makes the snowballs melt.

- Go on a nature walk in your neighborhood or park and look for worms. They like to come out just after rainfall. Or get a spade and dig a little. Let the children gently touch and feel the worms. Talk about how worms get their food from the dirt and enrich the soil.

Science Activities for Preschoolers

- Growing seeds is an engrossing activity for any age, but preschoolers are especially entranced by watching sprouts emerge and the plants grow.

  If you have garden space outside, you're in business. Beans and peas germinate and grow the fastest. Squashes, like pumpkin or zucchini, are popular, since they grow quite large. Another fun plant is the sunflower. It is large and dramatic, and you can roast and eat the seeds in the fall.

- An inside variation on this activity is to "plant" an avocado pit or sweet potato in a jar of water. Stick three toothpicks into the midsection and rest the bottom third in water. Watch the roots grow in the water and leaves sprout on top.

- Preschoolers love to play with magnets. You can extend their learning by providing opportunities for them to explore which objects are attracted to a magnet and which are not.

    Put together a shoebox of items that are made of iron and steel (e.g., paper clips, keys, crochet hooks, and metal buttons) and then include some nonmetal items (e.g., plastic buttons, wooden pencils, crayons, and toothbrushes).

    Have the children take turns holding the magnet and choosing something from the box. Talk about why the magnet picked up the object or did not. *Note:* Make sure the materials for this activity are only accessible to children who are old enough to play with them safely.

Learning Games

This is a broad category, but in general, the best learning games for children include a combination of the following elements:

- They promote problem-solving. Good learning games encourage children to think and solve whatever fun problem is at hand.
- They encourage cooperation. Group activities are more fun when there are winners only and no losers. You can accomplish this by offering games that require teamwork toward a common goal.
- They foster self-esteem. When children succeed at a game, they feel good about themselves and confident in their ability to meet challenges.
- They require communication: verbal, nonverbal, or both. Children improve and practice their language skills when they play games—especially cooperative ones.
- They allow children to be physical and become aware of their bodies; children discover what their bodies can do, and they learn to be respectful of others' bodies.

Of course, the most important element in learning games is *fun.* The more children enjoy an activity, the more they will participate and learn. Once again, be accepting of any children who choose not to join in; find a safe place for them to observe, but don't force them to play.

Learning Games for Babies

- Babies love faces. Peekaboo, that tried-and-true game that's been around forever, is still as relevant to babies' learning as ever. Peekaboo helps babies learn that something (or someone) still exists, even when they can't see it. It's also one that the older children can play with the babies in your care. Peekaboo can be played by covering your own face or by gently, momentarily, covering the baby's face with a soft cloth and then removing it.
- By playing mimic games with the older children (or with mirrors), you can help babies learn where certain body parts are, as well as concepts such as "on" and "off."

  Sit down with the baby in front of a group of two or three older children. Have the older kids put hats on their heads. Say, "The hats are *on* their heads!" Point to the hats. Put a hat on the baby's head. Let him take it off and put it back on. Watch the baby try to find his head.
- This game is the very start of learning to count. Bring out a six-cup muffin tin and six tennis balls (or whatever safe object you have six of). Give the baby the muffin tin. Have a preschooler show the baby how to place one ball into each hole. Let the children take turns putting the balls in and taking them out.

Learning Games for Toddlers

- Toddlers love to play with balls. You can teach them to roll balls back and forth to each other, toss them in boxes, and catch them. These activities help them develop gross motor skills and eye-hand coordination. The younger ones like the larger, lightweight balls, like beach balls; older toddlers can play with smaller, heavier balls. You can make your own cloth balls out of socks or pantyhose. Cut off the toe part and stuff it with the rest of the sock, then stitch it securely closed.

- You don't have to buy expensive wooden puzzles for children. Make simple puzzles out of heavy cardboard. For the youngest toddlers, circles are the easiest shapes to begin with. Using sharp scissors or a knife, cut a circle from the cardboard (make the edges as smooth as you can). Color the circle piece.

  Show the toddlers how to put the circle in and take it out. Let them practice it over and over again. Older or more experienced toddlers can graduate to other shapes. Watch them carefully; if they're not ready for a more complicated puzzle, they can get very frustrated. If this happens, put the new puzzle away and let them practice some more on an old one.

- Block play is the beginning of learning math and science skills. Boys tend to be more drawn to block play than girls, but it's important for all children to get a chance to experiment with and use blocks. This game is cooperative and includes everyone.

  Have the children sit in a circle with a box of blocks in the middle. Go around the circle having the first child put a block down and the others build on it. Keep going around the circle until you've used up all the blocks or the block building falls down.

Learning Games for Preschoolers

- Making a spiderweb out of string is fun for four or more preschoolers. Sit in a small circle. Have the children take turns rolling a ball of heavy string to a person sitting across the circle. Help them learn how to catch and roll with one hand and hang onto their string ends with the other hand. A web will begin to form. Remind them to hold the string ends tightly so the growing web stays taut.

  This is a good cooperative activity; if all children "hold up their end," a beautiful spiderweb will emerge. If you have a stuffed animal or puppet spider, it is fun to set it in the middle of the web.

- Balloon play, inside (in a large space) or outside, helps children learn to work together toward a common end. Have the children sit in a circle. Depending on how many children you have, give them one or two balloons. Have one child toss the balloon in the air. All the children are responsible for keeping the balloon in the air—tossing it up when it gets close to the ground. Encourage the children to work together so everyone has a turn. If you like, time how long they can keep it in the air. If they wish to, they can play again and try to beat their own time. *Note:* Make sure that infants and toddlers have no access to balloons. Many tiny tots have eaten or inhaled pieces of popped balloons and suffocated.

- "Simon Says" is a fun game that helps children learn to listen and follow directions. You can be the leader and then turn the role over to one of the children. Take turns being the leader.

    Here are a few starter lines:

    Simon says touch your nose.
    Simon says tug your ear.
    Turn around. (Simon didn't say!)
    Simon says hop on one foot.
    Simon says pat your neighbor on the back.
    Now pat your head. (Simon didn't say!)

    Praise the children when they follow the directions correctly. Smile and laugh if a child does it wrong, but don't exclude her or him from the game. Just say, "Let's try it again."

Movement Activities

Babies, toddlers, and preschoolers are learning to master their bodies and discovering how much those bodies can do. It's important to provide both structured opportunities for children to move in different ways and free play in which they can simply run around. These activities make use of the gross motor muscles, are a wonderful way to burn off children's normal energy, and can help children work through their emotions.

Movement Activities for Babies

- Gently touching and moving a young baby's arms and legs help the baby begin to learn that there are two sides to his or her body. Here is a quick activity that you can do during diaper changes.

    Lay baby on his back. Gently touch his palms together over the middle of his body. Bring his toes up to touch his nose. Carefully stretch his arms above his head. Bend his legs at the knee, one after the other, as if he were riding a bicycle.

    Talk about each body part as you move it. For example, "These are your toes. Now they're going to touch your nose."

    Kiss and blow on the baby's tummy and hands. Stick out your tongue and wiggle it left to right. Some babies will stick out their tongues back at you.

- After you've changed a baby, take a minute or two and pretend the baby is an airplane. Pick her up and hold her firmly around the chest, facing you. Lift her up above your head. Say, "Baby goes up!" Lower her down. Say, "Baby goes down!"

    Then hold her away from you. Say, "Baby goes backward!" Pull her back toward you. Say, "Baby goes forward!" Hold her away from you and turn around. Say, "Baby goes around!"

    This game will help baby's body awareness as you move her around in different directions.

Movement Activities for Toddlers

- Toddlers love to dance, especially with scarves. Collect big, sheer, diaphanous scarves in a variety of colors. (If the scarves are too long or big, tie a knot in the middle; you don't want children tripping on them.) Turn on some classical music with a strong beat, and let the children dance, twirl, and toss the scarves around. Scarves are fun to incorporate into other activities too, such as dress-up or building forts.

- Simple jumping can occupy toddlers for a long time. Consider getting out an old crib mattress (or you could purchase one at a garage sale). Place it on the floor, cover it with a crib sheet, and let the children jump away. Make sure the jumping space is safe. You don't want children tumbling off near sharp edges or corners.

- Make a simple obstacle course for toddlers to follow. You can use a small table to crawl under, a chair to sit on, a bench to crawl over, masking tape on the floor to walk a straight line, a broom to jump over, and a pile of pillows to jump in at the end. Demonstrate the course for them at first. Explain that one child at a time may follow the course.

Movement Activities for Preschoolers

- Have two children stand together on a sturdy, large, hardcover book. The fun is in balancing together, holding only onto each other. See how long each pair can balance before slipping off the book. Give everyone a few chances to succeed. This is a good activity to practice balance and cooperation.

- Create a caterpillar out of preschoolers. Have them all get down on their hands and knees in a line, then show each child how to grasp the ankles of the child in front of him or her. The "head," or leader, decides where the caterpillar will crawl. Tell the children to try not to let go of each other's ankles, so they don't break up the caterpillar. Let children take turns being the head.

- Traditional movement games, such as "Ring Around the Rosy" and "London Bridge Is Falling Down," are tried-and-true favorites of young children. The nice thing about these games is that children can play them with a group of just three or four. A bonus is that they are simple enough to include toddlers (whom preschoolers love to direct).

A Moving Activity

The pop-up tent toys (with attachable tunnels) are extremely popular with young children and a great indoor/outdoor large-muscle activity. Here's the trick: Bring it out only once a month. If it's too available, children will quickly lose interest.

Cooking and Snack Activities

Children love to spend time with you in the kitchen. It takes some careful planning, eagle-eye supervision, and more cleanup, but you can successfully integrate learning and cooking. And the best part is that children love to eat what they make.

A baby's contribution in the kitchen is mostly limited to exploring props and foods, but toddlers and preschoolers will enthusiastically participate in any phase of food preparation you allow them to.

Remember, kids in the kitchen require your constant and careful supervision. Try to limit their participation to safe areas and tasks (keep them away from hot stoves, ovens, and dangerous appliances such as mixers or food processors). Many children are fascinated with knives, so be careful to keep yours well out of reach. Older preschoolers, however, can often be taught to safely use a knife with a rounded, dull point. This, of course, would require your strict supervision.

Kitchen Activities for Babies

- For older babies, pots and pans are not cooking tools but fun puzzles. When a baby learns to put a lid on a pot, he or she is discovering how shapes fit together. This is an easy way to occupy a baby—and still keep an eye on him or her—while you are preparing lunch.
- Babies are very interested in how some objects fit inside one another, and they will try to push together some objects that don't fit. Many kitchen items are perfect for this game. You can use measuring spoons on a ring, measuring cups that nest inside one another, or pots and pans that fit inside one another.
- Everything that comes within a baby's grasp goes into his mouth. Take advantage of this. Set the baby up in a high chair. (This is a pretty good place for him while you're working on a cooking activity with the older children.) Give the baby two foods to gnaw on that have opposite tastes—for example, sweet and sour (banana and pickle) or salty and bland (saltine cracker and unsalted cracker). Watch the baby taste the foods. Which tastes does he prefer?

Cooking Activities for Toddlers

- Make a salad with toddlers. They are champions at ripping and tearing and will eagerly go after a head of lettuce. Give them a big, unbreakable bowl to put the greens in. They can dump in other vegetables you wish to add (precut by you) and mix it all up.

- A simple cooking activity older toddlers can do for themselves is to make their own sandwiches. Spreading peanut butter, tuna fish salad, cream cheese, and other soft spreadables is fun for toddlers. Give them blunt table knives, whole-wheat bread, and a choice of fillings.

- Part of learning to cook is learning to use kitchen tools and utensils. Get out the Play-Doh and give the children rolling pins and spatulas for making "bread" and "pancakes."

Cooking Activities for Preschoolers

- Making and eating cookies are high on most preschoolers' lists of favorite things to do. Choose a low- or no-sugar recipe. Preschoolers will learn to measure ingredients, mix and stir, and most fun of all, spoon out cookie dough onto the baking sheet. Young children love to taste the batter. Tell them at the outset that no tasting will be allowed until the baked cookies have cooled. Serve the cookies with milk at lunch or snack time.

- Making butter is a classic preschool cooking activity. Seat the children in a circle. Pour ⅓ inch of heavy cream (do not add salt) into a baby-food jar. (Give each child his or her own.) Shake or roll the jars five to seven minutes (rolling will take longer). Sing songs while you shake the jars. You can also talk about the cream's appearance and texture: a heavy creamy liquid; then a lumpy, swishy mixture; and finally, a watery liquid and a lump of butter.

  At snack time, have the children spread the butter on banana bread or crackers.

- Buy several types of pasta: elbow macaroni, shells, spirals, wheels, bow ties. Put all the pasta shapes in a big bowl in the middle of the table. Have the children sort the pasta by type (muffin tins work well for this). Then have them choose which types of pasta they want included for lunch.

Note: Scrupulously clean hands are important in all cooking activities.

Music Activities

It's a rare child who doesn't enjoy some kind of music. There are lots of fun ways to incorporate music into learning games and to incorporate learning into music.

Babies are learning to distinguish different sounds, rhythm, and rhyme. Toddlers and preschoolers are beginning to sing and move to music and to make music themselves. Now is a wonderful time to expose young children to many types of music and to encourage them to create their own.

Music Activities for Babies

- Drums are a fun way to make music or just plain old noise. Tape or glue the lid back onto an empty oatmeal box. It will make a very nice drum. Babies love to make sounds when they hit the drum with their hands or spoons.

    A good time for drum play is when the older children are making music as well; the babies will mimic them.

- Babies love lullabies. At naptime a very natural music activity with babies is to sing to them (or play a tape of quiet songs). Try any of the following: "Twinkle, Twinkle, Little Star," "Hush, Little Baby," "Rock-a-Bye Baby," and "Lullaby, and Good Night."

- One way babies learn about their world is by listening to the sounds around them: voices, music, water running, bells ringing, and much more. The daily sounds you and the other children make are interesting to babies. Watch their faces to see which kinds they like.

- Hang a wind chime near the baby, low enough that a young child can reach it. Every time you approach, tinkle it gently. Allow the children to ring it occasionally. Watch the baby turn her or his head toward the sound.

Music Activities for Toddlers

- Toddlers are born mimics and love songs that include movement or finger plays. The following are tried-and-true toddler favorites: "The Itsy-Bitsy Spider," "I'm a

Little Teapot," and "If You're Happy and You Know It." See the appendix for sourcebooks on songs and finger plays.

- Bring out a full-length mirror. Find an upbeat song on the radio, or play a tape you like. Line the children up and have them dance in front of the mirror. Call out a few directions, like "Dance high! Touch the ceiling!" or "Dance low, like a snake." Have the children take turns in front of the mirror.

- It's fun to bring out some "jingle bells" and tie them to toddlers' shoes. When you turn on some music, they can make their bells ring as they dance. This is especially fun to do as the winter holidays approach.

Music Activities for Preschoolers

- Collect some good children's music to listen to, dance to, and sing along with. Some good children's artists are:

    John Archambault and David Plummer—*Chicka Chicka Boom Boom and other Coconutty Songs* (2 Dad Music)

    Joanie Bartels—*Sillytime Magic* (BMG/Special Productions)

    Raffi—*Singable Songs for the Very Young; The Corner Grocery Store; Evergreen, Everblue* (Rounder)

    Leonard Bernstein—*Children's Classics* (Sony)

    There are many more. See your local librarian or bookseller for more suggestions.

- Have the children make their own instruments and create their own band. (Toddlers will enjoy playing these instruments too.) Here are a few ideas for instruments:

    A drum made from an oatmeal box.

    A banjo made from a shoebox. (Tape the lid on. Cut a hole in the top. String three rubber bands across the hole. Tape a paper towel tube to the end of the box for a handle.)

    Rattles and shakers made by putting beans, rice, or popcorn into tightly sealed plastic containers, clean yogurt containers, or clean plastic soda bottles.

    A set of cymbals made by crashing two metal pot lids together.

    A horn made with a paper towel or toilet paper tube. Punch a few holes in the sides and then cover one end with waxed paper (secure it with a rubber band). Blow and hum through the open end.

- Play musical statues. Choose a lively song to play on the radio, or select a tape. While the music is playing, the children dance. When you turn the music off, the children must freeze in whatever position they are in, then stay still and quiet until the music starts again. Vary the music you choose, from upbeat songs to rap to slow, soothing tunes.

Art Activities

Creativity takes many forms, and art projects are one of the best ways to exercise it, no matter what the age. Early childhood educators agree that what is important for young children is the *process* of creating art, not the product itself.

Young children learn by "doing." More learning about creativity takes place in the act of creation than in the finished product. For example, the mushing, squishing, and pounding of clay are more valuable to the child's creative growth than is the "dinosaur" it turns out to be.

Along with messy, process-oriented art, it is also fun to mix in some traditional structured art projects, such as construction-paper flags on Flag Day.

Here are a few tips to help children enjoy creating artwork:

- Never, never draw on, finish, or touch up a child's artwork. Anything the child makes is already good enough.
- When you talk with children about their artwork, do not focus on content. Instead of asking what the picture is of, describe what you see—for example, "I see bright red circles with three yellow lines going through this one." Another good conversation starter is "Tell me about your picture/sculpture."
- Be sincere with your praise. Children know when you're blowing something out of proportion—for example, "That's the best picture I ever saw." Instead, be specific about what it is you like—for example, "I like the soft green color you used in the sky part of the picture" or "I can see you spent a lot of time poking holes over here."
- Occasionally children want to tear up their artwork. Sometimes they just get frus-

trated trying to achieve a certain effect, and sometimes they are simply finished with the picture and don't want it anymore. Respect what they want; the artwork is their creation, and they have a right to keep, display, or dispose of it.

- Remember, unless you're making structured art with a set product expected, keep your involvement to a minimum; children will learn more that way.
- Pay particular attention to safety when you're making art. Choose products that are nontoxic, washable, and safe for children to create with. Supervise them carefully.

Internet Tips

Here are a couple of useful Web sites that offer free art activity ideas for young children:

- Child Fun, www.childfun.com. A smorgasbord of ideas— including lists of themes and accompanying activities.

- National Center for Children's Illustrated Literature, www .nccil.org/activities.html. Art activities based on selected well-known illustrators' work.

Art Activities for Babies

- Young babies like to see simple pictures of people's faces. Their favorite part of the picture is the eyes.

  Using either a thick black felt pen or brightly colored marker, draw a simple, bold picture of a Mommy face on one piece of white paper. Draw a picture of a Daddy face on another piece of white paper. Glue these pictures onto two pieces of cardboard. Cover with clear contact paper.

  Enlist the older children's help in taping one picture to the inside of the baby's playpen or crib for the baby to look at. With very young babies (ages newborn to six months) make sure the picture is placed down low on the inside of the crib. If the baby turns her head to the side, she should be able to see the picture no more than 12 inches away.

  After one week, change to the other picture. Babies like simple patterns too, like bull's-eyes and checkerboards. You can also tape these designs inside the crib.

- A "touchy-feely" board is a sensory toy that helps babies learn about colors, shapes, and textures. It is fairly easy to make and can easily be a cooperative project that involves the older children. You will need several brightly colored fabric scraps of different textures. Some good fabrics are velvet or velveteen, dotted swiss, brocade, carpet scraps, satin, wool, corduroy, terry cloth, fake fur, and quilted fabric.

Cut out 5-inch squares of material. Glue them onto cardboard in rows of three or four.

Let the baby feel one square at a time. Watch and see which ones he likes to feel the most. The older children will enjoy watching the baby play with their creation.

- The faces babies are most familiar with are those of family members but they should also know the faces in your day care well—and their names. This is a fun project for the older children to help make and a fun game for the baby to show off skill at identifying familiar faces.

Gather together two empty, washed milk cartons; some newspaper; clear contact paper; glue; and photos of yourself and the children in care.

Cut the milk cartons in half, 5 inches or so from the bottom. Stuff the two bottom halves with newspaper. Push the two halves together to form a cube.

Glue pictures of yourself and the children onto each side. Cover the cube with clear contact paper.

Rotate the cube and show the baby the pictures. If he is old enough to point, ask him to point out you and each of the children pictured. For fun, point to yourself and ask, "Is this Jason?" The baby will enjoy the joke.

Art Activities for Toddlers

- A classic introduction to painting is to give toddlers a bucket of water and some wide paintbrushes and have them "paint" your fence or even the side of your house. You will be amazed at how long this will hold their attention. Talk about the brush strokes they are making and how the water makes things look dark.
- Older toddlers like to make collages. Put a handful of each of the following items in a muffin tin: sequins, dry beans, cinnamon, sand, small discarded buttons, elbow macaroni, potpourri, or anything else that might be fun to stick down.

Give each child a square of clear contact paper, sticky side up. Show them how to sprinkle items onto the sticky surface. When they are done with their designs, cover the collage with another piece of contact paper, sticky side down. This will seal the artwork and preserve it.

- Toddlers are tactile creatures and like to know how things feel. Paint is no exception. Finger painting allows them to explore the medium of paint while they create pictures. Use washable tempera paint (available in craft stores and some toy stores) in shallow containers. Provide primary colors (red, yellow, blue) for them to combine to make other colors. Have some water available for them to wash their hands before trying another color. Provide large pieces of butcher paper to paint on.

    Do this activity outside (near a hose for cleanup) or inside on lots of newspapers. Old adult-size T-shirts make good smocks for children to wear over their clothes.

Art Activities for Preschoolers

- Preschoolers love to make dough, goop, and other kinds of clay. The following recipe makes "Fun Pucky," which is similar to Silly Putty but has its own consistency and color. The children can watch you. In one bowl mix two cups Elmer's School Glue with one cup water. In another bowl mix one tablespoon Borax with one cup water. Pour the two mixtures together and watch them react to form Fun Pucky. Mix it with your hands until it's dry enough to play with. Give each of the children a piece to explore and mold. Fun Pucky will keep a week or so in a ziplock bag.

- Painting is more fun if you explore color mixing first. Make this a group activity and have the children gather around. One child chooses a primary color and generously dabs it on the paper with a thick paintbrush. Another child chooses a color to add. What color results? Do this again and again. Let the children start to do their own individual color mixing. Don't be discouraged if they consistently make a muddy brown color—this is how they learn.

- Printing with objects is an engrossing art activity for preschoolers. Give them some tempera paint and heavy paper, and then provide a wide variety of objects in different shapes.

Some fun objects to print with are potato pieces, apple pieces, small balloons partially filled with water, sponges, corncobs, or plastic berry baskets (from the produce department of your grocery store).

Personal Safety Activities

Teaching children skills to keep them safe is as important as any other activity you will do with the children. A recent study in the United States shows that, of the abuse cases investigated by authorities, more than 60 percent are victims of neglect, almost 20 percent are physically abused, 10 percent are sexually abused, and 5 percent are emotionally mistreated.* The youngest age group—birth through three years—is the most at risk. As a child-care provider, you are mandated by the government to report any suspected or observed child abuse or neglect. Some states require you to give handouts to the parents with information on abuse prevention and statistics. You can go beyond these requirements and do even better for the children. You can work with them to build their personal safety skills.

This section focuses on increasing children's self-esteem, identifying and expressing feelings, building body awareness, and increasing decision-making skills—all things that help protect children from potential abuse.

Many adults are hesitant about teaching personal safety skills to children, fearing that the information will scare them. Research has shown, however, that the informed child is the safer child. Abuse prevention will not scare children if it is presented matter-of-factly and is appropriate for the child's developmental level.

The following activity suggestions are all child-tested and serve to educate and protect children. *Note:* This is a sensitive topic, and you would do well to let parents know when you present personal safety activities. You might send a note home describing the activities and encouraging parents to reinforce the safety information at home.

Personal Safety Activities for Babies

- Part of an infant's job is to learn where her body ends and the rest of the world begins. She is exploring her body and finding out what it can do. This is the time

* Statistics from the report *Summary Child Maltreatment*, Administration for Children and Families, www .acf.hhs.gov.

adults and older children can start practicing respect for a baby's body. This means watching the baby carefully to see what kinds of touching she likes and what kinds she doesn't like or is overstimulated by. Asking questions of the older children will teach them to be sensitive to the baby's needs and likes. Some questions you might try: When you pat or kiss the baby, what does her face look like? How do you think she feels? If a baby is uncomfortable, how does she let us know? (Emphasize body language here—does the baby cry, fuss, kick, or turn her head away?) If a baby doesn't like something that she really needs (e.g., having her diaper changed), how can we make it more pleasant for her?

- Everyone has feelings. Babies watch you and the older children express feelings of happiness, sadness, frustration, or pride every day. You can start to give babies words for simple feelings. And you can help them learn that people's faces show what they feel.

  Draw simple faces on paper showing the feelings: happy, sad, surprised, excited, or angry.

  Have the older children help you glue the pictures onto a large piece of cardboard. Set it up where the baby can see it. Say, "Let's make a happy face." Point to the happy face on the board. You and the older children make happy faces and grin at the baby. Prompt the baby to look at you and the children and then at the picture.

  Repeat with the other pictures. See if the baby will copy you.

- Fostering good self-esteem begins at birth. You can foster babies' emotional health by providing affirmations—that is, positive statements that encourage them to grow. Developmentally, babies need consistent affirmations, even though they don't always understand every word being said. There are two kinds of affirmations we all need: (1) for being and (2) for doing. We need to be affirmed for who we are and for what we can do. Some sample affirmations for babies are as follows:

  I like you. (being)
  Your needs are OK with me; I will take care of you. (being)
  What a terrific smile you have! (being)
  Wow, you can cry really, really loud! (doing)
  Look at that, you can sit up all by yourself! (doing)
  I like the way you explore these toys. (doing)

Fun Activities for Children

Affirmations are appropriate with all ages. You need them as much as the children do. The appendix lists some resources by educator and author Jean Illsley Clarke that will give you lots of information, props, and ideas on how to make affirmation-giving a natural part of your day for all the age groups present.

Personal Safety Activities for Toddlers

- Establish a Touching Code for your child care. Teach this to children beginning at one year of age. Make the rule simple, such as: Everyone must touch gently; no hurting allowed. Or, if someone is touching you in a way that makes you uncomfortable, say, "Don't touch me! I don't like it!"

  Then enforce the rule. If a child says, "Don't touch me! I don't like it!" to another, then the other child *must* stop. It's important that everyone follow this rule (including the adults); if you enforce it only occasionally, then children will conclude that it's not really a rule.
- If, when restraining a child, you find he tries to use the code on you to get you to let him go, just say, "There is no hurting allowed here. I can't let you hurt yourself or anyone else. I'll keep you safe until you're ready to be calm."
- Practice decision-making skills with toddlers. There's not a whole lot in their lives they are able to control (going to child care, having a bath, etc.), but there are myriad small decisions it is appropriate to give them control over. Whenever possible, offer them a choice between two options. For example: Would you like to sit on the green or the red mat? Would you like to take a nap or just rest quietly? Which doll would you like to play with, this one or that one? Would you like to play with the construction toys or make art with the rest of us?
- Read books that enhance and teach personal safety skills with the older toddlers.
- Read *Loving Touches* by Lory Freeman (see appendix). Talk about what loving touches are and why we need them. Practice giving each other different kinds of loving touches. (Remind the children that anyone who doesn't wish to be touched has the right to use the Touching Code.) Usually, a flurry of big hugs will result.
- Read the Feelings for Little Children series of board books by Elizabeth Crary and myself (see appendix). These are rhyming books you can sing to the tune of "When

You're Happy and You Know It." The text offers toddlers several fun ways to express the common emotions of happy, shy, mad, and silly. It's good practice for identifying and expressing feelings—an important personal safety skill.

Personal Safety Activities for Preschoolers

- Read the book *It's MY Body* by Lory Freeman (see appendix) with the children. They will enjoy practicing saying, "No, don't touch me. It's *my* body," and "No, I won't touch you. I don't like it."
- Have the children practice the Safety Yell. Explain that if someone is bothering them, trying to touch them in a way that's uncomfortable, or trying to get them to go with him or her without a parent's knowledge, then they need to use the Safety Yell and run away. Have the children practice looking you straight in the eye and then yelling as loud as they can (good words to yell: *NO! Mommy! Daddy! Stop it!*). Then have them run to the other side of the room. (*Note:* Some children may giggle or think this is a silly activity. Don't allow any giggling, and have the children practice yelling until they produce a good, strong yell.)
- Present some "What would you do if . . . ?" scenarios. Here are a few sample situations: "What would you do if a big kid took your toy car away from you and said he was going to keep it?" (You could say, "No! It's not yours!" in a loud voice, or find a grown-up to help.)

  "What would you do if your aunt wanted to kiss you goodbye and you didn't want her to?" (You could say, "No, I don't want to" and shake her hand instead.)

  "What would you do if a man stopped his car and offered to give you a puppy?" (You could yell, "*No!*" in a loud voice, run away, and then tell a grown-up.)

  "What would you do if your sister were tickling you and you didn't like it?" (You could say, "Don't touch me, I don't like it!" or call a grown-up for help.)

  "What would you do if you lost your mom in the grocery store?" (You could find a clerk or ask a woman with small children for help.)

  Children are more likely to react safely in dangerous situations if they've been taught what to do and have practiced doing it. This activity is a good one to repeat several times throughout the year.

- A critical part of abuse prevention is teaching children to tell the difference between secrets that are hurtful and secrets that are fun surprises. If they can do this, then they will be able to decide when to keep and when to share a secret.

  First read the book *The Trouble with Secrets* by Karen Johnsen (see appendix). It presents several situations in which preschoolers are commonly asked to keep a "secret"—for example, a bird's nest no one should know about, a sibling's birthday presents, the hiding place for your house key, and secret passwords. The book also covers scarier situations in which keeping a secret isn't appropriate—for example, someone hurts you and warns you not to tell, or maybe one parent tells you not to tell your other parent something.

  Make very clear to children that the way you decide to keep or share a secret is by thinking about how the secret makes you feel inside. If it's fun and exciting, like a surprise birthday party, then it's OK to keep. If it hurts or worries you, like uncomfortable touching, then you need to tell a safe person (as will be discussed shortly). Encourage children to talk about the secrets they've kept and shared in the past.

  Second, have the children draw pictures of at least three or four safe adults in their lives. A safe adult is someone you can tell a scary secret to. Possibilities include parents, you—as the child-care provider—grandparents, close neighbors, Sunday school teachers, and so on. When they're finished drawing, you should label each picture with the safe adult's name. Emphasize that if the child has a scary secret to tell and the first person she or he tells doesn't listen, then the child must keep on going down the list. The children should learn to keep telling until they find someone who will listen.

  Send the drawings home with the children, and explain to the parents what their purpose is.
- Identifying and talking about feelings can be valuable on many levels. When it comes to personal safety, the child who is able to recognize his or her own feelings of discomfort and warning is not likely to mistake abusive overtures as friendship or caring.

Start by identifying the feelings the children may be experiencing. For example: "Jason fell down. He feels hurt and sad." "When people ignore what I say, I feel frustrated." "Look at Amanda jump for joy. She's really excited." "Boy, I can see that you're really mad we're not going to watch *Sesame Street* today." "You feel happy when your mom comes to pick you up."

Draw some expressive faces on paper or cardboard. Make happy, sad, scared, excited, surprised, mad, and proud faces. During circle time, lay them all face down. Have the children each pick one up and name the feeling.

Fire Safety for Preschoolers

Although your child care will keep matches and lighters safely locked away, it is very good sense to teach young children fire safety. Children age five and younger are more than twice as likely to die in fires as are older children and adults.* Teaching fire safety can save lives.

Teach children the following:

- *Matches and lighters are for adults only.* Tell children these are tools for grown-ups only. Children should never touch them. If they find them, or see another child touching them, they should tell a grown-up right away.
- *You can't hide from fire.* Many children die in fires because they try to hide from the smoke and flames rather than escape. Tell children they cannot hide, but they can get out. Role-play with them your own fire escape plan. Teach them the phrase "Get out and stay out." Tell them never to reenter a burning building.
- *Know what a smoke alarm sounds like.* Children need to recognize the sound of a smoke alarm and react immediately. Conduct a fire drill, using a smoke alarm to signal the escape.
- *Have an escape plan.* Hold fire drills frequently. Encourage parents to do so at home. Everyone should know at least two ways out of every room

> ### Internet Tip
> National Fire Protection Association's children's Web site, www.sparky.org. This site offers fun fire-safety information, coloring pages to download, and materials for educators.

* Statistics from the National Fire Protection Association, www.nfpa.org.

and be familiar with all exits, including windows. Decide on a meeting place outside where everyone should gather.

- *Stop, drop, and roll.* Teach children the classic remedy for burning clothes:

  Stop where you are. *Don't* run.

  Drop to the ground.

  Roll. Cover your face with your hands and roll over and over or back and forth to smother the flames.

  Show how to use a coat or blanket to smother flames on another person's clothes. Role-play this procedure.

- *Crawl low under smoke.* Teach children to find another exit if they come up against smoke or flames while trying to escape a fire. Teach them to crawl low under smoke, with their heads 1 to 2 feet above the floor. To simulate smoke during a fire drill, you can stretch a bedsheet 2 feet above the floor and have the children crawl under the "smoke" to the exit.

- *Conduct fire drills.* The National Fire Protection Association recommends the following role-plays:

  "Pretend you wake up and there's smoke in your bedroom." (Practice crawling low under smoke.)

  "Pretend you're helping in the kitchen and your sleeve catches fire." (Practice stop, drop, and roll.)

See the appendix for a more extensive list of recommended resource books for providers and teachers.

Chapter Six
Positive Guidance Tools

Caring for children is both rewarding and wearing. Part of the frustration and weariness can come from dealing with conflicts between you and the children (No! I won't take a nap!) and conflicts among the children (I had it first! She hit me!). As the adult in charge, you must keep these conflicts from getting out of control and creating an unpleasant environment for everyone.

If you have children of your own or you've worked with kids before, then you know that no one guidance method works with every child all of the time. The reason for this is that at any given time, many, many things contribute to a child's uncooperative behavior:

- The child's developmental stage
- The match of child and caregiver in temperament
- Circumstances in the child's day (being overtired, sick, etc.)
- Inconsistent or differing rules and expectations at home and in child care
- Disparity between the child's ability and the caregiver's expectation
- Desire for attention
- Experiences in the child's life (new sibling, divorce, illness in the family, etc.)

This chapter offers you some basic, child-tested guidance tools. Some of them will seem like common sense to you, while others may elicit an "Aha! Why didn't I think of that?" Millions of experienced and loving parents and educators have grappled with this problem before you—and many of them have written about it.

Children's Developmental Ages and Stages

Tremendous growth and development go on in a child's first five years of life—more so than in any other time in the life span. Nothing will help you more in keeping the children in your care safe and happy than a solid familiarity with children's "ages and stages"—that is, the developmental phases all children pass through during the first years of life. There are many areas of development (physical, emotional, social, cognitive, etc.) and all are in interplay at any given time.

Sandy, a relatively new provider, talks about how knowledge of development makes a difference:

> When I first started doing child care, I was a new mother. My baby was three months old and not giving me much trouble (apart from sleep deprivation!). I began caring for a couple of two-year-olds and instantly had my hands full. Every five minutes there would be a fight over a toy. Mitchell would scream "Mine!" and protect his dinosaur from Katie, who would then beat on Mitchell to try and get the dinosaur. I was ready to strangle them both trying to get them to share. In desperation, I picked up a guidance book on toddlers. Lo and behold, I found that, developmentally, toddlers do not yet have the skills necessary to share on a regular basis. I changed my tactics, and now I don't put out any especially attractive toys unless there are two of them. When they get closer to three, I'll introduce sharing again.

Internet Tips

There is a wealth of information on development and guidance on the Internet. Two helpful sites are:

- Parenting Press, Inc., www.parentingpress.com/weeklytips.html. The Parenting Tip feature (written by yours truly) offers a free article every week. See their large archive of past articles on common guidance issues.

- Educarer World of Infants, www.Educarer.com/ lnk2answers.htm. The Quick Articles page offers just that on a variety of development topics. Despite the name of the site, the articles cover ages birth to five years.

A good knowledge of development will also help you in planning age-appropriate activities for children, thus avoiding unnecessary frustration on their part and the accompanying headaches for you. The following is a brief chart of the characteristics of the stages of development for children ages newborn through five. Keep in mind that every child is unique; no child will fit perfectly into every category. A child who talks early may walk late and be average in other categories. There is no one right age for any developmental milestone, only an age range of what is considered typical—one educator calls this "the wide range of normal."

The characteristics given for various ages are by no means complete. I would strongly encourage you to read books and magazines and to take classes in children's development. The more you know, the easier caring for young children will be on you and them.

Birth to six months

Sets own schedule (sleeping, eating, etc.)

Listens to sounds and voices—particularly parents' voices

Reaches for, bats at, and grasps objects

Imitates actions and sounds

Stares at bright colors

Rolls over, sits with support

Begins to develop eye-hand coordination

Six to twelve months

Sits alone

Babbles

Creeps and crawls

Knows the difference between a strange and a familiar face

Knows own name

Learns by watching others

Uses fingers and thumbs

Knows that objects still exist, even when they can't be seen

Is sometimes frightened of strangers

Plays simple games

Puts everything in the mouth

Twelve to eighteen months

Shows wants without crying

Drinks well from a cup

Responds to spoken requests

Initiates action on own

Plays alone

Scribbles on own

Crawls down stairs backward

Walks

Manipulates objects

Solves simple problems

May strongly prefer mother

Builds tower of two blocks

Uses simple words, names

Shows increased awareness of own body

Positive Guidance Tools

Eighteen to twenty-four months

Takes off clothes
Likes to explore
Makes believe in play
Utters two-word sentences
Mimics family
Names many objects
Builds tower of four blocks
Runs and climbs
Kicks ball
Can point to named body parts
Tests and resists rules
Knows what he or she wants but can't
  always express it
Is easily frustrated
Is often aggressive
Has short attention span
Likes to have choices offered
Begins to learn to sing
Plays alongside other children

Two years old

Puts on loose-fitting clothes
Begins to follow rules
Uses short sentences
Builds tower of eight blocks
Tosses ball overhead
Has tremendous curiosity and desire to
  explore
Can solve problems
Begins to separate by saying "No!" a lot
Pedals tricycle
Enjoys showing off strength and daring
Copies drawings

Gives first and last name
Uses plurals
Displays sense of humor
Is often very persistent and determined
Protects toys from other children

Three years old

Likes routines
Dresses with supervision
Separates more easily from mother
Is usually toilet-trained
Learns colors and numbers
Can balance on one foot
Understands prepositions (*behind,
  under, over,* etc.)
Likes playing with one or two friends
Starts to understand concept of time
Is now able to share
In drawing becomes more representa-
  tive of actual objects
Begins to play cooperatively with
  friends
Enjoys imaginative play
Can make multiple-word
  sentences
May have nightmares

Four years old

Dresses without supervision
Gives up nap
Draws person with three parts
Hops on one foot
Talks well and frequently
Catches bounced ball

Understands time better

Is interested in body parts and gender differences

Enjoys creative projects

May name artwork or creations

Brags

Plays cooperatively with friends

Five years old

Draws person with six parts

Enjoys and needs playtime with friends of own age

Likes organized games

Insists on following rules when playing

Skips

Plans own play and activities

Needs to feel respected

Likes true stories

Knows the alphabet

Counts to ten

Is interested in death and what it means

Discipline/Guidance Techniques

Part of being a young child means finding out where the limits are. Setting a limit is another way of saying "drawing the line" with regard to children's unacceptable behavior. It is developmentally normal for young children to test your rules and limits again and again in order to see if they are still enforced. Children vary in how much testing they do. The more consistent you are, the faster they will learn, for example, that "people are not for hitting," "food is not for throwing," or "flower beds are not for stomping."

But some days, even consistency doesn't seem to work. The key to minimizing misbehavior is having lots of options open to you. This section will cover communication and attention techniques, teaching consequences, and fostering good social skills in children. These techniques will stand you in good stead in many, many situations, but it's up to you to choose the tool and follow through. If one technique does not work, try another.

Communication Techniques That Help Children Behave

Shouting "No! Don't do that!" seems to come naturally to most adults who care for children. The trouble is that although it may stop the misbehavior, it doesn't keep it from happening again. Here are three techniques that address problems and help keep them from recurring.

Active Listening

Children usually have their own reasons for what they do, and some feeling behind it. Let's say an eighteen-month-old child begs for milk and then, when she gets it, decides she wants grape juice instead (like her friend). You refuse and she tosses the milk on the carpet.

In this case, the child loves milk but gets distracted by her friend's juice. It's a much prettier color than her milk. When she demands juice and you set a limit and insist she keep her milk, she gets angry and dumps the milk.

Your response might be to remind her of the rule "Milk is for drinking, not for spilling." And then you might acknowledge the feelings involved: "When someone spills milk on my carpet, I feel very mad, because I have to clean it up" (your feelings); or, "Boy, you feel real mad that you can't have juice. But remember, milk is for drinking, not for spilling" (her feelings).

You can use active listening even with a preverbal child. It consists of noticing what the child is feeling and reflecting it back to her or him. No questions are asked and no solutions are offered. This is easiest to do when the child's feeling is intense, like anger or frustration, and harder to remember when the behavior is positive, such as curling up with a book (contentment) or jumping for joy (happiness). Here are a few examples of providers using active listening:

> Cassie, age three, and Michelle, age three and a half, were painting pictures. Michelle got upset when Cassie wouldn't share the blue paint. She began to whine and hit Cassie's picture with her brush. Cassie responded by coming to me crying. "Looks like there's a problem here," I said. I looked at Cassie and said, "It's disappointing when someone splashes paint on your picture." Then I said to Michelle, "You feel mad when Cassie won't share the paint. Hmmm, what can we do here?" Without any input from me, they decided they would each put a little blue paint in their own baby-food jars to use. It was amazing to me how they calmed down when I talked about their feelings. I think it freed them up to solve the problem.

> Joshua is fairly new in my child care. Although it's normal for kids to cry a lot during the first two weeks when their parents leave, this two-and-a-

half-year-old seemed more distressed than usual when his mom dropped him off. One day I rocked him for a few minutes and said, "You feel really, really sad to say good-bye to your mommy today, don't you?" He looked up at me, cried a bit more, and then in about five minutes, got off my lap and went to look at the block tower the other kids were making.

Debbie, an experienced provider who has already raised her own family, often has younger parents asking her for advice.

I had a mom ask me about a problem she was having with her three-year-old daughter. She and her husband had recently separated, and Sarah was acting out quite a bit. Mom and Sarah were having a power struggle over Sarah going to bed. Mom picked her up, struggling, and put her in bed. Sarah bounced back up and announced, "I'm going to get a gun and shoot you!" The mom was horrified. I told her for this age, unfortunately, comments like that are pretty typical. Three-year-olds are very impressed with power and the symbols for it. I recommended that she ignore the gun specifics and respond to the feeling Sarah was expressing. Mom decided that next time something like that happened, she would calmly say, "Boy, you're really mad at me right now."

Children really do respond well to having their feelings identified for them. If you know how you feel, you can better decide what to do about it. Children don't always have words for what they feel, so if adults are accustomed to naming feelings for them, they will become more at home with their emotions, make better decisions about how to act, and become more sensitive to others' feelings.

You will be communicating that *all* feelings are OK to have and that limits are placed on how we express those feelings (e.g., being mad is OK, but hitting is not). Active listening works best as a prevention tool. You'll find it most effective when the child has a problem, rather than when you have a problem with the child's behavior.

Try to make active listening a regular way of relating to the children. This means reflecting feelings in ordinary, nonconflict situations as well as the more emotionally charged situations. Here are a few examples:

You look so cozy and contented when we read stories together.
(To an infant) You're crying because you feel hungry.
You feel excited when we talk about Santa Claus coming.
Daniel feels happy when he talks about his dad coming to see him this weekend.
Wow, look at that block tower you made! I'll bet you feel proud.

Active listening is just a matter of noticing a feeling and matter-of-factly mentioning it to the children. You don't have to ask questions, tell the child what to do, or solve the problem. Often, just reflecting the feeling is enough for the child to come to a resolution (There, somebody understands how I feel!) or to solve the problem on his or her own (like Cassie and Michelle did in the earlier example).

One word of caution: When talking about feelings, try to avoid the phrase "makes you feel" or "makes me feel." We're all responsible for our own feelings and actions. For example, when you say to Caitlyn, "Amanda made you mad when she took the doll away," you imply that her feelings can be manipulated by others. What would work better would be a response like "Amanda took your doll away. You feel mad." Skip the "makes me" or "makes you" part and go straight to "I feel" or "You feel." This slight change in response implies more strongly that the child is responsible for her own feelings.

I-Messages

After you have active listening down, start to practice I-messages. Remember the example of the toddler who spilled her milk on the carpet? When the provider said, "When someone spills milk on my carpet, I feel very mad, because I have to clean it up," she was using an I-message.

These statements have three parts:

- *When* . . . (describes in a nonjudgmental way the offending behavior)
- *I feel* . . . (describes your feeling)
- *Because* . . . (gives the effect the behavior has on you or others)

Here are a few examples of effective I-messages:

- When *you won't stay in your car seat,* I feel *scared* because *I know you're not safe without your seat belt.*
- When *children don't help pick up toys,* I feel *tired and frustrated,* because *I'll have to pick them up myself.*
- When *you interrupt the sharing time,* I feel *mad* because *then no one else gets a turn.*

I-messages clarify a problem situation for children. Oddly enough, many children know when a behavior will irritate a parent or caregiver but don't know why. An effective I-message will help them understand why the behavior isn't OK. It will also model for children how you take responsibility for your own feelings.

Pay particular attention to the "when" portion of the I-message. Do not use blameful language or overgeneralize. For example, "When you act obnoxious, I feel mad, because it isn't respectful" is simply name-calling, because it doesn't let the child know exactly *what* she or he did that you don't like.

A Better Way

This technique, developed by Dr. Haim Ginot, is especially effective with preschoolers whose language skills have developed enough so they can negotiate with you. (Indeed, some preschoolers' language ability is so skilled that you wonder if you're dealing with a small version of a lawyer or car salesperson!) It is most useful if you use this technique to avoid a power struggle.

There are three parts to A Better Way: (1) State what the child wants; (2) state what you want; and then (3) ask the child to come up with a better idea that works for both of you.

Lisa recounts one successful use of this technique:

> I wanted Chelsea, age three, to finish her lunch. She had refused her morning snack, and her mom reported that she wouldn't eat much breakfast. She had a cheese stick and half a sandwich left to eat. She had heard me use A Better Way with the older kids, so I decided to use it on her. "Chelsea," I said, "your way is not to finish your lunch. My way is for you to eat it all up. What's a better way?" Chelsea thought about it and then suggested, "I eat two cheese sticks?" I was delighted with this solution, and Chelsea happily ate up two cheese sticks.

A Better Way works only when the child is clear on the fact that the suggestion must be something you *both* like. If a child suggests something that is reasonable but impractical, try to incorporate as much of that suggestion as possible. For example:

Provider: Your way is to stay up and play. My way is for you to take a nap now. What's a better way?

Child: Mommy sing me a song first.

Provider: Your mom won't be here till three o'clock. I could sing you a song, or Cecilia (assistant) could sing you a song.

Child: Cecilia needs to sing "Twinkle, Twinkle, Little Star."

Provider: That's fine. Let's ask her if she will.

A Better Way is a simple form of problem-solving. It allows the child some control in the situation, avoids an all-out power struggle, and teaches the child simple negotiating skills.

Increasing Good Behavior

Believe it or not, "catching them when they're being good" is far more effective than disciplining them when they're misbehaving. This section looks at three useful ways to notice, compliment, and positively reinforce children when they're behaving well.

Praise

The technique of praising children for good behavior is based on a theory that says we *learn* to behave the way we do. Praise reinforces the behavior that immediately precedes it. The best thing about praise is that it's always available; it just takes your noticing the child behaving well and commenting on it. You don't need special stickers or treats to positively reinforce good behavior. And truly, sincere praise from you will be more valuable to the child than anything tangible you could give him or her.

To be effective, praise needs to:

- Follow the good behavior immediately. If you say two hours later, "I liked the way you played with Molly in the block corner," it won't work as effectively.

- Be specific. If Johnny, who has a history of running in the house, walks calmly from the doll corner to the table for lunch, your saying, "I like the way you walked to the table, Johnny" is far more effective than simply saying, "Good job, Johnny."
- Be sincere. Kids can tell if you're being overly lavish with your praise or if you don't really mean it. For example, a calm statement like "I saw the way you shared Duplos with Annie; that's great" is much better than "Wow, you're the *best* cooperator in the whole place!"

Sometimes, when dealing with a particularly challenging child, it's difficult to praise the one thing that child does well when eighty-five other things have gone wrong that day. You might be tempted to say, "Finally, you shared a toy!" rather than "I like the way you shared the dinosaur with Andy." Keep in mind that any negative comparison will completely negate the praise. The following are a few classic misused praise statements:

Good. You picked up your toys. Try to remember to do it tomorrow.
That was a great throw for a girl.
That's a nice drawing. Why didn't you finish the top part?

Remember, when using praise, be specific, immediate, and sincere. The rewards, shown in children's self-esteem and behavior, will follow.

Attention

One parent educator I know is fond of saying, "You don't get to choose whether or not you give children your attention. You only get to choose how." It's true. If children don't get your attention by behaving well, they'll get it by behaving badly. If an appropriate bid for attention goes unnoticed or unattended to, it will most likely turn into a bid for attention that cannot go unattended to. Brenda gives an example of how children may choose to get negative attention rather than no attention:

It was a rainy day and the children couldn't go outside to play, as we usually do. Two of them asked me for a story instead. I was busy getting the afternoon's art activity ready and told them to find something else to do.

The next thing I knew, they were beating up on the dog. Upon reflection, I wish now that I'd read the story, or told them when I'd be available to read. It would have been a lot easier than calming the children and the dog down.

It's important to realize that attention can be positive or negative, verbal (praise or scolding), physical (a hug or a spanking), or nonverbal (listening or smiling). What kind of attention children prefer depends on their temperament, the type of attention they are accustomed to getting, and their skill level in asking for attention. Lisa talks about how the children in her care like to receive attention:

> At four and a half years old, Danielle is very active. She likes me to watch her climbing on the jungle gym and performing various tricks. Her favorite way to ask for attention is, "Lisa! Watch me!" She doesn't seem to want me to say anything, just to watch. Now her younger brother, Zach, age twenty months, likes physical attention. He wants me to hold him on my lap and read or just rock. Often he'll signal this need by clinging to my leg. Both of them, however, are quick to get my attention by fighting with each other if I'm initially unavailable on the attention front.

Teach children acceptable ways to ask for your attention. Some simple ways are:

- Saying, "I need a hug."
- Asking for help.
- Saying, "I need some attention."

You can decide what will work best for you and your mix of children.

Rewards

A reward is used to reinforce good behavior. It is given just following the behavior you want to see and immediately reinforces it. The reward has to be something the child really wants, or this technique won't be an effective reinforcer. Here are two examples of providers who've successfully used rewards.

I watch each day to see who settles down cooperatively at naptime. The child who does this quickly and well gets rewarded by being the one to "wake up" the other children by tapping them gently with my magic wand. I whisper to this child before he goes to sleep. I rotate this reward so no one child gets it all the time, and sometimes no one gets it and I do the wake-up duty.

My children have a hard time paying attention to directions. Listening carefully is something we're working on. When I observe a child really paying attention, I remark on it right away and reward him by naming him "lunch helper" for the day. The lunch helper gets to help me serve lunch.

The most powerful reward for a toddler is an adult's time and attention. Preschoolers like to get special privileges (e.g., those described earlier), stickers, treats, or other kinds of special tokens. Try to rotate the rewards. If you use the same one all the time, then you give that item or privilege an exaggerated importance. It is also true that after a while, children become satiated with a reward and it begins to lose its attraction.

Be careful not to confuse rewards with bribes. A reward *follows good behavior* and reinforces it. A bribe is given beforehand or afterward to *avoid misbehavior*. While bribes will usually work if you use them on the same situation all the time, they provide only a short-term solution. It is far more effective to reinforce the behavior you want to see.

Andrea describes the following common example of a bribe:

I had one mom who would tell her daughter, Anna, age two and a half, that if she didn't cry when she was dropped off at child care, she could have candy when she got home. It didn't work. Anna would cry anyway, and half the time the mom would still give her candy. Finally, I talked with the mom about developing a good-bye ritual to help Anna with the transition. She still cried for about three weeks, but after that she settled down into the routine of child care.

If the mother in this example wanted to switch to a reward system, she could have asked Andrea to give Anna a sticker each time she went through the good-bye ritual with her mom calmly.

As opposed to bribes, the techniques of attention, rewards, and praise have the added advantage of emphasizing the behavior you want. Children are much more likely to behave the way you want when they know *what* it is you want. Many children can tell you what behavior will get them into trouble, but they are far less clear on what adults want them to do.

Decreasing Difficult Behavior

When you put even just two children together, there's no shortage of difficult behavior. Providers—and parents—cite daily struggles with:

- Sharing
- Hitting
- Refusing to cooperate with normal requests
- Following rules (e.g., no running inside)
- Eating
- Napping

As we've said before, reinforcing good behavior is the most effective way to get children to continue it, but when you've got a child who just can't seem to function in one area, then it's time to pull out a few tools to help him or her along.

This section will look at three techniques: ignoring, time-out, and setting consequences. We will also look at two techniques that are particularly effective with toddlers: changing the space and redirection.

Ignoring

This is an appropriate technique to use when a behavior is simply annoying (e.g., crying to get attention) rather than a safety problem (e.g., hitting). The idea is that you completely, absolutely ignore the offending behavior and it will die out from the lack of attention from you.

Brenda describes a successful case of ignoring:

> Tenisha, age three, went through a phase where she would screech at the top of her lungs to get attention. This didn't seem to bother the other children, but it drove my assistant and me nuts. We decided that the reason she

did it was to get our attention in order to solve her problem (usually boredom), so we decided to ignore it. The next time it happened, we were out on the deck, watching the children play. Tenisha got bored with her truck and tried to take another child's toy. He refused. Tenisha screeched as loudly as she could. My assistant and I continued to talk normally over the noise. We didn't make eye contact with her or even look at her. She turned her head to see why we weren't responding. We felt a little silly but started an intense discussion about the gate 3 feet ahead of us. We talked about that gate like it was the most important thing in the world. Tenisha screamed louder. And louder. After three minutes of this, she gave up and went to join two other children playing with a train. We had about two more incidents like this and then she stopped screeching altogether.

Ignoring works only if it is used every time the behavior occurs and absolutely no attention is paid to the child (even a glance). Don't try to distract the child by offering her a toy or treat.

Lisa shares her ignoring technique:

When I ignore an annoying behavior, I go to a nearby toy corner and interest myself busily in playing. I might build an amazing block tower or talk to a doll. I don't pay any attention at all to the child while he is whining, crying, or whatever. But when he stops and gets interested in what I'm doing, I will gently involve him in it and leave him to play on his own.

You may find certain behaviors so annoying that you can't help but give in and pay attention in order to stop them. If this is the case, don't use ignoring to decrease the behavior; try another technique.

Time-Out

This is a technique whose purpose is to remove a child from a conflict situation in order to give her or him a chance to calm down and try again. It is *not* a punishment.

Time-outs work best starting when a child is between two and a half and three and a half. The child needs to understand the concepts of "waiting" and "quiet." With toddlers, the time-out should last one minute or less. Use the one-minute-for-each-year-of-age rule for preschoolers. Here's a step-by-step description of how time-out is intended to work:

1. Misbehaving child is removed from conflict, rule is repeated ("No hitting"), and adult announces it's time for a time-out.
2. Child is brought to a quiet, calm spot (e.g., a couch or hallway) not too far away from the action and told to sit quietly.
3. Child sits quietly for the duration of the time-out (the timing begins *after* the child has stopped crying, whining, or talking). Adult does not talk to, comfort, or discipline the child during this time.
4. At the end of the time-out, the adult thanks the child for sitting quietly, explains what kind of behavior is appropriate ("Touch gently"), and invites the child to rejoin the play.
5. Adult watches and compliments the child when she is playing appropriately.

You will need to walk the child through this process one or two times before she or he understands how it works. After that you should be able to tell the child to take a time-out and have her or him go to the time-out spot. Remember not to start timing until all fussing has stopped.

This is a useful technique in child care because it allows the child a chance to calm down and then gives another opportunity to practice appropriate behavior. Do not abuse or lengthen the time-out period; several one-minute or shorter time-outs are more effective than one long time-out. The more chances a child has to practice appropriate behavior, the faster she or he will learn. Andrea describes how time-out works in her child care:

> All the kids in my care are very experienced with time-out. Some of them even seem to welcome the chance to take a break from the group and quiet down. Just yesterday Christopher was acting up during circle time. I told him to take a time-out. When I signaled him to return, he told me politely, "I'm ready to control myself now." And he was!

Be consistent with time-out, and use it appropriately. It is fairly common for caregivers or parents to misuse time-out by allowing themselves to argue, being swayed by tears and promises to do better, or just responding angrily to rudeness. Here's an example:

It seems as if you're half as effective with your own kids as with the child-care kids sometimes. I can do time-out letter-perfect with the little kids, but when it comes to my own six-year-old, I blow it every time. He just knows how to push my buttons. When I send him for time-out, he goes, but he makes obnoxious comments on the way about my mothering and by the time he gets there, I'm yelling enough to need time-out myself.

If you can't disengage from the conflict long enough to facilitate a time-out, the child won't be able to either. If you find yourself doing this, try another technique that works better for that child.

Setting Consequences

There are two kinds of consequences you can use with young children to decrease difficult behavior: natural and logical. Consequences are different from punishments; they are directly related to the child's behavior and always offer the child an opportunity to take responsibility for the misbehavior. Setting consequences works like this:

- *Natural consequences* happen automatically. If it's raining and a child doesn't put on her shoes when she goes outside, her feet will get wet and cold. If a child doesn't eat his dinner, he will get hungry before breakfast. These consequences are natural and don't need you to make them happen; they happen as a result of the child's action. They are valuable learning tools for young children who are just learning about cause and effect.

  Make use of natural consequences by pointing out what they will be. Chris describes how she does this:

  It was a bright, hot day and we were going to the beach. All the four-year-olds have child-size sunglasses to wear. I instructed each of them to put his or her sunglasses in the beach bag before we went. Tanya refused to cooperate; she was busy with a block tower. I told her, "If you don't bring your sunglasses, you'll get bright sun in your eyes." She ignored me, so we went without them. Sure enough, the bright sun bothered her and she was jealous of the other kids' sunglasses. She complained to me about it. I sympathized about the bright sun but reminded her that she chose not to bring her sunglasses. She was unhappy, but since then she has never failed to take her sunglasses to the beach.

Natural consequences allow children to take responsibility for their actions and learn from them. Chris was wise not to solve the problem for Tanya (buy her another pair, let her borrow another child's pair, etc.) but let her experience the natural consequences of her own decision.

Of course, allowing children to experience natural consequences is not appropriate in safety situations, such as stepping out in front of a car. Be on the lookout for opportunities where children can safely experience natural consequences.

- *Logical consequences* are created and administered by you. They should be related to the misbehavior, acceptable to you, and carried out immediately. For instance: "No splashing kids' faces in the wading pool. If you splash again, you'll have to get out." The consequence is related to the misbehavior and is one the provider is willing and able to carry out immediately.

    The following is not an effective logical consequence: "No splashing kids' faces. If you do it again, you won't get a story later." The consequence here is not related to the offense and feels more like a punishment than a consequence.

I would caution you not to overuse consequences. They are most effective when used sparingly. If a misbehavior occurs repeatedly, then take some time to think about the problem. Choose three techniques you think might solve it. After you've tried those things, if the misbehavior still happens, then set a consequence.

The following are some commonly used consequences for ages three through six:

Send child to another room.
Withhold play privilege for five minutes.
Ten minutes earlier naptime (or rest time).
Twenty-minute time-out for toy.
Loss of planned outing (park, walk) after one warning. (Do this only if you or another assistant is available to sit with the child.)

Making amends is a very good, logical consequence. When you make amends, you repair any damage you've done to another, or try, in some way, to make it up to him or her. Amends can be made for any number of transgressions that infringe on the rights of others.

I like using this technique because it teaches children to think about the needs and rights of other people. It works like this. Let's say three-year-old Taylor has torn four-year-old Kane's artwork.

> *Provider:* Taylor, you tore Kane's paper. What can you do to fix this?
>
> *Taylor* (looking at shoes): I don't know.
>
> *Provider:* Can you think of something that would help him feel better?
>
> *Taylor:* We could tape it.
>
> *Kane:* No! It's ruined. (Cries.)
>
> *Provider:* What else can we do to help Kane?
>
> *Taylor:* I could paint him a new picture. Or he could have mine.
>
> *Provider:* Kane, does that sound OK to you?
>
> *Kane:* OK, she can paint me a rainbow.
>
> *Provider:* Great. I'm glad you two worked this out.

The amends must be willingly offered by the perpetrator, and acceptable to the victim and you. If these attitudes are not present, use a different discipline technique to deal with the problem. Everyone, including you, needs to be satisfied with the amends. Helping a child make amends takes your time and direct involvement, so reserve it for the serious misbehaviors.

Changing the Space

Altering the physical environment works well with young children, particularly toddlers. This is something that most providers do naturally. You lock up the knives, put the stereo equipment in rooms they don't go into, or keep the dog outside. But changing the space is also a useful tool for solving specific behavior problems. Here's an example.

> I had trouble with children climbing over and bouncing on the couch. No amount of reminders helped them stop—it was just too much fun. After

some thought I decided to make the couch much less convenient to get to. I rearranged the room so that the couch was off in a corner near the books and blocked by other interesting, active toys. It wasn't so easy to run across the room and bounce onto the couch—they had to walk around inviting items to get to it. Gradually, the couch became used for storytime and the active play was confined to the middle of the room and outdoors.

You can cut down on chaos and problems by restricting certain activities to specific areas. For example, we eat only in the kitchen, make art only at the table, or play with sand only outside. In this way, you limit the environment.

You can also manipulate the children's space so that they can function more independently. A child-size stool and low towel rack in the bathroom will free you up from constantly assisting with hand-washing. Easy, low-level access to toys is also necessary.

Redirecting Children

Oftentimes a child does something unacceptable for the sheer joy of it. For example, toddlers enjoy ripping paper. Ripping up books, however, is unacceptable. In these kinds of cases, providing the child with an acceptable alternative is very effective. The toddler may not rip up a book but could rip up old newspapers. One provider gives an example of redirecting:

> Tyler, age three, loves to whack things. Inside or outside, he tends to find a bat, a stick, whatever, and whacks away. I worked very hard with him to help him learn that whacking inside is unacceptable. Outside, he can whack weeds or tree roots. Once we found an OK place for him to whack, the inside problems went away.

Toddlers will often easily accept this kind of substitution, but they will also test to see if you really mean it on Mondays, or when a parent is present, or if you're gone and your partner is in charge. This is normal. Be aware of such testing, and firmly remind the child what the rule is.

There are many, many ways to redirect children's play and exploration in acceptable ways. Train yourself to help children find better ways to explore.

Fostering Good Social Skills

All providers and parents want children to play together cooperatively, or at least without bloodshed. Some children have good instincts for getting along with others, whereas other children need more teaching and guidance.

Concepts like sharing, negotiation, and problem-solving are appropriate to start teaching when children are about age three. Before that children do not have the cognitive skills necessary to deal safely with conflict without your intervention. The beginnings of teaching problem solving can be found in the technique A Better Way (described earlier). Children who are familiar with this tool will learn problem-solving more easily.

You can do joint problem-solving with a young child, and you can help children begin to learn to solve their own problems. Elizabeth Crary, in her book *Kids Can Cooperate* (see appendix), describes the following problem-solving approach, which she calls SIGEP:

1. **S**top. Calm yourself and the child(ren) down.
2. **I**dentify the problem and feelings. State what the problem is in a factual, non-judgmental way. Then state the feelings involved, using I-messages.
3. **G**enerate ideas. Both adult and child(ren) think of all the ideas they can to solve the problem. The adult writes all the ideas down, even the silly or unworkable ones. Do not evaluate the ideas while you're thinking them up.
4. **E**valuate the ideas. Talk about why each one might work or might not. Cross out the ideas that won't work.
5. **P**lan. Together, pick one of the ideas you both like and plan how you will implement it. If it doesn't work, go back to your list and pick another idea.

Debbie talks about how she used this approach with a child who had a very hard time separating from her mom in the morning:

> Corrie, age three and a half, cried every morning after her mom left. Most of my kids will quickly get interested in playing after their parents leave, but Corrie was sadder than most, I think. She would cry for half an hour sometimes. I decided to try some joint problem-solving with her. I rocked her for a few minutes and then said, "You feel really sad when your mom

has to go to work." Corrie nodded and kept crying. "Hmmm," I said, "how could we solve this problem? Let's think of ways for it to be easier for you to say good-bye to your mom." Corrie just continued to cry.

"You could keep a special picture of your mom in your pocket," I suggested. The crying quieted a bit as Corrie got interested in what I was saying. "Or," I went on, "we could ask your mom to call you at snack time in the morning."

"We could stay home," Corrie insisted.

"That's one idea," I responded. "What's another idea?"

"She could play a game with me before she leaves," Corrie offered.

"Or," I said, "you could ask me for a hug if you feel sad. That's a lot of ideas. I don't think your mom can stay home from work all the time, so that won't work. Which of the other ideas do you want to try?"

Corrie decided she wanted her mom to play a game with her before she left and to call at snack time. I spoke with the mother that evening, and she agreed to arrive ten minutes earlier for a game and to check in on Corrie by phone.

Joint problem-solving is especially effective because it offers the child some control and "say-so" in how the problem is solved. If a child has helped choose a solution, then she or he has much more invested in seeing it work than if it was handed down from above.

Research shows that when faced with a conflict, the more alternatives a child (or adult) can come up with, the more likely she or he is to choose a solution that works well. There are three easy ways to model the problem-solving process for children.

First, you can model the process by using it to work out your own conflicts. For instance, one provider consistently uses problem-solving with her own older children in front of the children in care. It's also helpful to "think out loud" about problems in order to model solving them. For example: "Let's see. Maria wants me to help her wash her hands and Josh needs me to watch him on the monkey bars. That's two children who need me at the same time. I can't be two places at once, so what can I do? I could make Maria wait for help, make Joshua wait for me to watch, ask Lily (the teenage helper) to help Maria, or I could help Maria and watch Josh from the bathroom window. I think I'll try that. Is it OK with you if I watch from the bathroom, Josh, or would you like to wait?"

Second, you can model the process with puppets, dolls, or stuffed animals. Pick any problem you commonly see the children having, like sharing a toy, and have the puppets act out the problem. Talk about their feelings. Then ask the children for ideas on how the puppets might solve the problem. Listen to all the ideas, being careful not to discount any (if a child suggests something inappropriate, e.g., "Smash him in the face," then redirect the energy by saying, "Hitting and smashing are hurting ideas. What are some helping ideas?"). Then have the children choose one idea. Have the puppets act out the solution. If it doesn't work, point that out and have them choose another idea. Remember to keep talking about each of the puppets' feelings as they try different solutions.

Third, you can use children's books to illustrate problem-solving. There are many excellent books that specifically use this process and others that are easily adaptable to it. Elizabeth Crary's series on problem-solving is especially useful; it covers the common conflict areas of sharing, waiting a turn, entering a play group, name-calling, getting lost, and separating from a parent. Sarah, an experienced provider, shares this story about using Crary's book *I'm Lost* with her group:

> My kids weren't used to these kinds of problem-solving books at first. At the beginning of the story, the main character gets separated from her dad at the zoo. "What can Amy do?" I read. One little girl eagerly raised her hand and suggested, "She could give up and go live with the gorillas!" It was hard to keep a straight face, but I said, "Well, that's one idea. What else could she do?" We continued on, and the children quickly caught on to the real-life nature of the story.

Traditional stories can also be used to model problem-solving. One provider liked to use the classic story *Curious George*, by H. A. Rey, to do this.

> George gets into a lot of mischief. I'd point out the problem as he got into it and ask, "How does George solve the problem?" The children (who have read this book seventy million times) would tell me exactly what will happen. "What else could he have done?" I would ask. After a while they got into thinking up new ways for George to escape whatever trouble he was in.

The appendix lists several books that are helpful in fostering good social skills in children.

Where to Go When a Child Needs More Help than You Can Give

All children have behavior problems from time to time. Some children, however, exhibit behavioral disturbances that require help past what you can provide. Typically, these children are asked to leave several child-care settings due to chronic acting-out behavior. (Most parents of these children will not inform you of the child's history.) The difficult behavior might include hitting, screaming, constantly refusing to cooperate, biting, spitting, using foul language, and so on. Also of concern is a child who is extremely introverted or fearful. There is usually a physiological or psychological reason for a child's continued difficult behavior—and since you are neither a physician nor a therapist, it is better to refer the family to someone trained to help.

Although it is much more common for children to be excused from family child care due to problems with the parents, you may occasionally ask a child to leave for behavioral reasons. In general, it is wise to refer parents to your local Resource and Referral agency. The agency can direct them to other professional help or a therapeutic day care, if appropriate. It is also wise for you to call the agency and advise them that you've dismissed the child and for what reasons; this protects you as well as helps the agency properly refer the family.

Ten Common Guidance Problems

The following is a description of ten typical guidance problems that providers deal with. After each sample problem, I will point out factors you need to consider and offer three ideas for solving the problem based on the techniques presented in this chapter.

1. **Grabs Toys from Other Children**
   Ryan, age two and a half, is an active child, and actions speak louder than words with him. About five to six times a day I have to break up a conflict wherein he grabs something another child has. For instance, today I heard Chelsea screaming, "He took my train! He took my train!" and saw Ryan playing calmly with it on the track, ignoring Chelsea's cry.

What do you want Ryan to do?

I want Ryan to share the toys and wait for his turn.

What to think about:

At two and a half, Ryan is not yet able to share without adult assistance. His temperament is physical, and it makes sense that he would choose a physical way of solving his problem (grabbing).

Possible solutions:

1. Changing the space. Since forcing Ryan to share before he is developmentally ready to do so probably won't work, the easiest thing to do is to provide at least two of the same toy. You could either give Chelsea another train or put out two in the first place.

2. Active listening. Help Ryan see how his actions affect others. Say, "Ryan, look at Chelsea's face. How does she feel?" He probably won't answer, but point out, "She feels very sad and mad when someone takes her toy." Doing this every time a conflict occurs will help Ryan begin to be sympathetic to the needs and feelings of others.

3. Problem solving. State the rule "Children in this house have to wait their turn." Explain to Ryan that grabbing a toy isn't waiting for his turn. Help him think of ways he can wait while Chelsea finishes playing with the train. Some ideas: Sing a silly waiting song, set the kitchen timer for five minutes, or play with another toy.

2. Whines

Rebecca, age three, is my resident whiner. When she doesn't get something she wants, she whines to me about it. If she has to do something she's not excited about, she whines. Sometimes she's just bored and she whines! I think it's a habit more than anything else, but it drives me crazy.

What do you want Rebecca to do?

I want her to use a normal voice.

What to think about:

Whining is common in young children, usually among girls more than boys. They learn to do it because it gets your attention fast. Many do it automatically, not really aware of their voice quality. Others do it when tired or hungry.

Possible solutions:
1. I-message. Say calmly, "Oh, that voice hurts my ears" (cover your ears) and "Can you use a different voice?" You may need to model what a pleasant voice sounds like for her, and ask her to repeat it after you. Use this reminder every time she whines. Don't respond to her complaint until she uses a better voice.
2. Attention. Whenever she uses a pleasant voice, respond promptly to her requests. Say, "That's such a nice voice you used. I like to hear that."
3. Logical consequences. Tell her, "Ask me in a nice voice, or the answer is no."

3. Doesn't Follow Directions

Benjamin, age four, marches to his own drummer. He likes to do things his way, all the time. He gets along all right with the other kids but resists me a lot. For example, yesterday when we were finishing up an art activity, I said, "OK, everybody put their paintbrushes in the water jar and go wash your hands." Benjamin ignored me and continued to paint. A few minutes later I again told him to finish up. He scowled at me and said, "I'm not done!" When I tried to force the issue, he threw a tantrum.

What do you want Benjamin to do?
I want him to follow the same directions the other children do. I don't want the other kids thinking he gets special treatment all the time, but neither do I want to fight with Benjamin every day.

What to think about:
Some children have persistent temperaments. Although persistence is a wonderful adult trait, it can be difficult to deal with in a child. Also keep in mind that transitions from one activity to another are often hard for young children to navigate smoothly.

Possible solutions:

1. A Better Way. Ask Benjamin, "My way is that you finish up right now. Your way is that you keep painting. What's a better way?" He might respond, "I'll finish it after lunch" or "I'll just finish the sun part of the picture." If he offers anything workable, try to accommodate his suggestion.

2. Natural consequences. Let him take longer to finish his artwork. When he finally gets washed up and comes for snack, point out matter-of-factly, "When children come late for snack, there aren't any cheese sticks left. I guess you'll have to have carrots."

3. Avoiding the problem. Five minutes before it's time to clean up, announce that you are setting a timer and, when it goes off, they will start cleanup. This sort of advance warning helps children make the transition from one activity to another.

4. **Cries at Naptime**

Sarah, age two, cries every day at naptime. I believe she's the same way at home when she needs to go to bed. It's disturbing for the other children when she screams, and no one can settle down.

What do you want Sarah to do?

I want her to settle down to naptime calmly; she doesn't have to sleep, but she needs to be quiet.

What to think about:

You can put a child to bed, but you can't make her sleep. Realize that your control here is limited. It's also possible that she's experiencing separation anxiety and is afraid to go to sleep. She may also be overtired.

Sleepytime Reading

A quick list of good books to use with a naptime ritual:

• *The Napping House* by Don & Audrey Wood (also available as a board book, audio CD, and big book versions)

• *Goodnight Moon* by Margaret Wise Brown (also available as a board book)

• *Hush Little Baby* by Sylvia Long (also available as a board book)

• *Time for Bed* by Mem Fox (also available as a board book)

Possible solutions:

1. Offer a choice. Say, "Sarah, you can either lie down and go to sleep or you can just rest your bones on the couch and read a book to yourself." If she chooses to go to the couch, make sure she stays there quietly. If she gets down, tell her she has to go back to her napping place.

2. Establish a naptime ritual. Read *The Napping House* by Don and Audrey Wood before putting the children down, or conduct some other quiet, settle-down activity. If Sarah's been having fun at some activity just before, it may help her with the transition to nap.

3. Change the space. Move Sarah to another room for naptime so the crying won't disturb the other kids.

5. Calls Other Children Names

Rachel, age three and a half, calls the other kids names when she gets mad or frustrated. Today she got angry at Sam for winning a game and called him a "poo-poo head." Sam burst into tears, and Rachel began chanting "crybaby" over and over again.

What do you want Rachel to do?
I want her to deal with her feelings without hurting others.

What to think about:
Young children are usually very attracted to the power of name-calling. They seldom think about others' feelings. Regardless of how you choose to handle the problem, it is always appropriate to remind children of your rules about name-calling. In addition, you can work with both children to help them find better ways to cope. The child who is being picked on has options too.*

Possible solutions:

1. Logical consequence. Remind Rachel of the rule "We don't call names in this house." Give her a consequence: "Since you're not treating others kindly, you will have to sit out the next game on the couch."

* See the children's book *My Name Is Not Dummy* by Elizabeth Crary, listed in the appendix.

2. Active listening. Say to Rachel, "It's disappointing when you lose a game. It's OK to feel disappointed, but I can't let you call Sam names."

3. Problem solving. Ask Rachel, "What are three things you can do when you feel sad or disappointed about the game?" If she doesn't offer any ideas, say, "I can think of three things you could do. You could come ask me for a hug. Or you could tell yourself, 'I did my best. Next time I'll do better.' Or you could go play at something you do well—like Pickup Sticks."

6. Won't Pick Up Toys

Nathan, age four, refuses to help pick up toys during cleanup. He's quite clever—manages to be in the bathroom, or in the middle of a book, slips outside, or says he doesn't feel well when I say it's time to pick up. When I enforce the cleanup rule, he begins to cry and says, "I want my mommy!"

What do you want Nathan to do?

I want him to make some kind of effort toward cleanup. I want him to learn that part of the privilege of playing with toys is the obligation to pick them up.

What to think about:

Preschoolers don't make good maids. Most children are not capable of picking up after themselves until they are four, and then only with help. (The average age children pick up after themselves without help or reminding is twelve.) Expect resistance and what for an adult would be a "poor performance." How cooperative children are probably depends on how much their parents have required them to help clean up at home. Again, don't expect much at this age. It is reasonable, however, to start teaching children this skill.

Possible solutions:

1. Use praise. Whenever you see Nathan pick up anything and put it away, notice it and praise him. Say, "Wow, you put that toy away! I sure like that." Try to catch him doing this at least once a day.

2. Make cleanup a game. Set the timer for three minutes and tell the children to find anything with red on it and put it away. Repeat the procedure for blue, then green, and so on. Try to "beat the clock."

3. State a logical consequence. Establish a rule. For example, you could say, "Any child who does not help with cleanup does not get to play with [a particular toy] tomorrow."

7. Hits Other Children

Peter, age two and a half, is quick to hit. He does so when another child takes his toy, calls him a name, or won't let go of something, and then, of course, he hits back when someone hits him first.

What do you want Peter to do?
I want him to use other ways to solve his problems besides hitting.

What to think about:
Two-year-olds are famous for using their fists to express what they're not quite yet able to articulate in words. Since they do have some language skills, it is a perfect time to start teaching them other avenues of self-expression.

Possible solutions:
1. Time-out. In the midst of a conflict, it is often useful to remove a two-year-old from the scene and give him a chance to cool down. As you take him out, say, "People are not for hitting. Touch gently."
2. Active listening. Help give him the words for his feelings. For example, say, "You feel really mad, but I can't let you hurt Tyler. Next time, come get me."
3. Rewards. Give Peter a gold star every time you see him touching someone gently. It will help him notice the difference between gentle touching and hitting and the effect it has on others.

8. Cries When Parent Leaves

Megan, age two, cries every day when her mom or dad drops her off. This has been going on for months. She usually settles down within ten or fifteen minutes, but I'm starting to be concerned about her. She seems to be happy the rest of the time.

What do you want Megan to do?
I'd like her to be less distraught when her parents leave.

What to think about:

Crying at drop-off is very common the first few weeks a child is in child care. After that the child should settle into the routine and separate more easily. Discuss any prolonged distress with the parents; there may be other stresses in the child's life that are affecting her. If a child is truly inconsolable and remains so, advise the parents to reevaluate whether she belongs in child care.

Possible solutions:

1. Devising a good-bye ritual. Encourage the parent to establish a good-bye ritual to ease the separation. Perhaps Megan's mom could help her hang up her coat and start a play activity, then a hug and a kiss. Sometimes the promise of a midday phone call will help a child as well. (The parent must follow through with the phone call or it won't work.)

2. Active listening. Hug Megan. Say to her, "You feel very sad to say good-bye to your mommy. Would you like to sing the 'My Mommy Comes Back' song?"

3. Problem-solving. Once the child is calm, offer a few alternatives to crying (at three years or older, the child can help think up ideas). Here are three ideas: (1) Keep something of Mom's while she's away (a sweater or scarf to cuddle), (2) ask the provider for a hug, and (3) play a fun game.*

9. Complains "No One Will Play with Me"

I have one child, Madeleine, age four, who continually comes to me and says no one will play with her. There are ten children in my care, several her own age, so there's no lack of opportunity. I wonder if she's bored or if she just lacks the skills to join in the play.

What do you want Madeleine to do?

I want her to enter play groups without relying on my help.

What to think about:

Some children seem to be born with good social skills; they interact easily with everyone. Others have to be deliberately taught how to get along socially. Observe the child in a group. Is she shy, hanging back and waiting to be invited to play? Or is she trying to control the play, and turning other children off?

---

* See the book *Mommy, Don't Go* by Elizabeth Crary, listed in the appendix.

Knowing where the problem is will help you teach her what to do.

Possible solutions:

1. Try problem-solving. Help her brainstorm ideas on how to find a playmate. Say, "Hmmm. What have you tried?" (Most children either haven't tried anything or have simply asked if they can play.) "Let's see, you could start a fun game and invite someone else to join you. Or you could read a book to the littler kids. Or you could play by yourself."

2. Read a book. Read *I Want to Play*, by Elizabeth Crary (see appendix) with Madeleine.

3. Talk to the parent. Encourage Madeleine's mom to make play dates with the other kids outside of child care. Perhaps this way Madeleine will make friends more easily.

10. Is a Picky Eater

Adam, age three, is a picky eater. It's not uncommon for him to go all day without eating anything more than a few crackers. It worries me that he's hungry, but he doesn't want anything I offer him.

What do you want Adam to do?
I want him to eat enough of the food I offer to be nourishing.

What to think about:
Many preschoolers are fussy or inconsistent eaters. They eat a lot at one meal and practically nothing at the next. Nutritionists say that many young children end up eating a balanced diet when you look at it over the span of several days.

Possible solutions:

1. Involve Adam in food preparation. If he helps make it, he may be more motivated to eat it. It's also helpful to get a children's cookbook and to make some of the "fun-looking" recipes, which children are more likely to eat.

2. Ask his parents what he will eat. If it's nutritious, add it to your menu.

3. Add another snack time to the schedule. Fruit-juice Popsicles outside are an easy pick-me-up for the children. Or maybe tortilla chips and salsa in the afternoon would tempt Adam.

## Chapter Seven

Back to Business

This chapter attempts to give you a broad overview of record-keeping and taxes. Since tax laws are continually changing, it is inevitable that some information will change during the print life of this book; readers should always check their understanding of tax rules with the IRS and/or other qualified professionals. The information conveyed here is not intended in any way to take the place of legal, accounting, or other professional services.

Three areas that are important to your business will be discussed: (1) generating enrollment, (2) setting up your office, and (3) record-keeping. A successful business depends, to some extent, on all of these.

Generating Enrollment

You can't run a family child care without the children, so one of your first orders of business should be to generate enrollment. The sooner you operate at your capacity, the sooner you will be profitable.

But before you begin recruiting children, it is helpful to know your potential "market" precisely. That is, the better you know the type of family you are after for your child care, the more successful you will be at attracting them to your business.

The questions in the following worksheet will help you focus on what type of family, parent, and child you wish to attract to your child care. Perhaps you live close to an aerospace company and would like to care for the young children of the parents who work there. Perhaps you plan to have a preschool curriculum in place and don't want the added responsibility of infants. Answering the following questions will get you started on narrowing down who you want and how to find them.

Sample Profile of Prospective Market

Part 1

Type of Parent

__ Employed (presumably)

__ Professional

__ Blue-collar

__ Traditional hours

__ Unusual hours

__ Works at particular company/organization: _____

__ Travels a lot

__ Other: _____

__ Other: _____

__ Other: _____

__ Other: _____

Type of Family

__ Single-parent home

__ Two-parent home

__ Families with two or more children

__ Income range of: _____

__ Values parenting/family time

__ Lives or works nearby

__ Other: _____

__ Other: _____

__ Other: _____

__ Other: _____

Type of Child

__ Age range of: _____

__ Special-needs child (medical, behavioral, etc.)

__ Ready for preschool curriculum

__ Able to go on field trips

__ Other: _____

__ Other: _____

__ Other: _____

__ Other: _____

Part 2

Brainstorm ways in which to reach these types of families. Come up with three to five ideas.

_____

_____

_____

_____

_____

_____

_____

_____

_____

_____

There are several ways to go about marketing your child-care services. We will go over several ideas, but keep this thought in mind: You need to be able to market your services in *more* than one medium.

- *Sign up with your local child-care Resource and Referral (R&R) agency* as soon as you are licensed. These agencies refer their callers to all appropriate child-care options in the area. You were probably put in touch with your local Resource and Referral when you went through the licensing process. If not, locate the nearest agency by contacting the National Association of Child Care Resource and Referral Agencies (NACCRRA—see appendix). You can ask someone from your R&R to come out, look at your child care, and offer suggestions for marketing. Perhaps your entryway needs a spring cleaning or flowers in the front flower bed would go a long way toward creating a more attractive first impression.
- *Hand out or post printed materials advertising your child care.* Many of us have the ability to make business cards on our home computers. You can buy special card stock to print them at home, or you can have some professionally made. Most communities have printing shops that offer a business card service. Black ink on a white card is usually the least expensive and can look very professional. If you have an artist friend, have her or him sketch you a logo in black ink to have reduced and put on the card. Keep in mind that you cannot reproduce just any drawing you find; most are protected by copyright. However, you can buy books of "clip art," drawings that are published with the express permission that they can be duplicated. Ask for this kind of book at your local bookstore or library.

The following is an example of a provider's business card:

> **Internet Tip**
>
> You don't actually have to be your own designer when it comes to a logo for your business, nor do you have to scout out a graphic design firm in your neighborhood. Go to www.Logoworks.com and take a look at their services. Starting at $299 they will access their pool of designers and solicit logos for your business based on your specs. You choose from the resulting submissions.

Carry a few business cards and hand them out everywhere you go—especially when you're out with the children for a walk or on a field trip.

- *Another printed piece you can create is a flyer that advertises your service.* This flyer can be posted in dozens of locations in your community (with permission), including the local grocery store, church or synagogue, children's clothing or book stores, restaurants, beauty salons, laundromats, personnel offices of large employers in your area, and so on.

    When preparing your flyer, try to focus on the *benefits* a parent will receive by coming to you—such as discounts for more than one child—rather than listing features (such as your big backyard). Your background in early childhood education and your program content are features that contribute to a clear benefit: children who learn. Start by looking at how other providers have put together flyers. Your local or regional child-care association can help you collect some of these.

    Make sure you include, in large letters, directions for what an interested parent should do. For example, the flyer for the Sunshine Family Child Care tells parents to "CALL NOW!" and gives the phone number in big numerals.

    You can have flyers typeset and printed at your local printing shop. If you (or a friend) have a nice desktop system, you can typeset the flyer yourself. When getting ready to print the flyer, take time to look over the selection of papers and inks. Ask to see samples of how certain color combinations work together. If you've seen a flyer you especially like, take it in as a sample and ask the printer for an estimate on printing your flyer with the same or similar paper and ink. Always, always get an estimate before you place a print order. Keep in mind, too, that every change you make as you progress will cost you extra money.

- *Name your business with marketing in mind.* Think about the area where you are located and the families you will service. The two child cares represented thus far have very different types of names. "Bakeman Family Child Care" is straightforward and would appeal, say, to those in a university community. If you are competing with several child-care centers in the neighborhood, something like "Sunshine Family Child Care" is more eye-catching. Here are some other examples of business names:

Andrews Family Child Care

The Strawberry Patch

Kiddie Corner Day Care

Rainbow Kids Child Care

The Happy Kids' Place

Your choice of a name depends on how you want your business to be perceived. I recommend choosing a name that communicates child care and warmth but sounds like a business. Brainstorm a few possible names and then run them by your neighbors, friends, and associates before you make a decision.

Something else to keep in mind is that in the event of an audit, the IRS typically responds better to businesses that operate in a businesslike fashion and have a name that sounds like a business. If you are operating without a business name, you will appear more as a babysitter to the IRS than as a businessperson.

- *Put your business name on your checks.* Even if your bank account is in your name, you can add "dba" (doing business as) and the child-care name—for example, "Susan Townsand, dba The Secret Garden Child Care." Deborah, a longtime provider, talks about this method of marketing:

> I've always put my child-care name on my checks. You'd be surprised how many clerks and merchants notice it, comment on it, and ask me about my business. Half the time they are looking for child care or know someone who is.

Sample Advertising Flyer

SUNSHINE
Family Child Care

A full-service family child care providing loving care for children ages birth through six years

- Fully licensed home child care (license #40073)

- Preschool curriculum program for ages three through five

- Flexible hours: 6:00 A.M.–5:30 P.M. Monday through Friday

- Participant in Federal Food Program

- Discounts for second child in care

- Convenient location

- Reasonable rates

- Owned and operated by former preschool teacher

- Member of the National Association of Family Child Care

Located at:
54322 Redondo Beach Drive
Santa Theresa, CA 92533

Proprietor:
Mary Nichols

Phone:
(808) 555–7765

CALL NOW!

Sample Naming Your Business Worksheet

1. Describe the family type you wish to attract to your business (e.g., professional, preferably siblings, live nearby).

    _____

    _____

    _____

    _____

    _____

    _____

2. Brainstorm all sorts of words (nouns, verbs, adjectives) that would appeal to this type of family.

    _____

    _____

    _____

    _____

3. List all the descriptive words you can think of to describe your business and the care you will offer (e.g., gentle, competent, countryside).

    _____

    _____

    _____

    _____

    _____

    _____

4. Now brainstorm all the business names you can think of. Write them down even if they sound silly. You're not evaluating here; you're just generating ideas. Write down a minimum of ten ideas.

_____   _____

_____   _____

_____   _____

_____   _____

_____   _____

_____   _____

_____   _____

_____   _____

_____   _____

_____   _____

5. Choose the top five ideas from your list. Type them up on a separate piece of paper. Quiz all parents of young children you know as to which business name appeals to them most. Ask parents who are most like the ones you wish to attract to your child care—try to get at least ten to fifteen responses. Make note of the choices and see if one or two particularly appeal to your test group. Make your decision.

Top five picks:

1. _____

2. _____

3. _____

4. _____

5. _____

- *In order to use a dba or business name (anything other than your own name), you must file a fictitious business name statement with your city or county.* Go to the bank where you'd like to open up your business checking account. They can advise you on how to proceed. In some communities the local newspaper handles the application for you; in other areas you need to go directly to a government office. You will be asked to fill out a form describing your business (answering, for example, Is your business conducted by an individual? Partners? Is it a corporation?) and to present identification. There will be a filing fee. In addition, you must take out space in your local paper that informs the public of your fictitious business name. Find out when your statement expires (generally, it's five years); you will need to refile at that time.

    As you go about this process, check to make sure that no one else is using the same business name. The business licensing people in your community or the staff at your local library can help you with this kind of name search. You can also do an Internet search for the business name in your locale. Be aware though, an Internet search is not necessarily exhaustive.

- *Talk up your business:* Word of mouth is, perhaps, the very best way to fill your child care. Tell everyone you know that you are opening a child care or have spaces to fill. Inform your relatives, friends, former colleagues, neighbors—anyone you come in contact with. Word will spread.

    One provider describes how this approach works for her:

    > When I first started doing child care, I began by caring for a few friends' children. I expanded with referrals from my R&R and from my church and soon was filled up to my capacity. Now I get calls at least twice a month. I prefer to take referrals from my group of parents; I trust their recommendations more than any other referrals I get.

- *Network with other family child-care providers in your area.* Keep a list handy of their numbers and agree to refer any callers to them if you are full; in turn, they will refer to you when they are full. You can get in touch with other providers through your local child-care Resource and Referral agency and your local family child-care association.

- *Parents of the children currently in care.* Once you've been in business a while, this will be perhaps your best source of referrals. If you have an opening, let all the parents know.
- *Classified or display advertising* is also an option. Providers' opinions vary on how effective this really is. In general, it is better to advertise in the small, local weekly papers in your community than in the large dailies. An even better option is your community's parenting newsletter. When placing a classified ad (the most cost-effective), remember that every word costs you money, so be concise. Here is a sample classified ad:

> **Family Child Care**: openings for kids 1–5 yrs. Licensed, experienced provider. 7 am–6 pm M–F. Valle Vista area. Call 555–8222.

If you are placing a small display ad, scan the publication for other ads the same size that catch your attention. Make sure the service you offer (family child care), the area you are located in, and your phone number are prominent.

- *Have sweatshirts or T-shirts printed*—for yourself, your assistant, and the children—with your business name and logo on the shirts. Wear them when you go out on field trips or even to the grocery store. People will notice and comment on them. An added benefit is that wearing matching shirts helps you keep track of the children while you're out. (*Note:* Do not put children's individual names on the shirts—it makes them vulnerable to abduction.)
- *Halloween marketing.* Attach your business card to the treats you hand out at Halloween. It's an easy way to advertise to those right in your neighborhood.
- *Keep your child care clean and tidy.* When parents come to visit or to drop off or pick up their children, a clean environment will help you keep them enrolled. A messy or dirty child care will not reassure parents or encourage them to place their child with you.

Camille talks about her system for keeping things tidy when parents walk in:

I make cleanup part of the daily schedule. I vacuum early in the morning before anyone arrives. The children help my assistant and me to pick up before circle time (about 1:30 P.M.). Then at 5:00 P.M. we have mandatory video-watching in the study while my assistant quickly picks up the main playroom and vacuums. The parents arrive at 5:30 P.M. I really feel the clean play area helps sell parents on family child care.

This strategy works well for Camille. Some parents, however, may object to mandatory videos—however educational they may be. Be sensitive to parents' priorities in this area. Again, someone from your R&R can help you cast a critical eye over your facility and point out areas that need attention.

Not all of the marketing ideas described here will work for you, but some of them will. Undoubtedly, you will have ideas of your own. Faye, a relatively new provider, shares the methods that worked for her:

I wish now that I'd started advertising the business the minute I started the licensing process. It's taken me about nine months to fill up to capacity. The things that worked the best were (1) big posters posted on utility poles (made with thick black felt markers on neon-orange-colored poster board), (2) referrals from our R&R, and (3) an ad in the *Eastside Parent* newspaper. We also ran an ad in the local daily paper, but that didn't get even one call.

Many providers also report that spring is a good time to generate enrollment. There are a few reasons for this: Some providers close for the summer, many schools are ending their school year, and families often move in the late spring and summer.

Screening Parents and Children

Experienced providers often recommend some kind of screening process once you've attracted potential customers. If possible, you want to avoid "problem" parents and children (e.g., parents who have left a previous child care with unpaid bills, are chronic offenders of the late-pickup policy, or neglect their children, or children who have behavioral problems beyond your ability to cope with them).

Sample Provider Screening Questions and Checklist
(for provider use only)

1. Child's name and age:

   _____

   _____

2. Where was your child last placed in care?

   _____

3. Why did you leave? (Press the parent to be as specific as possible. If a parent replies vaguely, "It didn't meet our needs," then probe further: "What specifically didn't you like?" or maybe, "From what you said earlier, it sounds like there might have been a personality conflict. Was that it?")

   _____

   _____

   _____

   _____

4. My hours of operation are _____. My closing time is really not flexible due to my own family obligations. Does my schedule pose any problem for you with pickups?

   _____

   _____

   _____

   _____

5. Does your child have any special needs?

   _____

   _____

6. Where do you (and your spouse, if applicable) work? What are your hours?

   _____

   _____

You can screen prospective clients by inviting the parent and child in one evening (after child-care hours) for a brief meeting and tour of the child care. You'll want to get some important information from the parents. The sample checklist in this chapter includes some possible questions or points to cover in your meeting.

The screening questions are not comprehensive. You will undoubtedly have more to ask as you observe the parent and child. Some providers routinely ask for one or two former child-care references in writing. If appropriate, suggest that the child and parent spend an hour or two one morning with you and the other children; this way you can observe how the child interacts with others.

If you are considering two or more children for one space, let the parents know; if you decide against one family, it is a more graceful way to decline enrollment.

Last, remember to advise parents of your probationary period for all children (see chapter 3). If you and the family are a poor match, there's an automatic way out for both of you.

Setting Up Your Office

Many new providers are so enthusiastic about setting up the space for the children that they neglect to set up office space for themselves. You won't need a lot of space or equipment, but having a space specifically designated for your after-hours business work will help you stay organized and on top of the paperwork.

A desk in the study, kitchen, or bedroom can easily do the trick. One provider uses her formal dining room as a business and planning space. This area needs to be clearly off-limits to the children and possibly off-limits to your family as well.

Answering Machine/Voice Mail

It is almost essential for you to have an answering machine or voice mail for your telephone. When you are caring for the children, they are your first priority—not the telemarketer, neighbor, or relative on the line. Deborah, an experienced provider, describes her use of an answering machine:

I couldn't get along without it. My message goes something like this: "Hi, this is the Strawberry Patch. All hands are on deck right now, but if you'll leave your name and number, I'll get right back to you." I tell all the parents that if they call during the day, they will most likely get the machine. I check the calls regularly and return them as promptly as possible. I haven't had any complaints from the parents.

Not only do answering machines or voice mail allow you to focus on the children; they help with your marketing: Prospective parents who call don't have to hear the noisiness of the children—you can return the call during a quiet time of day, and you can be sure you won't miss the call. A polite message on the machine also reminds your friends and family that you are at work and not available for visiting on the phone.

Filing System

You will be keeping track of many pieces of paper in the course of running your business. You will need to keep attendance records on each child, as well as medical consent forms, immunization records, meal records, and so forth. When the state inspector comes to visit, she or he will want to look at your files on the children. If the IRS pays a call, they will also want to see that you've kept your receipts and information for tax deductions in a systematic, orderly manner. The moral of this story is: You need easy access to this information in some kind of file cabinet.

Many of us have a home filing system already. If not, you can buy small file cabinets new or used or purchase cardboard or plastic file storage boxes. It is easiest to set your filing system up at the outset, rather than creating it as you go. To start out, prepare file folders as listed on the next page. Some of these categories we've gone over in detail already; others—the expense and tax categories—we'll cover in depth later in this chapter.

Computer and Printer

Expensive hardware and elegant software are not "must-have" items. You can run your child care efficiently with an old-fashioned typewriter and a nearby copy shop. But if you

Sample List of File Folders

Children's Files

1. Attendance records (including dates when care began and ended).

2. Parent-Provider Agreement (signed!). This agreement should include child's full name, address, age, birth date, parents' home and work phone numbers and addresses, and any special needs the child has.

3. Medical consent form (see samples in chapter 2, which should include an adult emergency contact if both parents are unavailable).

4. Signature list of those authorized to pick up child.

5. If you do not carry liability insurance, you need a signed statement from the parent acknowledging this.

6. Copies of any correspondence or notes you've taken on the child's care.

7. Copies of any W-10 forms given to parents for the year.

Business Files

1. Record of income by week (can be combined with child's attendance records).

2. Meal records (for USDA Child and Adult Care Food Program [CACFP]):

   A. Number of children who ate breakfast/snack/lunch/dinner each day.

   B. Record of money reimbursed to you by the food program.

   C. Copies of your menus.

3. Record of miscellaneous income.

4. Records of expenses by quarter:

   A. Direct expenses.

   B. Indirect expenses.

   C. Capital expenditures.

   D. Start-up expenses.

   E. Food receipts for child care.

   F. Family food receipts.

5. Quarterly tax file (for copies of finished forms).

6. Tax record archive (this will more than likely be a box you store in an out-of-the-way place).

7. Records of your business hours.

8. Bank statements, receipts, and returned checks.

9. File for licenses or permits that are not required to be posted.

have a home computer, you can make good use of it. Most providers with access to computers use them in the following ways:

- Typing up a handbook of child-care policies for parents
- Creating templates for Parent-Provider Agreements
- Creating flyers or notices of special events, schedule or rate changes, and so on, for parents
- Using home-office invoicing software to bill parents
- Using home-office accounting programs to keep track of expenses and deductions
- Creating banners and other graphics for the children to enjoy
- Browsing the World Wide Web for information and sites relevant to your business
- Receiving and sending e-mail

Providers vary in what kinds of computer programs they like to use. Most use the word-processing program they learned before they started doing child care. *Microsoft Word* and *WordPerfect* are two popular word-processing programs. When it comes to the nitty-gritty of home businesses, many providers like to use Intuit's *Quicken* (which includes a check-writing program for paying expenses) or, from the same publisher, *Quick Books* (which differs in that it offers an invoicing feature).

You do not need to invest in complicated software systems designed specifically for child-care programs if you are first starting out. However, as you establish your child care and decide to stay in the business, it is smart to look to the future. And you may decide that a software system for child-care programs would be beneficial to your business. If you do, keep the following points in mind as you shop for software:

- *Will it meet your needs?* Know ahead of time what you want the software to do: billing, keeping attendance records, daily schedules, and so forth. Don't be distracted by peripheral features. To be considered, the program needs to meet your primary needs.
- *Will it be easy for you to learn and use?* You won't have a lot of time to sit in front of the computer terminal and worry each step through. All programs advertise themselves as easy to use, but we all have different learning styles and speeds. The best way to answer this question is to try the system out; get a demo disk or find

another provider or center that uses the program and ask for an overview.

- *Does the program provide customer service support?* In other words, when you get stuck, is there someone at the company you can call? All reputable programs provide customer support and, if you're lucky, a toll-free number to access it. You'll need support the most when you install and start using the program.
- *Is the program guaranteed?* Make sure you get a written warranty that protects you if the software is defective or turns out to be completely wrong for your child care.
- *Can you really afford the program?* Many programs are costly, and some will require you to buy hardware you do not already own. When shopping, get the full estimate of what the system will cost you and weigh it against your income and expense projections for the year.

See the appendix for additional information on software designed specifically for family child cares.

Record-Keeping

Well-known family child care tax specialist Tom Copeland says, "Taking care of children is only half of your job. The other half is taking care of business." This section will look at the most important business records you will need to keep.

There are two umbrella categories to pay scrupulous attention to: *records of income* and *records of expenses*. Family child-care providers are not exempt from paying taxes. You will need complete, accurate records of what money you bring in (income) and how you spend it (expenses) in order to file a tax return.

How much time you spend on keeping income and expense records accurate and up to date (as you incur them) will dramatically affect your profitability as well as your mental health come April 15 each year.

Some Good Advice

Tax consultants who work with family child-care providers are unanimous in their recommendation to keep business and personal records as separate as possible. Providers (and other home-based businesses) need to be particularly careful about this. The IRS views any crossover of personal and business expenses with suspicion. There are many ways you can safely separate your family expenses and income from those of your business. Here are a few tips for starting out:

- Open a separate checking account for your business. Deposit all business income in this account. Pay as many business expenses from this account as you possibly can.

    For those occasions when the expense is shared by your business and your family (e.g., food), pay for it out of your family account, and then reimburse your family account with a check from your business account (properly documented).

    When you pay yourself, write a check from your business account to your family account. Document it as a transfer of funds.

    Keep all your bank statements and canceled checks for both accounts.
- Many providers have a credit card that is exclusively dedicated to business expenses. This is a good idea. Some companies provide you with monthly reports of expenditures. Keep all your statements and reports.

The government varies in its rules for how long to save ordinary receipts and paperwork. A good rule of thumb is four years. Check with your accountant if you have questions about specific records. If you buy something and do not get a receipt (or lose it), make a receipt for your own records, as shown in the following example.

Sample Cash Receipt

Date:	6-4-06
Name:	South Prarie Used Book Sale
Address:	442 Main Street, South Prarie, WA
Purchase:	five books at $1.00 each
Paid:	$5.00 cash

Income

The majority of your income will come in as payments from parents. For each payment received, you need to record:

- Child's name
- Amount paid (along with check number or receipt number if paid in cash)
- Dates of care covered by the payment
- Date payment was received

Most providers use a simple payment record. An example of a monthly record follows. A blank one you can adapt to your needs is located in the appendix.

The provider in the following example cared for three children during June. She collected $160 a week for the full-time children, Sarah and Eric, and $79 a week for one part-time child, Jonathan. For the most part, the parents paid with checks; however, Eric's mother paid in cash the weeks of June 5–9 and 19–23 and the provider noted the number of the receipt given her. We can see that our provider collects payment each Monday for the week she's providing care.

More sophisticated calendars are available for keeping combination records of your income and the children's daily attendance. Specifically, I recommend *Calendar-Keeper: A Childcare Record Keeping System,* published by Redleaf Press; this calendar allows you to

Sample Monthly Payment Record

Child	June 5–9	June 12–16	June 19–23	June 26–30
Sarah Anderson	$160/ck 458 pd 6-5-06	$160/ck 466 pd 6-12-06	$160/ck 472 pd 6-19-06	$160/ck 477 pd 6-26-06
Jonathan Carr	$79/ck 222 pd 6-5-06	$79/ck 238 pd 6-12-06	$79/ck 245 pd 6-19-06	$79/ck 253 pd 6-26-06
Eric Gray	$160/rcpt 45 pd 6-5-06	$160/ck 876 pd 6-12-06	$160/rcpt 49 pd 6-19-06	$160/ck 912 pd 6-26-06

keep very specific track of each child's attendance, payment records, and meal plan participation all in one place. There is also an online version on this product for use on your home computer. (See the appendix, "Software.") Combining some of these records, once you understand what is required of each, can save you time. One provider's combined time sheet and billing form for charging by the hour (which she chooses to do, since she cares for many part-time children) is shown on the next page. A sample invoice for Laurie-Anne's Family Child Care is shown on the subsequent page. A blank invoice you can adapt to your use is located in the appendix.

The second source of income you will receive is money from the CACFP. It functions like a reimbursement (you are paid a certain amount of money per child, per meal), but the IRS views it as income, and it is therefore taxable. The records you will be required to keep in order to participate in the food program will be very useful to you come tax time. Report the food program reimbursements as income and report the food served to child-care children as business expenses. Your food program sponsor will likely send you a 1099 form at the end of the year reporting how much you were paid or reimbursed for food. The RNI recommends that providers report and label their food program reimbursements as

Sample Attendance/Billing Sheet

Name: _____   Billing month: _____

Date	Time In	Initials	Time Out	Initials	Total Time
13					
14					
15					
16					
17					
18					
19					
20					
21					
22					
23					
24					
25					

Billing calculation

1 _____ hours (days) x $_____ per hour (day) = $_____

2 _____ absent/short days x $_____ min per day = $_____

3   Subtotal $_____

4   Previous balance $_____

5   Total of lines 3 & 4 $_____

                        New balance $_____

"CACFP Income" on the Schedule C tax form. Although the IRS does not specifically require providers to separate it out this way, RNI asserts that you are less likely to be audited if the IRS can see a clear distinction between food income and food expenses on Schedule C. (*Note:* Reimbursements you receive for meals your own children eat are not taxable income and should not be included.)

Other forms of income you may receive are bonuses or gifts from parents or grant money from local or governmental organizations for buying equipment or other business items. Some providers care for low-income children and are paid by the state instead of the

Sample Invoice

Laurie-Anne's Family Child Care
800 Campbell Street, Mesa, AZ 86458
(602) 555–9987

Bill to:	Date	Invoice #
Sarah Roberts 44689 Citrus View Drive Mesa, AZ 86458	6-1-06	6-36

Number of Days	Child's Name	Rate	Amount
10	Jonathan	$30.00 per day	$300.00

parents. Income from any of these sources must be recorded and described as well.

At the end of the year, many of the parents will ask you to fill out IRS Form W-10: *Dependent Care Provider's Identification and Certification.* This form asks for your social security number or tax identification number. Many parents are eligible for a tax credit on their child-care expenses and will report how much they've paid you for the year. The W-10 does not ask you to report how much each parent has paid you; however, it is in your best interests to have your income figures match the parent's expense figures for child care. (The IRS will be tempted to investigate if parents report spending more than you report earning.) Many providers routinely give (or mail) each parent a report and receipt of their total child-care expense for the year and have it signed by the parent. This helps ensure that everyone's figures are accurate. Another good idea is to routinely give parents a W-10 at the end of the year, whether they request it or not.

Some providers fear that parents will not be honest and will inaccurately report how much money they pay you in order to gain a higher tax credit. If this is a concern, explain to the parent that if your figures do not match, there is a strong likelihood that both you and the parent will be audited.

Expenses

There are three kinds of expenses: *direct business expenses, indirect business expenses,* and *capital expenditures.* You will have all three, and you may deduct all three on your taxes. You will want to claim as many deductions as you are legally entitled to, because this will reduce your taxable income. There are, however, specific rules for what you may and may not deduct, and the IRS is continually changing its guidelines. This section will give you a broad overview but does not attempt to cover every question you might have—for that, you'll have to consult an accountant. The RNI, along with its director Tom Copeland, is one of your best resources for family child-care business and tax issues. I *highly* recommend you purchase Copeland's tax workbook before filing your taxes (RNI brings out a new edition for each tax year). The RNI and other resources for figuring your expenses and taxes are listed in the appendix.

There are two main tax forms you will use to report your income and expenses at the end of the year: Form 8829: *Expenses for Business Use of Your Home* and Schedule C: *Profit or Loss from Business* (Schedule C accompanies Form 1040). Your record-keeping throughout the year should be designed to give you accurate information to fill out these two specific tax forms. I will refer to them frequently throughout this chapter.

Many providers are confused by the similarities in Form 8829 and Schedule C—and indeed, many of the expenses look the same. It helps to think of Form 8829 as pertaining to expenses related to your home itself (utilities, real estate taxes, repairs to built-in appliances and fixtures, etc.) and Schedule C as concerning expenses related to your personal property (liability insurance, repairs to things like toys or furniture, insurance on personal property items, etc.). An accountant experienced in family child-care taxes can help you with these distinctions.

Before you do your first set of taxes, you will need to calculate your Time/Space Percentage. This figure tells you what percentage of your home is used for business. The IRS considers it a reliable figure for determining what percentage of your home expenses are deductible as business expenses.

Time/Space Percentage

This is a figure that helps you calculate how much of certain expenses shared by your business and your family (with the exception of food) can be deducted on your business taxes. For example, if your Time/Space Percentage is 25 percent, then you may deduct 25 percent of your mortgage interest, rent, utilities, and other household expenses. Later in this chapter we will look specifically at what you can deduct using the Time/Space Percentage.

To figure out your Time/Space Percentage, you need the following information:

- *The number of hours your home is used for business in one year.* You can calculate this figure by adding up the total number of hours you spend caring for the children, planning activities, cleaning for the business, keeping records or doing paperwork for the business, working on generating enrollment, and so forth. In short, you count any time you spend *in your home* working on business.

Since you are just starting out, it will be easy for you to keep a daily log of time spent on business. A sample day's time record might look like this:

Tuesday 6-13-06		
7:00–7:30 A.M.	Cleaning	.5
7:30 A.M.–5:00 P.M.	Caring for children	9.5
5:00–5:30 P.M.	Cleaning	.5
7:00–7:30 P.M.	Activity planning	.5
7:30–8:00 P.M.	CACFP paperwork	.5
Total hours		**11.5**

Keep these kinds of records for every day you work in your home. Should you ever be audited, you will have highly accurate records of your time to back up your figures.

I recommend separating out the categories (child care, cleaning, planning and preparation, etc.) and adding up your total hours every month (just as in the foregoing example) for two reasons: (1) At tax time you will simply need to add up the total twelve months' worth of time to figure your time percentage; in the event of an audit, you can show that you really did spend this much time on business and exactly what it entailed; (2) you can scan these figures each month to make sure that the time you are putting into your business in each area is reasonable for the amount of money you are making.

Now take the total number of hours worked in your home for the entire year and divide it by the total number of hours in a year. For instance, let's say you worked in your home 2,765 hours for the year. Your time percentage would look like this:

2,765 (hours worked)

8,760 (hours in a year) = 31% time percentage

- *Number of square feet in your home used for child care.* Count every room in your house that is regularly used by your business. Most providers use their family room/playroom, living room, kitchen, bathroom, laundry room, storage rooms, some bedrooms, and space such as entryways, hallways, and attached porches or decks. You may count your garage if you use it for storage of child-care items. You may not include your lawn, swimming pool, patio, or driveway. See IRS Publication 587: *Business Use of Your Home* for more information.

"Regular use" is usually interpreted as consistent, customary use whenever your business is open, though regular use does not necessarily mean every day. If you use your spare bedroom three of the five days you are open, then that constitutes regular use. If you use it only once or twice a month, that is not regular use.

You may already know the square footage of each room in your home. Or you might be like the rest of us and need to measure the rooms. Do this by getting out your tape measure, then multiply the length (in feet) of the room by the width; this will give you the area in square feet. Add the size of all the child-care spaces together. Then divide that figure by the total square feet in your home. For example:

1,450 (square feet used for child care)
2,000 (square feet in home) = 72.5% space percentage

The provider in our sample has a time percentage of 31 percent and a space percentage of 72.5 percent. To get her Time/Space Percentage, she needs to multiply these two figures:

31% x 72.5% = 22.5% Time/Space Percentage

The provider may thus deduct 22.5 percent of her relevant household expenses from her taxes.

You will need to recalculate your Time/Space Percentage every year. Report it on Form 8829.

Exclusive-Use Rooms

Here's a footnote to your space percentage. If you happen to have a room in your house you use *exclusively* for business (i.e., you do no more than walk through it to get to another room when your business is closed), then you have an "exclusive-use room" and need to calculate your space percentage a little differently. This room is typically a special playroom used only for child care. Here's how to calculate your space percentage:

1. Divide the square feet of the room by the total square feet of your home:
$$300 \div 2{,}000 = 15\%$$
2. Divide the square feet of all the other rooms you use regularly for business by the total square feet of your home:
$$1{,}550 \div 2{,}000 = 77.5\%$$
3. Multiply the space percentage of the shared rooms by your time percentage:
$$77.5\% \times 31\% = 24\%$$
4. Add the percentages from Step 1 and Step 3 to get your final Time/Space Percentage:
$$15\% + 24\% = 39\% \text{ Time/Space Percentage}$$

Notice that this Time/Space Percentage figure is decidedly more favorable than the figure for the example provider I used earlier who does not have an exclusive-use room. If you do have such a room, it is in your best interest to do the extra math here and use it in your Time/Space Percentage.

Actual Business-Use Percent

For the majority of cases, you will use your Time/Space Percentage to figure your shared business and personal expenses. In a few cases, you are allowed to figure the "actual business-use percent" of an expense. The tax results of doing this are usually more favorable to you, so when it's allowed by the IRS, take the time to figure the expense this way. Here's how to do it. Let's say it cost you $100 to fix the plumbing in a room you use 75 percent of the time for your business. In this case, you can claim 75 percent of the repair cost, or $75. Be aware that you must keep receipts and clear records of how you figured the actual business-use percent of any particular item or expense. Keep these records with your tax information; if you are ever audited, they will help you justify your expenses with the IRS.

Direct Business Expenses

The IRS defines a *direct business expense* as an "ordinary and necessary" cost of running your business. Family child-care providers commonly have expenses that fall under these categories listed on tax form Schedule C.

- *Advertising.* This includes most of your marketing: ads, flyers, posters, buttons, and so on. (Business cards fall under office expenses.)

- *Bad debts.* A bad debt occurs when you deposit a check in one year (and claim it as income) and then that check bounces in the following year. Unfortunately, you cannot claim an unpaid bill by a parent as a bad debt. But if a parent does not pay you, be sure not to report this unpaid money as income.
- *Car and truck expenses.* You can deduct car expenses in two different ways. Most providers prefer to use the standard mileage rate method. At the time of this writing, the standard rate was 48½ cents per mile. This figure covers all costs associated with using a car for business: gas, repairs, maintenance, and insurance.

To use this method, you keep track of where you go, the total miles traveled that trip, and the date. Use a calendar to keep track of where you drive to. A sample calendar week could look like this:

JUNE						
4	5	6	7	8	9	10
	Safeway grocery	Bank			Ace Hardware	

Let's say it's a 5-mile round-trip to Safeway, a 2.5-mile trip to the bank, and a 2.5-mile trip to Ace Hardware. At the end of the year, add up the number of trips you have taken to Safeway and multiply it by five. Your total mileage for these three destinations might be:

Safeway:	46 trips x 5 miles	=	230 miles
Bank:	24 trips x 2.5 miles	=	60 miles
Ace:	19 trips x 2.5 miles	=	47.5 miles
		Total:	337.5 miles

Multiply the mileage by the current standard rate (right now it's .485) for your deduction:

337.5 miles x .485 = $163.69 (your deduction)

You may not claim the costs of business car insurance or repairs for damage caused by business driving. You may, however, deduct parking fees, tolls, and ferry fees, and bus, subway, and train fares for business trips. You may also deduct your business-use percent of your vehicle loan interest and vehicle property tax. Multiply these expenses by your business-use percent for your car (your business miles for the year divided by your total miles for the year) to arrive at the deduction.

This method is more time-intensive but may yield you a higher deduction. You must calculate the number of miles you drove your car for your business and divide that figure by the total number of miles you drove your car in the entire year; then multiply that figure by 100. For example, if you drove your car for 1,000 business miles and 10,000 miles total for the year, then your business use is 10 percent (1,000 ÷ 10,000 = .10 x 100 = 10%).

You may then deduct 10 percent of all your car expenses. You may also depreciate the cost of your car with this method; consult your accountant if you wish to do this. *Note:* If you choose the actual-expenses method for the first year you use your car for business, you are then locked into this method for as long as you own that car.

- *Employee benefit programs.* It is unlikely you will be starting off hiring employees and giving them benefits (health, life, or disability insurance), but if you do, you may deduct these costs.

- *Insurance.* Smart providers carry liability insurance for their businesses, whether they are required to by the state or not. You may deduct 100 percent of this expense. If you carry workers' compensation insurance for yourself or your employees, it is also 100 percent deductible. (Renter's and homeowner's insurance are covered elsewhere on Form 8829.) Car insurance is not deductible unless you use the actual car costs method of figuring your deduction (as described above).

    Rules regarding health insurance change often; consult your tax accountant before claiming this. Disability and life insurance are not deductible.

- *Interest.* You may deduct 100 percent of interest charged on items you've purchased for exclusive business use. Use your Time/Space Percentage to calculate deductions on any items purchased for joint business and personal use. (Report mortgage interest on Form 8829.)

- *Legal and professional services.* A tax preparer or consultant you hire for your business taxes provides a professional service. Other services included here are legal fees and services and accounting/bookkeeping services. All of these expenses are deductible. (Report your tax preparer's fee for your personal taxes on Schedule A. If your tax preparer is doing both your personal and business taxes, ask him or her to calculate how much of the fee is attributable to family or business.)

- *Office expenses.* A host of expenses comes under this category. Some of the more common office expenses are bank service fees; office supplies, such as paper, pencils, and envelopes; postage; resources for your business use, such as software, books, and magazines; supplies for record-keeping, such as calendars, forms, receipts, and ledgers; training and classes; photocopying costs; and membership dues in professional organizations, such as the National Association for Family Child Care (NAFCC) or the National Association for the Education of Young Children (NAEYC).

  If in doubt about the eligibility of an office expense, consult your accountant or tax adviser.

- *Rent or lease.* This covers the rental of items for business use, such as DVDs or a pressure washer to clean your desk—not your monthly house or apartment rent. (Enter your home rent on Form 8829.)

- *Repairs and maintenance of personal property.* "Repairs" refers to repair of items damaged by your business. For instance, if one of your children in care hides M&Ms in your VCR, the repair bill is fully deductible. If your own child did it, then you may use your Time/Space Percentage to deduct the business percentage of the bill.

  Maintenance refers to all cleaning and maintenance supplies for your home that are necessary to run your business. A list of all the cleaning supplies you probably need would take up the rest of this book, but the top five might be cleansers and detergents, soap (dishwashing and hand), paper towels, toilet paper, and mops and brooms. Highlight these supplies on your grocery and drug store receipts to separate them from food. It is a good idea to separate out cleaning supplies as its own category; enter it as "Cleaning Supplies" on one of the blank lines on Part V of Schedule C.

  Home maintenance and repair costs (such as seasonal servicing of your central heating or repairs of your plumbing) are entered on Form 8829.

- *Supplies.* This is a big one. You will be purchasing many supplies for children's activities and care over the year. If they are used exclusively for business, you may deduct 100 percent of the cost (e.g., children's books). If you purchase an item that you use after hours for the home (e.g., a booster seat), then you need to use your Time/Space Percentage to figure your deduction.

    "Supplies" is an umbrella category that covers the following types of expenses: children's activities (craft items and games), items for children's care (cribs, bibs, potty seats, etc.), and kitchen supplies (dishes, utensils, garbage bags, and small appliances).

    Keep records of all these purchases and how you determined the deduction.

- *Taxes and licenses.* Fees you incur during the licensing process (permits, fire inspections, license fees, etc.) are 100-percent deductible. If you hire an assistant and pay payroll taxes, then those are also deductible. (Your property taxes can be entered on Form 8829.)

- *Utilities.* Most of your utilities (electricity, gas, water, sewage, and garbage) are deducted on Form 8829. The only utility that should be listed on Schedule C is phone service. The IRS will not allow you to deduct the monthly cost of your first phone line into your house. A second, separate business line is 100 percent deductible. If you use the second line also for personal calls, then deduct your business-use portion. On both lines, you may deduct long-distance business calls, services like call-waiting, and phone repairs, using your Time/Space Percentage.

- *Travel, meals, and entertainment.* When you travel away from home, overnight, to a conference or training session, you may deduct the full cost of your transportation by car (using the standard mileage rate), plane, bus, or train, as well as lodging. You can claim meals on these trips in two ways. Either save every receipt and claim the actual amount spent, or claim the standard meal allowance set by the IRS. At the time of this writing, the standard allowance was $39 per day. If you use the standard meal allowance, you must use it for every trip taken in that tax year.

    For other types of business meals (i.e., not associated with overnight trips), you may deduct 50 percent of the cost.

- *Wages.* This covers the wages you pay to employees (your assistants). Do not include in this category independent contractors: the clown you hired for the birthday party or the graphic artist who designed your business cards. (The graphic artist's fee is a legitimate business expense and would be included in the advertising category. The clown may or may not be deductible—check with your accountant.) Do not include the money you pay yourself. You may include wages you pay a family member to assist you in the business.

  You must report wages on Schedule C, while payments totaling $600 or more per year to independent contractors are reported on Form 1099-Misc: *Miscellaneous Income.* If you are confused about whether you have an employee or an independent contractor on your hands, consult your accountant right away; there are serious penalties for failing to file correct forms and pay taxes on employees.

- *Other expenses: food, household items, toys, yard supplies, activity expenses.* Food is one of your major expenses. It is also, for the vast majority of providers, a shared expense between business and home. Household items include things like safety barriers, tools, fire extinguishers, and bed linens. Yard supplies would be items such as garden hoses, sandboxes, and lawn mowers.

- *Food.* Historically, when conducting an audit of a family child-care provider, the IRS would zero in on your food records right off the bat. They did this for two reasons: (1) They couldn't quite believe your own family wasn't gobbling up all the food while the children were brown-bagging it; and (2) many providers were lax about keeping their family grocery receipts and thus could not document the difference between their family and business food expenses. Be aware that only food eaten by the children in care is deductible as a business expense. Any food eaten by you, your own children, or any other member of your household is not deductible. The food your employed assistant eats (if she works both before and after a meal) may be deducted.

  Family child-care providers may use a standard meal allowance rate to claim food deductions (whether or not you use the federal food program or not). The standard meal allowance rate works on a per child/per meal basis (see page 45 for the Tier I and II reimbursement rates). Amounts on both tier schedules are slightly higher for residents of Alaska and Hawaii. Consult either your food provider or your tax preparer to see if you qualify for a Tier I reimbursement rate. Note that the federal food program will only reimburse you for three meals a day, that is, breakfast, one lunch *or* supper, and one snack. However, the IRS allows you a deduction for *every* meal the child eats, whether you were reimbursed for it or not.

All providers are eligible to use this standard meal allowance rate on their taxes, regardless of whether you are licensed, registered, or regulated by your state. You do not even have to be participating in the food program to use this easy method of deduction. If you are receiving reimbursement from the food program on the Tier II schedule, you still may claim the Tier I rate on your food expenses for your taxes. Unless you spend massive amounts of money on food for the child care, this method of deduction will increase your profitability.

Here's how to claim the deductions:

— To use the standard meal allowance, and I strongly recommend that you do, you must maintain records that include:

  ✓ name of each child
  ✓ dates and hours of attendance in care
  ✓ number of breakfasts, lunches, dinners, and snacks served per day

  Your food-program supplier will provide you with forms to help you track this information.

— Remember, you may not deduct food expenses for what you and your family eat. Even if the meals your own children eat are reimbursed by the food program, they still are not deductible on your taxes. (*Note:* These reimbursements for your own children's meals are not taxable income and should not be reported as such.)

— It's a good idea to purchase food for your business and for your home separately. If you must shop for food at the same time, then have the clerk ring up two separate purchases. Pay for the child-care food out of your business checking account.

— Some providers who live in high-cost areas may be better off using the actual-food-cost method of deducting food expenses. This is a very record-keeping-intensive method that requires you to keep *every* single food receipt for your business *and* your family. If you believe you are spending significantly more than the maximum deduction per child, per day, that the standard meal rate allows, then save all receipts for one to two months and compare the figures. The vast majority of new providers will be better off using the standard meal allowance. Also, be aware that using the actual-food-cost method puts you in greater risk of an audit by the IRS.

— *A reminder:* Keep records of *all* meals served, even if they're not being reimbursed. The IRS will look at this in the event of an audit.

- *Household items.* Save all receipts for items used for food preparation—such as aluminum foil, paper products, or food containers. Include these items in the "supplies" category.

- *Toys and gifts.* Keep careful, accurate records of your toy expenses. In other words, keep all your receipts. The IRS worries if it sees a big expense here—it thinks you might be buying toys for your own children and then passing it off as a business expense. To help justify your figures, keep all the receipts of toys purchased for your own children in a separate file; if you are audited, you can use this record to show that your business deduction is reasonable.

   Gifts can be deducted here. This refers to gifts you might give a parent of a child in care. If you give such gifts, you may deduct up to $25 per person each year. Again, keep the receipts. (Do not deduct gifts given to the children for birthday and holiday parties here; since these parties are regular activities in your child care, they are considered activity expenses.)

- *Activity expenses.* Activity expenses refer to fees for field trip activities—for example, admission to the zoo. Include the fees paid for the children in care, yourself, and your helper. You may not include the fees for your own children. This category also includes birthday parties and special activities.

You should report all the aforementioned direct business expenses on Schedule C.

Indirect Business Expenses

Also called "house expenses," indirect business expenses are specific costs you have in maintaining your home. Typically, you use your Time/Space Percentage to figure the deduction you may claim. Note, however, that you may not show a loss in your business for the year from claiming these expenses. These expenses should be listed on IRS Form 8829. (If you live on a military base and pay no house-related expenses, then you do not need to fill out Form 8829. If you spend your own money on a home repair or improvement, then you may claim the business-use percent.) The specific costs are described as follows.

- *Mortgage loan interest and real estate taxes.* If your Time/Space Percentage is 25 percent, then you may deduct 25 percent of your mortgage loan interest and real estate taxes for your business on Schedule C. The remaining 75 percent can be deducted on your personal taxes, Schedule A, if you itemize. (You may not deduct the principal of your monthly mortgage payment; it is accounted for in your house depreciation.)

- *Casualty losses.* A casualty loss is damage to or loss of property from events such as hurricanes, earthquakes, floods, accidents, or vandalism. This is what you have home or car insurance to cover. However, if you do not have insurance or the insurance has a deductible, your out-of-pocket cost from the damage or loss is an indirect business expense. Use your Time/Space Percentage to figure what percentage of the cost you may deduct.

- *Insurance on your house.* You may deduct your Time/Space Percentage of your home and mortgage insurance as an indirect business expense. If you purchased a business rider policy, it can be deducted here as a direct expense. Do not include any other insurance policy in this category.

- *Utilities.* Use your Time/Space Percentage to deduct the business portion of the money you spend on electricity, gas, water, sewage, and garbage; do this whether you rent or own your home. Certain telephone costs are deducted on Schedule C.

- *House repairs and maintenance.* All homes need yearly upkeep. Items in this category could include painting (inside and out), fixing broken windows, servicing the furnace, and so forth. Be careful not to include any repair or maintenance of personal property here, just what is pertinent to the useful life of your house. Major home improvements (adding on a room, enclosing a porch) are not covered in this category (see "Capital Expenditures" in the next section). Check each year for any cost limits on this category.

- *House rent.* If you rent your home, you may deduct your Time/Space Percentage for the rent. You may also deduct your Time/Space Percentage for any utilities you rent or pay for.
- *Moving expenses.* If you move to a new home, a portion of the moving expenses may be deductible. Consult your accountant on this. The IRS has specific requirements for the reason for the move (it must be closely related to your business or your spouse's business or employment) and for how you claim deductions.

Capital Expenditures

A capital expenditure is the purchase of any one item for your business that will last more than one year. For example, the following are often claimed by providers as capital expenditures: house, couch, computer, refrigerator, car, or adding on a new room.

A capital expenditure must cost $100 or more. Capital expenditures wear out gradually, year after year. Because you don't "use them up" all in one year, you may deduct only a year's worth of use instead of claiming it as a business expense. This practice is called depreciation. It is complex, and the government likes to change the rules frequently. Once you start depreciating a purchase under a certain rule, then you continue with that rule for the purchase until the item wears out.

Since you are just beginning your business, consult an accountant or tax preparer on current depreciation rules and practices. You will be able to depreciate portions of the following:

- *Your house.*
- *Major home improvements.* This category differs from a home repair in that the improvement increases—not just maintains—the value of your home. (*Note:* Some providers spend thousands of dollars remodeling a room under the mistaken impression they can write off the entire amount that tax year. Consult your accountant if you have questions about the tax consequences of your planned improvements.)
- *Land improvements.* These are permanent improvements that increase the value of your property (e.g., landscaping, fences, or tennis courts).
- *Personal property.* This category includes furniture, major appliances, playground/yard equipment, and so on.

- *Electronic office equipment.* This category includes computers, software, printers, fax machines, copiers, scanners, electric typewriters, and so on.

- *Entertainment items.* These are things like TVs, VCRs, DVD players, CD players, musical instruments, cell phones, and photographic equipment.

- *Start-up expenses.* Money you spend for start-up will fall into one of two categories: (1) Items costing more than $100 that you would depreciate: your home, equipment, appliances, furniture, etc. Simply begin depreciating them in the year you start your business. (2) Everything else, or more specifically, items that originally cost less than $100. You can claim up to $5,000 worth of category 2 start-up costs in the year you start your business. You will either use your Time/Space Percentage or your business-use percent to figure your deductions for these items. If you spent more than $5,000 on these items, the overage will be subject to depreciation. Consult your accountant on this.

- *Automobile.* You can depreciate the cost of your car if you are using the actual-expenses method instead of the standard mileage method of claiming expenses.

According to tax specialist Tom Copeland, the top five areas of IRS audits focus on:

- *Provider income.* An auditor typically asks to see copies of all your bank statements to search for unreported income. You can protect yourself by keeping an orderly record of all deposits, for example, "spouse's wages," "day-care income," "refund from oil company." You can note this information on your check register, on deposit slips, or in your check-writing program on your computer. Even if you maintain a separate bank account for your business, still keep careful records of *all* your personal deposits. Copeland recommends labeling each business deposit by the parent's name. If you can't account for a deposit, the IRS will assume it is child-care income and tax it.

- *Work hours.* As discussed elsewhere, you need to be keeping good track of all the hours you work, both during and after child-care hours. An auditor often questions the number of hours you work after your day care has closed for the day (time spent cleaning, in meal preparation, in record-keeping, etc.). You can substantiate your claims by keeping accurate records of these hours on your calendar for a minimum of two months.

- *Food deductions.* If you use the standard meal allowance and have kept accurate records of attendance and individual meals served, there will be little for the IRS to quibble with. If you use the actual-cost method of food deduction, you must keep *all* food receipts (business and personal), attendance records, meal counts, and menus, or the IRS will disallow any food expenses over your food-program reimbursement.

> **Internet Tip**
> I've mentioned the Redleaf National Institute (www.redleafinstitute.org or 651–641–6675) before, but it bears mentioning again that its Web site will help you with resource material on taxes along with a special section on audits. They also offer help by phone—very friendly folks out in Minnesota—so give them a call.

- *Supplies.* If you try to claim 100 percent of household supplies and toys and then use them personally, the entire expense will be disallowed. If you buy toys for your child care and also have young children at home, it is unlikely the IRS will believe you use them only for your business. Copeland recommends taking pictures of the children in care using the items.

- *Automobile expenses.* The IRS can't quite believe you're always going to the grocery store or hardware store just for business and often denies these business miles. You are, however, entitled to deduct these trips if the primary purpose is for business. Copeland recommends you save all your canceled checks from your personal trips to these stores to show you're not claiming them fraudulently. Also, save all receipts to show you bought more business items than personal ones on the legitimate business trips.

Reporting and Filing Your Taxes

We've covered income and expenses in the previous sections, including routine references to the federal tax forms you will need to report them. The following is a brief list of forms and publications issued by the IRS for you to gather as you get ready to file taxes.

Schedule C: *Profit or Loss from Business*

Schedule SE: *Self-Employment Tax*

Form 1040 ES: *Estimated Tax for Individuals*

Form 1040: *U.S. Individual Income Tax Return*

> Schedule A: *Itemized Deductions*
>
> Schedule B: *Interest and Ordinary Dividends*
>
> Schedule D: *Capital Gains and Losses*

Form 4562: *Depreciation and Amortization*

Form 8829: *Expenses for Business Use of Your Home*

Form W-10: *Dependent Care Provider's Identification and Certification*

Publication 334: *Tax Guide for Small Businesses*

Publication 583: *Starting a Business and Keeping Records*

Publication 505: *Tax Withholding and Estimated Tax*

Publication 587: *Business Use of Your Home*

If you hire employees (assistants):

Form W-2: *Wage and Tax Statement*

Form W-4: *Employee's Withholding Allowance Certificate*

Form W-3: *Transmittal of Income and Tax Statements*

Form SS-4: *Application for Employer Identification Number*

Form 940: *Employer's Annual Federal Unemployment Tax Return*

Form 941: *Employer's Quarterly Federal Tax Return*

Form 1099: *Miscellaneous Income*

Form I-9: *Employment Eligibility Verification*

Publication 15, Circular E: *Employer's Tax Guide*

Form 1040 accompanied by Schedules C and SE, and Form 8829 are the backbone of your taxes. The other forms deal with documenting and supporting your income and deduction claims and those taxes associated with having employees.

Lots of providers show a loss in the first year or two of business. This is generally due to a combination of start-up costs and a slow buildup of enrollment. Such a loss is considered normal. The IRS becomes concerned when you don't show a profit for three out of every five years. If you do show consistent losses, you are more likely to be audited; the IRS may decide that you are not serious about making money and merely have a hobby, not a business, and then disallow your business deductions.

There are several sections in this book dealing specifically with business concerns that will help you become profitable; consider carefully how they apply to you and your business. Family child care can be a successful and profitable career for you, but it demands that you function in a businesslike manner.

A Final Word about Taxes

Don't be daunted by the complexity of figuring and filing taxes. No one can know everything about tax law. As long as you keep accurate, orderly records, follow IRS instructions, and get help when you need it, chances are you will be just fine.

I recommend you attend workshops on record-keeping and taxes for family child-care providers. Find out about workshops offered in your area from your local family child-care support group, your local R&R, or your food program sponsor. I highly recommend the RNI books about this subject: *Family Child Care Tax Workbook and Organizer* (updated every year) and *Family Child Care Record Keeping Guide*. Of particular interest to new providers is a booklet from Redleaf, *Getting Started in the Business of Family Child Care*.

When you're looking for a tax preparer, try to find one who is thoroughly familiar with family child care. Ask your colleagues whom they use, ask your R&R for a referral, or visit www.redleafinstitute.org to access a state-by-state directory of tax preparers who are familiar with family child-care tax forms. Not all accountants and tax preparers are educated about the unique tax situation your small business is in.

Chapter Eight

Solving Common Problems

Every business has its problems, and family child care is no exception. This chapter will look at some common problems providers have in dealing with parents, with their own families, with the age mix of the children in care, and with interruptions by friends and neighbors.

Problems with Parents

Most providers rank parents as their top problem. As one provider put it, "It only takes two out of fifteen parents to make your life miserable." Problems commonly develop over communication, attitudes, guidance philosophy, late pickups, and nonpayment.

Communication and Attitudes

The best way to avoid communication problems is to have written policies that parents sign when you agree to care for their children. When conflicts over things like payments, pick ups, or sick children come up, you can state your position and refer them to the Parent-Provider Agreement.

Faye describes some parent communication problems she's had:

> I had one set of parents who were not very honest. They made a lot of excuses for not abiding by the terms of our agreement. One of my policies

is that parents will call me in the morning if a child will be late or absent. Somehow their daughter was late a lot without my being notified. These parents also would drop their daughter off in the morning and expect me to take her to a doctor's appointment if they couldn't make it. We had talk after talk about these problems, but to no avail. I finally had to terminate care.

Remember, too, a Parent-Provider Agreement is a two-way street. You must enforce your rules and policies or you will teach the parents to disregard them. For example, if it is your policy that children going through potty training not wear overalls and you find one child turns up every Thursday in his OshKosh B'Gosh specials, then you need to speak to the parent about it. If you don't, the parent learns that your policies can be ignored without repercussions. Other parents who love to dress their children in those cute little overalls will notice your permissiveness and resent it, or begin to follow suit. You do no one a favor if you allow parents to abuse your policies. If you find that a particular policy is no longer relevant, then put the policy change in writing and distribute it to the parents.

Parent Communication Tools

- ❏ Opening interview
- ❏ Your written policies
- ❏ Parent bulletin board
- ❏ Drop-off & pickup times
- ❏ Notes or flyers in child's cubby
- ❏ Phone calls
- ❏ E-mail
- ❏ Parent conference

An excellent tool for parent communication is a bulletin board near the entryway. Train parents to check this board for notices of forthcoming events, schedule changes, planned curriculum, licensing information, or even menus for the day.

Possibly most wearing on providers are parents who have "attitude problems" or, as one provider put it, "are just plain obnoxious." Camille describes the complaints she has fielded:

It always tends to be the same parents who gripe. They complain about another child having a cold, or about spilled paint on clothing, or that little Joshua said he was starving when he left child care the night before—it just goes on and on. I make it a routine to greet each child and parent at the door in the morning and then see them off at night. If little Joshua fell outside and scratched his elbow, then I tell the parent about it and how it happened. Likewise, if he comes in the next morning with a bump on his forehead, I ask how he got it. I don't want the parent coming in later and thinking that he got it here. And my state requires that I document such things.

The following is a parent complaint form you can use to keep track of what problems are coming up for parents. Some will be frivolous, but others may be quite legitimate and need attention from you. Keeping these on file will help you determine whether a pattern is developing. You don't need to fill out these forms in front of parents if you don't wish to.

A blank parent complaint form for your use is located in the appendix.

Besides complaints, which are usually straightforward, some providers report more subtle attitude problems. Faye, a provider and also the parent of adult children, runs a

Sample Parent Complaint Form

Date _6-12-06_

1. Parent's name: _Sandra Johnson_
2. Child's name: _Lindsay Johnson, age three_
3. Description of problem:

   Mom reports Lindsay says she's not getting enough to eat at lunchtime.
   Says she's always hungry during naptime and no one will give her any
   food.

4. Action taken (or will take):

   Advised Mom that Lindsay usually refuses to eat anything but her sand-
   wich at lunch—turns down fruit, veggies, and crackers. Snack time is two
   hours after lunch—I can't have all the kids snacking at different times. I
   asked Mom if she had any ideas. She said she'd talk to Lindsay about fin-
   ishing her lunch.

5. Other notes, observations:

   I could give Lindsay a small cup of fruit juice right before naptime—if I do
   it without getting the attention of the other kids. Or I could ask her mom
   what lunch foods she really loves; if they're nutritious, I could include them
   at lunchtime.

family child care with her partner and daughter-in-law, Tina, who is the parent of a two-year-old. The partnership works well for them in terms of their differing expertise and in sharing the workload. Some parents, however, show an inappropriate tendency toward age discrimination—they dismiss Tina as "not the adult in charge." Faye describes the situation:

> The way we have things organized, Tina arrives at my house at 6:00 A.M. to set up and cook breakfast. She greets the early-arriving children and parents. I don't come on duty until about 7:00 A.M. Some parents insist on speaking to me about a concern, even though we've repeatedly told them that we're partners and they can consult with Tina about anything.

Faye and Tina have dealt with this sort of subtle disrespect on an ongoing basis. They made a conscious decision to have Tina initiate discussions with parents on their children's needs, child-care policies, and other routine matters. They report that slowly but steadily, parents are showing more respect for Tina's role.

Some providers report that being older than the parents, and in many cases having raised their own children, places them in a more confident position. "Parents perceive you as having more authority," says Camille, "and you feel less intimidated by the parents when you've been through the child-raising years yourself."

Camille goes on to warn against giving advice routinely or encouraging parents to lean on you. Parents who are unusually stressed, emotionally needy, or just plain immature can drain you with requests for information and support. "Know your limits," she advises, "and don't get overly involved with any one family."

All providers report that if you think providing quality child care will cause parents to express appreciation, you're in for a resounding disappointment. One state inspector puts it this way, "Parents are not out to find wonderful child care, pat you on the back, and reward you handsomely. They're cheap and out to find a bargain." An experienced provider adds this: "Never, never do family child care as a favor to the parents; they will not appreciate you as they should. Charge enough money to feel amply compensated." Another provider agrees: "You have to learn to reward yourself; parents won't do it for you."

Most providers agree that the rewards in family child care are many, but they come in the form of the work you do with the children, the money you make, and the support you get from your colleagues—not in appreciation from parents.

Differing Guidance Philosophies

Ideally, your initial interview process and your written policies should help you sniff out any parents who have dramatically different philosophies from yours. But sometimes they slip by you. Lisa describes a time when this difference in philosophy became a problem:

> I cared for a special-needs child, Krista, age four, who has hydrocephalus and is in a wheelchair. I thought my guidance philosophy was clearly spelled out in my policy, but this child's parent decided that my policy didn't apply to a child with such health challenges. She lets Krista bite. Biting is not acceptable in my child care, so I brought it up with the mother. Her position was that the other children, who were not physically challenged like Krista, should be tolerant of her behavior. I was unwilling to change my policy on this for anyone, so needless to say, we soon parted ways.

Again, clear policies and quick communication when there is a problem will help you prevent and deal with situations like these.

Parent Conferences

There are two types of parent conferences. Some providers hold annual (or biannual) conferences to discuss the child's development and learning—much like elementary school conferences. A sample form for this type of conference can be found in the appendix. The second type of parent conference is held over a particular problem or concern that arises in the child's care. This is something of more importance than would be discussed at the door over drop-off and pickup. You can schedule parent conferences in the evenings or on weekends; they can also be done over the phone. The child should not be present. This is an opportunity for you and the parent to privately and calmly discuss the problem and brainstorm ways to solve it. The goal is not to terminate care but to preserve it.

On the following pages is a sample worksheet to illustrate the problem-solving process. A blank worksheet for you to adapt to your own needs is located in the appendix.

Sample Parent Conference Form

Date: 6-15-06

Child's name: Robbie Davidson
Parent's name: Alison Davidson

Description of problem:

Robbie, age three, uses foul language when he's upset, frustrated, mad, or just wants to show off. It's unacceptable to use such words in my child care, and his mom is distressed with it too. The other children are beginning to pick up the words, and the other parents are beginning to complain. Robbie's behavior otherwise is fine.

Other relevant information or circumstances:

Robbie tends to swear at me when he doesn't want to do something. He swears at objects or other children when he is frustrated. Mom says her husband does swear a lot at home. Neither Mom nor I think he's trying to be deliberately mean or bad; he just isn't choosing appropriate ways to express his feelings and likes the attention the bad words bring him, even though it's negative.

Ideas for solving the problem (just make a list here—the ideas can be good, bad, or silly):

1. Mom and Dad make a great effort to watch their own language at home.
2. Give Robbie some silly nonsense-words he can use instead of swearing when he's exasperated—for example, "Oh Crabgrass!" or "Snicker Snack!"
3. I could say, "My ears don't hear words like that" and walk away.
4. Make it clear that such words are not allowed in child care.
5. Set a consequence. For example: "If you use bad words, you don't get to watch videos for the day."
6. Say, "Think of three better words to use and then I'll . . ." (do whatever child is requesting).

7. Notice when he uses good words and praise him.

8. Tell him the "Good Word Fairy" doesn't like little boys to talk like that. Dress up as the Good Word Fairy one day (or have someone else do it) and explain to the children the importance of using good words.

9. Ignore the bad words—don't pay any attention to them.

Plan of action:

Mom and Dad will clean up their own language at home. Give Robbie some nonsense words to use and remind him to use them. Try dressing up as the Good Word Fairy and making it something the whole group can work on.

Date at which parent and provider will evaluate progress:

Two weeks from now we will get together and evaluate progress. I will keep track of how many "bad word" incidents Robbie has during this time.

Late Pickups and Nonpayment

No provider is immune to late pickups (from every once in a while to chronic offenders) and an occasional parent who doesn't pay the bill or who pays late. It's annoying, a headache to deal with, and it will happen to you.

Chapter 3 goes over suggested policies for handling these particular problems. The important thing to remember is to *do what your policy says you will do.* If you state that you will charge $5.00 for every minute a parent is late, then you must keep track of when the parent comes in and charge him or her, no matter how reasonable the excuse. If a parent bounces two checks and your policy states that he or she then must pay up front, in cash, then you must require that. If the parent fails to do so, then you must terminate care.

Don't be afraid to exercise the termination clause in your Parent-Provider Agreement. If a parent consistently abuses your policies or fails to pay you, then you have just cause to ask the parent and child to leave. It is not fair to you, your business, and your family to allow parents to abuse your time and services.

On the following pages are a sample dismissal worksheet for you to keep in your files and a sample termination notice to parents. A blank version of this worksheet is located in the appendix.

Sample Dismissal Worksheet

Date   _6/9/06_

Child's Name: McKenna Adams

Parent's Name: Michelle Orr

Termination notice given: 6/9/06

Last day of care: 6/23/06

✓   Provider's choice

___   Parent's choice   _____

                                        Parent's signature

Bill paid: _____

Balance of _$75_ due _on receipt_

Notes:

McKenna is too disruptive to the other children. There have been three separate instances where she has hurt (bitten, hit) the younger children and three separate parent complaints about her (attached). I believe she needs more one-on-one adult supervision than I can provide. I am referring her to the local R&R for specialized help.

___ R&R notified (if necessary)

Sample Termination Notice

Please be advised that as of _____ (date), I will no longer be able to provide _____ (child's name) with care. As it states in my child-care policies and agreement, I am giving two weeks' notice for you to find another child-care arrangement.

Sincerely,

_____
Provider's signature

When you are terminating care, always give written notice. It is appropriate to tell the parent why, although you do not need to state it on your termination notice. Always document the problem on your dismissal worksheet.

If a parent leaves angry or with an unpleasant attitude, notify your local child-care Resource and Referral agency; tell them exactly what happened and the reason why you dismissed the child. Keep written records of what happened (e.g., document the nonpayment on the specific dates, keep copies of written notices to the parent, and make notes of any discussions you have with the parent). Then if the parent goes to the Resource and Referral agency (R&R) with a complaint or accusation, you will have documented the events leading to your action.

Problems with Your Family

Chances are, even if you have involved your family in the planning of the business and brainstormed on ways to cope with the sacrifices all family members will have to make, you'll encounter a few bumps on the way. No matter how prepared you and your family are, there will be problems from time to time. This is normal. Experienced providers offer solid advice for coping with these times.

Complaints from Your Spouse

Most providers report their spouses to be wonderfully supportive of the business. These providers are also careful to structure the business day so that overlap with family life is minimal. Spouses' main complaints are about sharing space and your time with the business.

> My husband's beef about the child care was having kids around after my 6:00 P.M. "closing." I made my late pickup policy much more strenuous and enforced it more regularly. The late pickups subsided dramatically and my husband relaxed more.

Keeping work and family as separate as possible will prevent problems. Providers who expect their partners and children to constantly give up family time and space to the business after hours soon deal with serious problems. Try to strike a balance between their needs and yours. One provider describes her experience:

> We haven't had too many problems. At first, Bob resented the planning and paperwork time I needed in the evenings to organize the business. We worked out a deal where I confined my after-hours work to Tuesday and Thursday evenings from 7:00 to 9:00 P.M. while he looked after our kids' needs. Then after 9:00 P.M. I was available to him and the kids.

Problems with Young Children

Your own children are understandably not very happy to share you. Some adapt well and like the activity and interaction of the child care; others have a hard time adjusting to the invasion. Providers agree that the number-one problem children ages two to five have is sharing their mom. Here are two accounts from providers:

> Jason was four years old when I started my business. At first, he intensely disliked my paying attention to the other kids. Since the business was my way of being able to spend more time with Jason, we persevered. We talked about ways he could ask for my attention without resorting to tantrums and we also looked at the best times of the day he could have my time. I set up a star chart for him to reward him for the times he asked for atten-

tion appropriately. When he got ten stars I took him to McDonald's for lunch. After a while, things calmed down. He started to like the other kids better, although he was usually ready for them to leave by 3:00 P.M. instead of 5:00 P.M.

My five-year-old daughter had trouble sharing me. We worked out a special time just for her. When the kids in care were napping, she was allowed to choose a special game for me to play with her.

Like the provider in the second example, you may find it effective to establish a special time that your young child has exclusively with you, every day. It doesn't have to be during business hours, but it does have to be consistent and belong entirely to the child. Don't use the time to teach your child, and don't choose the activity yourself. Let the child decide what you will do together (even if you have to play Candyland for thirty days in a row), and follow his or her lead. If you consistently offer your child pleasant, focused time with you, his or her behavior at other times will generally improve.

Difficulty in sharing mom is followed closely by being asked to share toys. In general, children aren't developmentally capable of sharing until ages three to four. Forcing two-year-olds to routinely share their toys will buy you much misery and little peace. Providers vary in how they deal with this.

I make my own kids' toys off-limits to the day care. My kids are not allowed to bring them out into the playroom unless they are willing to share them with everyone (it rarely happens). Consequently, all the day-care toys must be shared—no exceptions. This has worked pretty well for us. For some reason, my kids are not territorial about their books; they're quite willing to share them, so that's not an issue.

My budget is not very big, so when I started the business, I planned to use my three-year-old daughter's "big toys" (kitchen center, ride-on toys) in the day care. We talked about which toys she was willing to share with the other kids. I didn't force her to share any toy she didn't want to—and she surprised me with how generous she was. All her nonsharing toys had to stay in her room. I also allowed her to change her mind about sharing a toy, but she had to make the decision at the end of the day when the kids were gone, not in the midst of play.

Issues of sharing parents and toys are very common with this age group. Be sensitive to your child's needs, and honor her or his preferences whenever possible.

Problems with School-Age Children

Your school-age child, ages six to eleven, is usually better about not demanding your constant attention, but sharing issues continue to crop up. School-age children are typically much more territorial about their rooms and toys, as described in the following accounts:

> My son is seven. We worked through his concerns for privacy and privilege by making his room private and off-limits to the business and by allowing him to choose his own snacks (but he always had to eat them away from the other kids).

> Jenny is eight. She likes the children in care, especially the younger ones, but is bothered by the older ones being in her room or playing with her things. I need to use her room for naptime, so we worked out a deal. I pay her "rent" for the time the other kids are in her room. All toys are off-limits and put away unless she decides she wants to rent a certain toy to the business. This way she has a concrete benefit when she's required to share.

School-age children also like having some attention when they arrive home from school. Adjusting your schedule—perhaps the other children can have free play at that time—will allow you to focus on your own child for a brief time.

There are many ways to deal with your children's concerns. Networking with other providers and discussing options will give you more ideas.

Problems with Older Children and Teens

Older children tend to ignore the child care in favor of their own agendas. Many providers report these kids are just "hardly ever around." Some of the same issues do appear, however.

One provider had trouble with her middle-school-age kids wanting to boss the little kids around. They felt their space invaded and attempted to maintain some ownership by controlling the children. The mom in this case solved the problem by encouraging her older kids to invite friends over (or visit other friends' houses) and socialize with them while the child care was open. This way their focus was on their friends, not on the children being cared for.

Another provider shares her story:

> I have three teenage sons. They like the kids and will occasionally help out. Their biggest complaint, though, is "You give all the good food to the day-care kids!" We addressed this problem by involving them in the family shopping so they could have some control over what food was available. I also worked out a system where, if nothing else appealed, they could take child-care food (I keep it separate) and write down what they ate.

The provider in this example not only had to record what food was eaten by her teens but then had to subtract the cost from her business expenses.

Coping with your own children's needs will take some creativity and flexibility on your part, but it is worth it. A happy, supportive family is something a family child-care provider needs in order for the business to be successful.

Problems with a Multi-age Mix of Children

We all know that life with young children can be easier if they have someone around their own age to play with. They play together better and their needs are similar. Life is not perfect, however, and you will undoubtedly not end up with conveniently matched pairs of children in care.

The Benefits

There are some definite benefits to having a multi-age mix of kids. First, you can accommodate siblings. It is important to many parents that their children be together in child care. This is a special feature that a family child care is equipped to provide. Child-care centers almost always separate children by age; *you* can have them all together in a home-like atmosphere.

Second, it is a good learning experience for children to be around other age groups. They can learn appropriate ways to play with younger children, and they can learn from the older children. It is a great self-esteem booster for children to be able to help and look out for each other, and family child care is an ideal place to foster this behavior.

The Challenges

A multi-age mix does bring with it certain problems. Experienced providers recommend that you carefully plan the age mix you accept for care. Accepting six children of different ages is asking for trouble. One provider recommends seeking children who are the same age as your child as a place to start. Another prefers to take children from ages two up to five (prekindergarten), although she'll take a child as young as twelve months if he or she is a sibling. She explains her age limit:

> I find the kindergartners are usually too big for many of the toys I have. They're also a bit more disruptive. I guess they feel they've outgrown the child-care setting.

Making rules based on ages is often effective for avoiding chaos. Lisa describes how she handles a mix of two- through five-year-olds:

> I don't let the younger twos do circle time with the others—they're just not ready for it yet. Another thing I do is put out toys and puzzles on two ends of my long play table: the younger toys at one end and the older toys at the other. I also find it's helpful to adhere strictly to the "only four kids playing with the housekeeping toys at one time" rule.

Another provider adds that she makes it a rule that the older children (ages five and six) not play with the smaller toys with intricate pieces around the children ages two and younger. They can play with these special toys during the younger children's naptime. You can use height to maintain safety as well. Put the activities with small pieces on a high table or bar. The older children can use this space while the height helps protect the toddlers from small pieces. Another useful safety tool is a baby gate; close off certain areas to the younger set.

The best advice most providers offer for handling a multi-age mix is to spend adequate time *planning* the daily schedule so that the different ages can mesh. For example, if the toddlers are napping, the preschoolers can be having quiet story time.

Assistants Come in Handy

Most providers agree that a broad age mix is most easily handled when you have an assistant or partner. Many advise against taking infants unless you do have an assistant, since babies take up so much more time.

Tina describes how she and her partner, Faye, handle their broad age mix:

> Since there are two of us, I take the older kids downstairs for more structured preschool activities and Faye keeps the younger ones with her upstairs. During the summertime, we all go outside together, where there's more space.

Deborah, a provider in a sunny climate, uses her outdoor play area on a daily basis.

> My assistant has storytime inside with the younger kids while I take the older ones outside for free play. Then we trade places.

Providing care on your own without an assistant does not automatically mean that you will go crazy with more than two age groups present, but it does mean that you will need to be very, very organized. A common problem time is when you need to prepare food or clean up and still watch the children.

Laura describes how she handles the problem spots:

Tips for a Multi-age Mix

- Use the concept of "centers." Have a block corner, a dress-up area, a reading "nest" area with pillows. Children can play independently while you "float."

- Circle Time should be broken into age-appropriate groups.

- Use large tubs to contain an activity—this is an easy way to transform the space. When you're done, store the activity in the tub out of sight.

- Use an area rug (or a blanket) to "anchor" an activity—for example, "All blocks stay on the rug."

I use my look-through window from the kitchen to the family room to keep an eye on the kids while I'm cooking or cleaning up. The secret is to keep food preparation quick and simple. I serve snacks that are easy to prepare and quick to clean up. Another thing I commonly do is put on a favorite video (about twenty minutes long) for the kids to watch while I'm preparing lunch; that keeps them quiet, occupied, and all together.

Minimizing Interruptions

If you've ever been home with children or worked out of your home, you already know that friends, family, and neighbors tend to interrupt at the least opportune time. When you have six young children to watch, you can't have Aunt Bernice calling up to chat about the family reunion or your neighbor dropping in.

Deborah, a longtime provider, addresses the problem:

> You just have to educate people. When they call or stop by, tell them that you can't talk while the children are in care and give them an option or two when they can call back or drop by again. Most family and friends are understanding once you explain it to them. I also highly recommend getting an answering machine and using it. Train yourself not to pick up the phone if you are involved with the children.

Family and friends can also e-mail you if they dislike answering machines. But be aware that neither answering machines nor e-mail will solve the problem if you don't get back to people in a regular and timely fashion.

Everyday problems in child care are inevitable. The good news is that some provider somewhere is sure to have experienced a problem like yours before. Belonging to your local and regional family child care association groups will put you in touch with other providers. Attend meetings and ask for help when you need it. Going to special seminars and other educational events will also help you solve these kinds of problems in ways that work for you.

Chapter Nine
Planning for the Future

P lanning is a natural part of a new venture. At the outset, however, many providers forget to plan for growth of their business. Even as you're starting out, you should think about if, or how, you want to expand. Business growth that simply mushrooms without careful planning will leave you overwhelmed and possibly ready to close up shop. Too much demand without a plan for meeting it has often been the undoing of many a small business. Healthy growth is a matter of making choices ahead of time and planning carefully.

Small versus Large License

After two years or so, many providers with a small license are often ready to upgrade to a large license (seven to twelve children); others are happy staying where they are. Staying small and growing larger each present benefits and trade-offs. Let's look at some of these.

Small License

Benefits

- No need to alter space for additional children

- Opportunity to raise fees regularly and improve certain features of the business

- No need to hire help and increase paperwork

- Less stress on own family

Trade-offs

- More of a cap on income—much reduced potential for income increase

- Less creative challenge as you become experienced with the business and its size; more potential for boredom

- Fewer "extras" for family due to smaller income

Large License

Benefits

- Increased income

- Opportunity to work with other adults (assistants)

- Increased creative challenge

- More flexibility with setting fees

- More flexibility to take part-time children

- More "extras" for family, due to increased income

Trade-offs

- Increased work

- Obliged to hire assistant and assume all the responsibilities of an employer

- Obliged to meet state requirements for large license (possibly increase space)

- Higher possibility of job burnout

- More stress on own family

These are some major concerns to think about; you will undoubtedly consider many more ramifications on your own. Start giving growth some thought now. Later in this chapter we will look at specific goals for providers as you go along.

At this start-up point, there are several areas you need to think about when it comes to planning for the future.

Your Physical and Emotional Well-Being

If you plan to care for young children day in and day out, then planning to be in good health and carrying out that plan is critical to the long-term success of your business. All providers agree that it is paramount you take good care of yourself and find support when you need it. "After a week with young children," says one provider, "you can feel it."

Working and living with young children require a high level of energy from you. Camille shares her thoughts on this:

> I would say that having lots of energy is even more important than liking children! (Especially if you are caring for babies.) I had to cut one of my assistants down from four to three days a week, just because physically, she was burned out by Thursday.

Faye agrees:

> The most important thing for me is getting lots of sleep. I used to work in
> child care some years ago and had to quit because I injured my back from
> lifting the kids too much. This time around I strictly limit the lifting—
> nothing too heavy. The changing table is set exactly for my height. I also
> make sure I get massages as often as possible—that helps me relax and stay
> in tune with my body.

Taking care of yourself means getting adequate sleep, eating right, and exercising regularly (by yourself, not with the children). In addition, find ways to nurture yourself, like having regular massages or manicures. Providers agree that you should *not* give up hobbies or activities that are special to you, like piano lessons, book groups, or playing on a softball team. Lisa talks about how she protects her leisure time:

> I have a fellowship group at church every Wednesday night. It's important
> to my mental well-being for me to go. I sent out a notice to all the parents
> letting them know that they must be on time to pick up their children on
> Wednesdays. I accomplished this by beefing up my late-fee schedule and
> then enforcing it strenuously on Wednesdays.

Another important way to be good to yourself is to take vacations and holidays. Don't give in to the temptation to work on your time off or take in just one or two kids. You need the breaks.

If you do not take good care of yourself, you may become ill or burn out on family child care. It is hard to keep your capacity up if you are continually getting sick and requiring parents to find substitute care. The parents and children need to depend on you to stay healthy and provide consistent care. You can do so only by paying good attention to your own needs.

Planning for a Substitute

There will be occasions when you cannot be at work. Going to an educational conference, dealing with a family crisis, and having the flu are just a few examples. You will, of course, attempt to keep these occasions few and far between. Instead of canceling child care for the day and forcing parents to fend for themselves, it is nice if you can provide a substitute.

One way to do this is to use your assistants (if you already have them), provided they are adults—you must always have at least one adult present with the children. Some providers have an arrangement with a friend, relative, or neighbor who is a stay-at-home mom; this friend agrees to substitute for your planned absences in your home for a daily fee. Additionally, she agrees to make herself reasonably available for your unplanned absences. Check with your licensing department on their specific substitute policy. A substitute is usually not required to be on your license, although if you use your spouse, as Deborah does in the following example, then it can be convenient to have his name on the license.

Deborah planned ahead for absences:

> When I upgraded from a small license to a large one, I put my husband on the license. He's not a daily part of the business but has agreed to substitute for me—as the responsible adult on the premises—when I need to be away for family child-care meetings. His job is such that he is able to take a day off here and there without any problem. All the parents know him, and it makes a fun change for the children once in a while.

Another option is a substitute service. These are similar to the substitute pools that schools use; they are not yet widespread, but they are growing. Your regional family child care association or your local child-care Resource and Referral agency can tell you if there is such a service near you.

Whenever you bring in a substitute, you need to leave her or him fully equipped to keep the children safe, fed, and occupied on a schedule that is as close as possible to your own. Make sure your substitute has a copy of your daily schedule, is familiar with your emergency route out of the house, knows the location of the fire extinguisher and emergency phone numbers, has a copy of the menu for the day, and is briefed on any special needs the children have.

Hiring an Assistant

When your child care is established and you are reasonably profitable, you may consider hiring an assistant. If you are expanding your license, then in most states you will be required to hire help. Having someone to help out and share the burden is usually well worth the extra expense and paperwork involved.

Julie, who has a large license, describes her assistants:

> I employ an adult woman in the mornings (I have two who job-share) and a teen helper in the afternoons. I had no trouble finding them. The women are stay-at-home moms who wanted to earn a little extra money; I found them via friends at church. I found my other helper by calling up my local high school home economics department and asking for possible candidates.

Regardless of whether you find your assistants through your personal network or advertise for them in the paper, all job applicants should fill out a standard application. A sample application follows this page; you can adapt it to your use.

An assistant can help you with many things. The following is a list of some ways that having an assistant will make your job easier and more enjoyable.

- You are free to go to the bathroom, answer the phone, and feel confident that the children are safe.
- An assistant can supervise the children while you are preparing food or cleaning up.
- An assistant can monitor activities in progress and help sense when it's time to move on.
- An assistant can help prepare art activities and assist the children as they do projects.
- You have someone to share with; children are always doing something charming and priceless, or challenging and obnoxious. An assistant is someone to celebrate and commiserate with.

Sample Standard Job Application

Name _____ Social security number _____

Address _____

_____

Phone _____

Position applying for _____ Date can start _____

_____ Referred by _____

Job objective/career goal _____

_____

Educational Background

High school _____

Year graduated _____ Or last year attended _____

College _____

Year graduated _____ Or last year attended _____

Degree received _____

Employment Background

Last position held _____ Special training _____

_____

Company _____

Duties include

_____

_____

_____

Supervisor's name _____

Phone _____

Date began employment _____ Date left employment _____

Salary _____

Reason for leaving _____

Previous positions _____

Company _____

Duties included

_____

_____

_____

Supervisor's name _____

Phone _____

Date began employment _____ Date left employment _____

Salary _____
Reason for leaving _____
Previous positions _____

Company _____
Duties included

_____
_____
_____
Supervisor's name _____
Phone _____
Date began employment _____   Date left employment _____
Salary _____
Reason for leaving _____
Previous positions _____

References (please give three)
1.   Name _____
     Relationship _____
     Phone _____
2.   Name _____
     Relationship _____
     Phone _____
3.   Name _____
     Relationship _____
     Phone _____

Activities (civic, athletic, etc.)

_____
_____
_____

In case of emergency please notify
Name _____
Address _____
Phone _____
Phone _____

_____   _____
Signature of Applicant   Date

- It's good for the children to have another caregiver around. Often you will have one child to whom you just don't relate well; many times your assistant will cope better with this child than you can.

This last point is illustrated by Laura, an experienced provider:

I have one little girl, Amanda, age four, who is prone to screeching when she wants something. I've had demanding children before but never one who gets on my nerves like she does. After some thought I realized that she reminds me a lot of my oldest son at the same age—it was a hard time for both of us. I asked my teen helper, Malia, to make a special point of attending to Amanda. This gave me a nice break in the afternoon, which allowed me to relax and tolerate Amanda a little better. She responded well to the attention from Malia, and her screeching diminished a bit.

When you go through the applications submitted, you might decide to interview three to five candidates. Legally, you need to treat all job applicants the same. So use the same basic questions for each applicant. The following list of questions is a place to start. Write down the person's answers as you talk with her or him.

Keep in mind that there are many questions you cannot legally ask a person—for instance, age or marital status. If the applicant offers such information (many people talk about their spouses and families), that's fine, but don't probe further. In general, it is safest not to initiate any questions of a personal nature; keep the discussion to the job at hand.

Hiring employees also brings with it certain responsibilities and challenges. If you've ever worked as a manager or business owner before, then you know firsthand all the snags that tend to crop up. By the time you hire an assistant, you probably will have settled on a style and daily routine that work well for you. Introducing a helper to your child-care day will change your pattern. Whether those changes will be for the good or the bad depends on how well you make your expectations known and how open you are to new ideas.

Sample Interview Questions

1. Why did you decide to apply for a job with my company?

_____

_____

2. What did you do at your last job?

_____

_____

3. Why did you leave?

_____

_____

4. Do you have any experience (job or otherwise) working with children? What ages? Working with parents?

_____

_____

5. What do you consider your greatest strengths?

_____

_____

6. What do you consider your greatest weaknesses?

_____

_____

7. (Discuss the job description.) Are these all tasks that you are willing, interested, and able to do? (If lifting children is involved, be explicit about this—some people have back problems.)

_____

_____

8. The hours for this position are _____. Are you available for these hours?

_____

9. Are there any questions you have for me about the position?

_____

_____

10. I am required by the state to have myself and all my employees subjected to a criminal activity screening and fingerprinted. Is this a problem?

_____

_____

11. When could you start?

_____

_____

Camille, an experienced provider who has assistants, shares the problems she's encountered:

> I wish my assistants would take a little more initiative in planning the daily activities and in seeing that something needs to be done and doing it without waiting for me to tell them to. I also have to watch that we don't end up with "dead time" where the assistant sits and listens to me during circle time or visits too much with the parents instead of working.

Job descriptions are helpful. They tell the assistant exactly what you expect, and you can refer to the job description when you meet with your assistant to review her performance. A sample job description for a part-time assistant follows.

When you are ready to hire an assistant, there are many places you can find good candidates. Like Julie in the example earlier, you can find people through your own personal network of family, friends, church, or other groups to which you belong. Mothers who are choosing to stay at home with children sometimes welcome the chance to earn a little extra money and still have their children with them (however, you need to have room in your capacity to accommodate these children). The early childhood or home economics departments in your local high schools, community colleges, and universities have job boards where you can list the position you have open. Your local Resource and Referral agency (R&R) also offers a job bank for those interested in working with children.

The hours you offer depend on your needs and the state's requirements. If you have a

Sample Job Description

Salary: $9.25 per hour

Title: Child-care assistant

Hours: 2:30–5:30 P.M., Monday through Friday

Description: Responsibilities will include assisting provider with:

- Preparing, serving, and clearing meals
- Preparing materials for art and other activities
- Leading certain activities such as storytime and selected games
- Accompanying children on outings to the park or more special field trips
- General crowd control
- Clean up of playroom, kitchen, and bathroom
- Planning of activities
- Ensuring the safety and well-being of all children in care

large license, then you are most likely required to have an assistant present when the seventh child arrives. Many providers have a morning and afternoon assistant, with little if any overlap. Wages for this position are generally paid by the hour and vary according to where you live. To avoid over- or underpaying assistants, network with other providers in your area to find out what they offer as a starting wage. Your local R&R agency may also be of help here. Also check federal and state minimum wage laws (if your state minimum wage is higher than the federal—and it usually is—then you need to meet the minimum wage for the state).

Most providers choose to hire one full-time assistant or a combination of two or three part-time assistants. Hiring one or more part-time employees is generally simpler and less expensive for your business than hiring a full-time employee (which is different from a full partner). Full-time employees are entitled to certain benefits, such as overtime wages and any benefits you provide for yourself (pension, vacation pay, health insurance, etc.).

Lastly, do not overlook the fact that when you hire an employee, the IRS requires you to deduct and pay social security and federal income taxes (together, these are known as payroll taxes). In addition, you must pay federal (and sometimes state) unemployment taxes. See Chapter 7 for the specific IRS forms you will need to file. There are payroll serv-ices who can handle all these tasks for you. Look in your phone book for one near you. If you handle the payroll yourself, you can refer to Tom Copeland's *Family Child Care Tax Workbook* (Redleaf Press) for a detailed and helpful discussion of how to correctly keep and file this tax information.

Evaluating Your Assistant's Performance

If you've hired an assistant, then you need to regularly meet with her or him and evaluate her or his performance together. I suggest meeting quarterly, or at the very least every six months. Use the job description to guide you in evaluating your assistant's performance. Following are some general questions, based on the previous job description, that you can adapt to your own purposes.

Discuss all portions of the evaluation with your assistant. Use the time to convey what you appreciate about your assistant's performance as well as what she or he can improve on. You can use the evaluations over the space of a year to assist you in deciding whether to raise wages.

Increasing Your Fees

Another key ingredient to long-term success is planning your fee increases. There are many reasons for raising your fees. The most common are:

- Rising expenses
- Increased expertise or education on your part
- Accreditation of your child care (discussed later in this chapter)
- Improvement of your facility or other improved features of the care you provide
- Upgrading to a large license and hiring an assistant

Right now, think about when you realistically might increase your fees. Set a date, per-haps six months from opening, to review your fee schedule and expenses and to calculate your profitability. If you are running in the red, you need to either reduce expenses or increase

Sample Performance Evaluation

1. List two things the assistant does quite well.

   _____

   _____

2. List two things the assistant could improve on.

   _____

   _____

3. Rate the assistant in the following areas. Make any explanatory comments below.

   E = Excellent, S = Satisfactory, U = Unsatisfactory

   ___ Meal preparation and serving

   _____

   _____

   ___ Activity materials preparation

   _____

   _____

   ___ Leading storytime and games

   _____

   _____

   ___ Supervising children outdoors or on field trips

   _____

   _____

   ___ Cleanup of playroom, kitchen, and bathroom

   _____

   _____

   ___ Planning activities

   _____

   _____

   ___ Ensuring safety of children

   _____

   _____

fees immediately. If the situation is not critical, but you feel a fee increase is appropriate, set a reasonable date for doing so. Give parents at least one month's notice of the fee increase. More than one fee increase per year is viewed unfavorably by parents, so figure your calculations and make plans carefully.

Plan to review your profitability on a regular basis. If you make your fee increases at consistent intervals (e.g., every year in June), parents will be more comfortable and less likely to leave you for other care.

Camille, a successful, longtime provider, increases her fees yearly.

> I notify the parents of the fee increase in June and then put it into effect in September. I find yearly increases, even as small as 50 cents a day, are more effective than a larger increase once every three years. Parents accept the smaller, regular increases more readily.

One month ahead of the fee increase, send all parents a notice. A sample notice is below. Have the parent sign and return it. This serves as an addendum of change to your contract with the parent. Similarly, if a parent contracts with you for five days a week of

Sample Fee Increase Notice

Notice to All Parents

Due to increasing costs, I find it necessary to increase my rates to the following amount:

_____

The new rate will become effective in thirty days (date _____).

Thank you for your continued patronage and goodwill.

Sincerely,   _____

Jane Provider   Parent Signature

---

care, then drops to two days, amend or change your contract in writing. You don't want the IRS assuming you're collecting fees for five days a week when it's only two.

Networking: The Importance of Being Well Connected

Plan to plug into your local, regional, and national family child-care networks. One very important source of support will come from your colleagues in the form of professional associations. No one will understand your problems and successes like another provider.

As discussed in chapter 2, joining the National Association for Family Child Care (NAFCC) is a good place to start. The NAFCC can put you in touch with your regional group; send you its newsletter, the *National Perspective*; and offer you resources to order by mail. In addition, the organization sponsors both national and regional conferences.

Another pertinent organization is the National Association for the Education of Young Children (NAEYC). Membership is open to those who work with young children in all types of settings—day cares, preschools, child-care centers, universities, and so forth. Like NAFCC, NAEYC has many regional and local branches and sponsors conferences and workshops on all levels. In addition, the group publishes a bimonthly magazine, *Young Children*. Addresses for both NAFCC and NAEYC are listed in the appendix.

It is not always practical to attend national conferences, but whenever they are held near you, make every effort to take a couple of days off and attend. They provide wonderful opportunities to hear nationally known speakers on early childhood topics, and a plethora of useful, practical workshops are there for the taking. In addition, these conferences almost always sponsor an exhibit hall of vendors who are eager to sell you books, toys, and teacher resources. Your expenses to attend such a conference are business expenses and may be claimed on your taxes. You may claim conference fees, travel costs (mileage or airfare), lodging, and meals. Consult your accountant for details on how to claim these expenses. If you live far away from any major city, chances are these national conferences won't be held near you, so look to your state and regional conferences. They are often just as helpful, though not as big.

Another organization worth knowing about, although you probably do not need to belong on the national level, is the National Association of Child Care Resource and Referral Agencies (NACCRRA). This is the umbrella organization your local R&R agency belongs to. Besides providing you with referrals from parents, your local R&R is a clearinghouse of educational material and information. These agencies sponsor and advertise local child-care events (fairs, exhibits, workshops) in which you can participate and promote your business. They can provide you with referrals for insurance companies, food-program sponsors, and other services you might need. R&Rs commonly serve as job banks for individuals looking for employment in child care as well. And they routinely sponsor trainings and workshops for providers. Your R&R is a friend indeed. You will be put in touch with your local agency as you go through the licensing process. I recommend you develop a real relationship with your local agency. Go visit them so they know you in person and will recognize you when you call. For those who are not required to be licensed or registered, phone the NACCRRA headquarters (see the appendix) or visit the association's Web site, www.naccrra.org, for a referral to your closest R&R.

Local organizations are also available to you as a source of workshops, networking, and training. Your local food-program sponsor, state and county department of education, vocational institute, YWCA, and community college or university all offer periodic classes and training for those who live and/or work with young children. Subscribing to your local parenting newsletter or magazine (such as *LA Parent*) will often gain you generous mailings of flyers and circulars advertising classes and workshops. The wider your network, the more opportunities will become available to you.

All of the aforementioned suggestions will help you become a part of the wider early childhood network. Nothing, however, can substitute for the support and information you receive by having your own informal provider support group. Most providers knew an experienced provider before they opened their own family child care. Networking and keeping in touch with this person are good ways to start your own informal group. Soon these informal groups grow and you find yourselves meeting once every month or so for tea and sympathy and, of course, exchange of information. The old adage "There's power in numbers" is true; a problem you've been struggling with will benefit from having two or three extra minds considering it.

In addition, it's always nice to have a provider or two nearby with whom you can share parent/child referrals. If you're up to capacity and get an inquiry, you can refer the parent to your provider friend. She or he can do the same for you. Some providers even "share" a part-time child (for example, the child is at one child care on Monday, Wednesday, and Thursday and at another on Tuesday and Friday).

Planning for Accreditation

As you become experienced at providing family child care, you may wish to apply for accreditation through NAFCC. The purpose of accreditation is to give professional recognition and an opportunity to heighten parents' awareness of the high quality of the provider's child care.

There are some eligibility requirements. You must have provided care for at least eighteen months in a home, be the primary caregiver for a minimum of fifteen hours per week (children are not left with a substitute more than 20 percent of the time), have at least three children enrolled and present, be at least twenty-one years of age, have a high school diploma or GED, and have completed ninety hours of documented training or education in the field. It is a process that involves self-evaluation and parent surveys, and then outside review, observation, and evaluation by an NAFCC-appointed child-care professional and an independent parent.

The NAFCC accreditation standards cover six categories: relationships, environment, activities, developmental learning goals, safety and health, and professional and business practices. Providers report that going through the accreditation process is a real learning experience and self-esteem booster. You find out what you're already doing right and become very focused on ways to improve your business. Standards for accreditation are higher than most state licensing regulations, so providers who become accredited feel very confident about citing their accreditation to parents as a special feature of their business. In states where there are no regulations, accreditation will make your child care a real standout.

Internet Tips

Two organizations that offer accreditation programs:

- National Association for Family Child Care, www.nafcc.org.

- National Association for the Education of Young Children, www.naeyc.org. NAEYC is the nation's largest organization of early childhood professionals working with children through age eight. Membership is open to all family child-care providers, licensed or not.

What It Costs

Accreditation through the National Association for Family Child Care requires membership ($35 per year) and the accreditation fee of $495 (prices current as of this writing).

Recognition and certification from a national organization also boost your image as a professional; they reinforce the fact that being a family child-care provider takes special skills—not just anyone can do it. Last, the accreditation process gets you energized and excited about the quality and potential of your child-care business and keeps the job challenging.

When you are ready, contact the NAFCC for the accreditation application forms, study guide, and fees.

Note: The NAEYC also offers an accreditation program. You may contact the association for more information (see the appendix).

Setting Goals

Making goals, reviewing your progress toward the goals, and reaching them are an integral part of any business. Highly successful people set goals and monitor their own progress on a regular basis. Here are three components of setting goals.

- The goal must be specific. "I will keep good records" is too vague. You must state exactly and specifically what you will do. For example: "I will keep accurate and organized attendance records."
- The goal must be measurable. A measurable form of the previous goal would be, "I will keep accurate and organized attendance records each month." At the end of the month, you can check to see if you have indeed kept accurate and organized attendance records.
- The goal must have a deadline. Studies have found that we achieve our goals far more consistently if we have a deadline to meet. So the first goal could further be restated, "I will keep accurate and organized attendance records to be completed by the last day of each month."

The following are some thoughts on where you might be one, three, and five years from now, together with some sample goals set by individual providers.

One Year

At the end of their first year in business, most providers are just catching their breath. This is a good time to take a day to sit back, look over the events of the year, evaluate your performance or success in specific areas, and set goals for the future.

As a general guide, evaluate yourself using the following worksheet; it should help you pinpoint areas that need work. Once you have identified trouble spots, you can include them in your goal setting.

The following are typical provider goals for the first year in business:

- By the end of the year, I will have turned a profit.
- By year's end I will have a preschool curriculum program developed and in use.
- By year's end I will have organized, easily accessible records on business expenses for tax purposes.

Three Years

After two to three years in family day care, most providers who are not suited to the business have gotten out and those remaining have developed a stable child-care program and a solvent business for themselves. This is a common time for many providers to expand to a large license and really make a financial success of family child care. The section earlier in this chapter about staying small or expanding to a large license describes some of the benefits and trade-offs of such growth.

Regardless of whether you expand or not, this is a good time for you to take another look at your skills and background and determine if there are still holes you need to fill. Some questions to ask yourself are:

1. Am I up to date on infant and child first aid and CPR?
2. Which curriculum areas in my program are tired and could use some new ideas?
3. Would a class or seminar on parent-provider relations be of use to me at this point?
4. (If you have assistants) Is there a class on managing others that would be useful for me to take?

Sample Self-Evaluation Worksheet

Rate yourself using the following scale:
E = Excellent, S = Satisfactory, U = Unsatisfactory
Make any explanatory notes or plans for improvement below.

__ **Overall record-keeping**
__ Am I maintaining accurate, timely, and well-organized records?
_____
_____

__ Meals (USDA Child and Adult Care Food Program [CACFP] records)
_____
_____

__ Attendance
_____
_____

__ Income
_____
_____

__ Expenses
_____
_____

__ **Overall daily activities**
_____
_____

__ Schedule—Is it working reasonably well for the children? For me?
For the parents?
_____
_____

__ Activities—Do I have an appropriate mix of free play and structured activities?
_____
_____

__ **Overall environment**
_____
_____

___ Does my facility adequately meet the needs of my business? What changes might improve it?

_____

_____

___ Safety—Are there concerns that have come up over the past year? How have I addressed them?

_____

_____

___ **Overall relationships**

_____

_____

___ Are my policies clear to the parents and children? Are they signed by each and every parent?

_____

_____

___ Are there children or parents who should be terminated?

_____

_____

___ How is my family reacting to and coping with the business?

_____

_____

___ **Overall business performance**

_____

_____

___ Have I made a profit?

_____

_____

___ Am I over budget anywhere?

_____

_____

___ How are my marketing tools for generating enrollment working?

_____

_____

___ Have I planned which marketing tools to discard or use again?

_____

_____

Sample Goal-Setting Worksheet

One-Year Goals

1. _____
    _____

2. _____
    _____

3. _____
    _____

Three-Year Goals

1. _____
    _____

2. _____
    _____

3. _____
    _____

Five-Year Goals

1. _____
    _____

2. _____
    _____

3. _____
    _____

5. Is it possible for me to attend the next national conference of the NAFCC or NAEYC?

The following are common goals for providers after two to three years in business:

- At the end of three years, I will have taken four courses in the areas of parent involvement, curriculum, and safety.
- At the end of three years, I will be earning enough money after expenses and taxes to pay for 50 percent of my daughter's yearly college tuition.
- At the end of three years, I will upgrade to a large license.

Five Years

The providers who have reached the five-year mark are truly professionals in early childhood care. Their programs are solid and their businesses are very stable and generally quite profitable. Looking ahead to where you want to be in five years, think long-term. Be ambitious in your goal-setting and tune in to the dreams you have for your career as a whole. It's never too early to set goals, but five years is a long time in the future to think about specific program questions.

- At the end of five years in business, I will have completed my early childhood education degree.
- At the end of five years, my partner and I will take the first steps toward opening up a commercial child-care center.
- At the end of five years, I will turn the garage into an extra room.

Don't neglect to do this kind of long-term thinking even if planning daily menus and activities is more fun; the more time you spend in business-planning now, the smoother the growth of your business will be.

Written Goals

People who write down their goals have a much higher rate of reaching them. Remember to make each goal specific and measurable and to give it a deadline. Review your goals at the end of each year and update them.

A Word about Professionalism

Unfortunately, when it comes to planning, you must also expect to encounter a certain amount of ignorance and lack of respect for your profession and decide how you will deal with it. You've already heard from other providers that parents will not shower you with appreciation and respect for the good job you do. In general, that is true of our society as a whole; people who work with children, especially young children, are viewed as paid baby-sitters rather than professionals. Sadly, this attitude is even more prevalent when you work in your home.

Combating this perception begins with you. The resounding advice from successful, experienced providers is *Develop an attitude.* Insist on respect for the vitally important service you provide. Deborah, an experienced provider, shares her thoughts on this:

> I wish someone had told me about the lack of respect. I'd worked in early childhood in center settings before I had children—but I really felt the disrespect when I opened my own business in my home. I felt it from parents, other professionals, and even some of my own family child-care colleagues who don't respect themselves. I found I had to take charge and demand the respect I deserved.

The language you use is important. Be sure to refer to your business in professional terms. For example, notice the difference in the following statements:

> *You say to your spouse, "After a day of watching the kids, I'm exhausted."*
> *Or,*
> *"A full day of child care takes a lot of energy."*

> *You say to the life insurance representative, "Tuesday isn't good for me—the children are here."*
> *Or,*
> *"I work on Tuesdays."*

Which comments sound like a babysitter's? Which ones sound like the statements of a professional? Be careful of how you label yourself. People will take their cue from you. If you have a healthy respect for your career and are not shy about saying so, it will encourage others to respect your career as well.

Lisa talks about self-respect:

> I was raised to be very modest and not blow my own horn. I do consider myself successful but was hesitant to say anything that might be construed as bragging. My husband helped me change what I thought was bragging into healthy respect. In groups he would refer to "Lisa's business" in little ways that would open conversations and clearly show that my business was every bit as important to our family as his job in management. In time I learned to speak just as confidently.

Susan points out that how you operate your business also gives others important cues as to how you want to be perceived:

> Be as professional as possible. Do what you say you will do: Bill the parents, charge late fees, enforce your policies. You own a business—run it like one.

In today's society there really is no place for any kind of discounting the importance of child care. Our children and their care are too critical to discount, belittle, undermine, or overlook. So get your attitude in order and communicate clearly to the world that family child care is your profession and a vital one at that.

A Wish for Success

Working with young children is not easy, but it is immensely rewarding. As you embark on your business venture and become embroiled in preparations and planning, don't forget to enjoy yourself. Caring for children is an important job, and you are to be congratulated for your choice. One provider described her job this way: "I'm in the business of socializing the next generation."

I wish you good luck and much success.

Appendix

Publications

Business Books

Copeland, Tom. *Family Child Care Audit Manual: Strategies for Protecting Your Business in an IRS Audit.* St. Paul: Redleaf Press, 2002.

———. *Family Child Care Marketing Guide: How to Build Enrollment and Promote Your Business as a Child Care Professional.* St. Paul: Redleaf Press, 1999.

———. *Family Child Care Business Receipt Book.* St. Paul: Redleaf Press.

———. *Family Child Care Record Keeping Guide.* 7th ed. St. Paul: Redleaf Press, 2004.

———. *Family Child Care Tax Workbook and Organizer.* St. Paul: Redleaf Press. (Available for each calendar year).

Redleaf Business Series editors. *Calendar-Keeper.* St. Paul: Redleaf Press. (New edition each year; also available in software form.)

Books on Activities to Do with Children

Bittinger, Gayle. *Exploring Water and the Ocean.* Torrance, Calif.: Frank Schaffer Publications, 1993.

Colgin, Mary Lou. *One Potato, Two Potato: Chants for Children.* Mt. Rainier, Md.: Gryphon House, 1991.

Crary, Elizabeth. *Feeling Elf Cards & Games.* Seattle: Parenting Press, 2003.

Dexter, Sandi. *Joyful Play with Toddlers: Recipes for Fun with Odds and Ends.* Seattle: Parenting Press, 1996.

Haas, Carolyn Buhai. *Look at Me: Activities for Babies and Toddlers.* 2d ed. Chicago: Chicago Review Press, 1987.

Hendrickson, Karen. *Baby and I Can Play & Fun with Toddlers.* Seattle: Parenting Press, 1990.

Kohl, Mary Ann. *The Big, Messy but Easy-to-Clean Art Book.* Mt. Rainier, Md.: Gryphon House, 2000.

———. *Mudworks: Creative Clay, Dough, and Modeling Experiences.* Bellingham, Wash.: Bright Ring Publishing, 2002.

Miller, Karen. *Things to Do with Toddlers and Twos.* Rev. ed. Chelsea, Mass.: Telshare Publishing, 2000.

Silberg, Jackie. *Games to Play with Babies.* 3d ed. Mt. Rainier, Md.: Gryphon House, 2001.

———. *Games to Play with Toddlers.* Rev. ed. Mt. Rainier, Md.: Gryphon House, 2002.

Steelsmith, Shari. *Peekaboo and Other Games to Play with Your Baby.* Seattle: Parenting Press, 1995.

———. *Theme-a-Saurus.* New York: McGraw-Hill, 1989.

———. *Toddler Theme-a-Saurus.* Torrance, Calif.: Totline Publications, 1991.

Books on Children's Safety

American Academy of Pediatrics. *Pediatric First Aid for Caregivers and Teachers—Resource Manual.* Boston: Jones & Bartlett, Inc., 2005.

Boelts, Maribeth and Darwin. *Kids to the Rescue! First Aid Techniques for Kids.* Rev. ed. Seattle: Parenting Press, 2003.

Freeman, Lory. *It's MY Body.* Seattle: Parenting Press, 1983.

———. *Loving Touches.* Seattle: Parenting Press, 1986.

Hart-Rossi, Janie. *Protect Your Child from Sexual Abuse.* Seattle: Parenting Press, 1984.

Johnsen, Karen. *The Trouble with Secrets.* Seattle: Parenting Press, 1986.

Web, Michael, ed. *American College of Emergency Physicians First Aid Manual.* New York: Dorling-Kindersley, 2004.

Books on Guidance

Ames, Louise Bates, et al. New York: Dell. 1980–1989.

> *Your One-Year-Old*
>
> *Your Two-Year-Old*
>
> *Your Three-Year-Old*
>
> *Your Four-Year-Old*
>
> *Your Five-Year-Old*

Briggs, Dorothy Corkille. *Your Child's Self-Esteem.* New York: Doubleday, 1975.

Clarke, Jean Illsley. *Self-Esteem: A Family Affair.* Center City, Minn.: Hazelden, 1998.

———. *Time-In: When Time-Out Isn't Working.* Seattle: Parenting Press, 1999.

Clarke, Jean Illsley, and Connie Dawson. *Growing Up Again.* Center City, Minn.: Hazelden, 1998.

Crary, Elizabeth. *Kids Can Cooperate.* Seattle: Parenting Press, 1984. A new edition is forthcoming; check your library.

———. *Magic Tools for Raising Kids.* Seattle: Parenting Press, 1994.

———. *Pick Up Your Socks.* Seattle: Parenting Press, 1990.

———. *365 Wonderful, Wacky Ways to Get Your Children to Do What You Want.* Seattle: Parenting Press, 1994.

———. *Without Spanking or Spoiling.* Seattle: Parenting Press, 1993.

Eyre, Richard and Linda. *Teaching Your Children Values.* New York: Simon & Schuster, 1993.

Faber, Adele, and Elaine Mazlish. *How to Talk So Kids Will Listen and Listen So Kids Will Talk.* New York: Harper Collins, 2004.

Samalin, Nancy, and Catherine Whitney. *Love and Anger.* New York: Penguin Books, 1992.

Steelsmith, Shari. *Go to Your Room: Consequences that Teach.* Hemet, Calif.: Raefield-Roberts, 2000.

Whitham, Cynthia. *Win the Whining War.* Los Angeles: Perspective Publishing, 2003.

Stories and Other Books for Children

There are literally thousands of children's books available. Here are just a few tried-and-true favorites. Ask your librarian or bookseller to suggest more.

For Babies

Hoban, Tana. *Black on White.* New York: Greenwillow Books, 1993.

———. *Red, Blue, Yellow Shoe: A First Book of Colors.* New York: Greenwillow Books, 1986.

———. *What Is It? A First Book of Objects.* New York: Greenwillow Books, 1985.

Kunhardt, Dorothy. *Pat the Bunny.* Racine, Wis.: Golden Books, 1976.

Oxenbury, Helen. *All Fall Down.* New York: Simon & Schuster, 1999.

———. *Clap Hands.* New York: Simon & Schuster, 1999.

———. *Say Goodnight.* New York: Simon & Schuster, 1999.

———. *Tickle, Tickle.* New York: Simon & Schuster, 1999.

Wells, Rosemary. *Max's Birthday.* New York: Dial Books, 1998.

For Toddlers

Ahlberg, Janet and Allan. *Each Peach, Pear, Plum.* New York: Penguin Books, 1999.

———. *Peek-a-boo!* New York: Viking, 1997.

Asch, Frank. *Just Like Daddy.* New York: Simon & Schuster, 1990.

Brown, Margaret Wise. *Goodnight Moon.* New York: HarperCollins, 2005.

———. *Runaway Bunny.* New York: HarperCollins, 2005.

Brown, Ruth. *A Dark, Dark Tale.* New York: Penguin, 1992.

Carle, Eric. *The Very Hungry Caterpillar.* New York: Penguin, 1994.

———. *The Very Quiet Cricket.* New York: Penguin, 1997.

Crary, Elizabeth, and Shari Steelsmith. Feelings for Little Children Series. Seattle: Parenting Press, 1996.

When You're Happy and You Know It

When You're Mad and You Know It

When You're Shy and You Know It

When You're Silly and You Know It

de Angeli, Marguerite. *Book of Nursery and Mother Goose Rhymes.* New York: Doubleday, 1954. (Out of print now, but check your library and used booksellers for it.)

Fox, Mem. *Time for Bed.* San Diego: Harcourt, 1993.

Hennessy, B. G. *Jake Baked the Cake.* New York: Penguin, 1992.

Long, Sylvia. *Hush Little Baby.* San Francisco: Chronicle Books, 1997.

Opie, Iona. *Here Comes Mother Goose.* Cambridge, Mass.: Candlewick Press, 1999.

Oxenbury, Helen. *We're Going on a Bear Hunt.* New York: Aladdin, 2002.

Pallotta, Jerry. *The Yucky Reptile Alphabet Book.* Watertown, Mass.: Charlesbridge Publishing, 1990.

Shaw, Nancy. *Sheep in a Jeep.* Boston: Houghton Mifflin, 1986.

Wells, Rosemary. *Bunny Cakes.* New York: Puffin, 2000.

———. *Max's Dragon Shirt.* New York: Penguin, 2000.

For Preschoolers

Bemelmans, Ludwig. *Madeline.* New York: Penguin, 2000.

Bingham, Mindy. *Minou.* Santa Barbara, Calif.: Advocacy Press, 1987.

Brett, Jan. *The Trouble with Trolls.* New York: Penguin, 1999.

Burleigh, Robert. *Flight: The Journey of Charles Lindbergh.* New York: Penguin, 1997.

Carroll, Lewis. *Jabberwocky* (illustrated by Graeme Base). New York: Harry N. Abrams, 1996.

Crary, Elizabeth. The Children's Problem Solving Series. Seattle: Parenting Press, 1996.

> *I Can't Wait*
>
> *I'm Lost*
>
> *I Want to Play*
>
> *I Want It*
>
> *My Name Is Not Dummy*
>
> *Mommy, Don't Go*

Greenfield, Eloise. *Honey, I Love: And Other Love Poems.* New York: Harper Collins, 1986.

Kirby, David, and Allen Woodman. *The Cows Are Going to Paris.* Honesdale, Penn.: Boyds Mills Press, 2002.

Leaf, Munro. *The Story of Ferdinand.* New York: Penguin/Putnam, 1976.

Mayer, Mercer. *There's a Nightmare in My Closet.* New York: Penguin, 1976.

Prelutzky, Jack. *The Dragons Are Singing Tonight.* New York: William Morrow, 1998.

Rey, H. A. *Curious George.* Boston: Houghton Mifflin, 1973.

Sendak, Maurice. *Where the Wild Things Are.* New York: HarperCollins, 1988.

Wells, Rosemary. *Voyage to the Bunny Planet Series: First Tomato; Moss Pillows; The Island Light.* New York: Dial Books, 1992.

Willems, Mo. *Don't Let the Penguin Drive the Bus!* New York: Hyperion, 2003.

Wood, Don and Audrey. *The Napping House.* New York: Harcourt, Brace, 1984.

Mail-Order Catalogs for Publications and Other Products

Chinaberry Book Service

"A Cozy Place for Buying Books and Other Treasures for the Entire Family"

2780 Via Orange Way, Suite B

Spring Valley, CA 91978

(800) 776–2242

www.chinaberry.com

Discount School Supply

Everything you might ever want to supply a preschool program.

(800) 627–2829

www.discountschoolsupply.com

Gryphon House Early Childhood Resources

Books on activities, curriculum, and teacher support. Some free activities on the Web site.

PO Box 207

Beltsville, MD 20704-0207

(800) 638–0928

www.gryphonhouse.com

Lakeshore Curriculum Materials Company

These folks also operate many retail stores. Check their Web site for one in your area.

2695 East Dominguez Street

Carson, CA 90895

(800) 778–4456

www.lakeshorelearning.com

Parenting Press Catalog

Many titles on specific guidance issues. Web site offers free parenting articles each week.

PO Box 75267

Seattle, WA 98125

(800) 992–6657

www.parentingpress.com

Redleaf Press Catalog

If you go nowhere else on the Web, go here. Tons of good information for family child-care providers.

450 North Syndicate, Suite 5

St. Paul, MN 55104

(800) 423–8309

www.redleafpress.org

School-Age Notes, Resources for After School Professionals

Lots of information and materials geared specifically toward after-school care.

PO Box 476

New Albany, OH 43054

(800) 410–8780

www.schoolagenotes.com

Software

CK Kids: The Online Calendar-Keeper, Redleaf Press, 10 Yorkton Ct., St. Paul, MN 55117, (800) 423–8309. Free thirty-day demo at www.redleafpress.org.

Quicken and *Quick Books.* Intuit. (Available in stores.)

Word. Microsoft Corp. (Available in stores.)

WordPerfect. Corel Corp., www.corel.com. (Available in stores.)

Professional Organizations and Associations

National Association for Family Child Care (NAFCC)

5202 Pinemont Drive

Salt Lake City, UT 84123

(800) 359–3817

www.nafcc.org

National Association for the Education of Young Children (NAEYC)

1509 Sixteenth Street NW

Washington, DC 20036

(800) 424–2460

www.naeyc.org

National Association of Child Care Resource and Referral Agencies

(NACCRRA)

3101 Wilson Blvd., #350

Arlington, VA 22201

(703) 341–4100

www.naccrra.org

National Child Care Information Center

10530 Rosehaven St., #400

Fairfax, VA 22030

(800) 616–2242

www.nccic.org

Redleaf National Institute (RNI)

National Center for the Business of Family Child Care

10 Yorkton Ct.

St. Paul, MN 55117

(651) 641–6675

www.redleafinstitute.org

U.S. Consumer Product Safety Commission

Washington, DC 20207-0001

(800) 638–2772

www.cpsc.gov

State Child Care Home Pages/ Information on Licensing

Alabama	www.dhr.state.al.us/page.asp?pageid=255
Alaska	http://health.hss.state.ak.us/dpa/programs/ccare/
Arizona	www.azdhs.gov/als/childcare/index.htm
Arkansas	www.state.ar.us/childcare/
California	www.ccld.ca.gov/
Colorado	www.cdhs.state.co.us/childcare/licensing.htm
Connecticut	www.dph.state.ct.us/BRS/Day_Care/day_care.htm
Delaware	www.state.de.us/kids/occl/occl.shtml
District of Columbia	www.dchealth.dc.gov/
Florida	www.dcf.state.fl.us/childcare/
Georgia	www.decal.state.ga.us/
Hawaii	www.state.hi.us/dhs/
Idaho	www.healthandwelfare.idaho.gov/
Illinois	www.state.il.us/dcfs/index.shtml
Indiana	www.childcarefinder.in.gov
Iowa	www.dhs.state.ia.us/dhs2005/ dhs_homepage/index.html
Kansas	www.kdheks.gov/bcclr/index.html
Kentucky	www.chs.state.ky.us/oig/
Louisiana	www.dss.state.la.us/departments/ os/Licensing_.html
Maine	www.maine.gov/dhhs/index.shtml
Maryland	www.dhr.state.md.us/cca/index.htm
Massachusetts	www.eec.state.ma.us/
Michigan	www.michigan.gov/fia
Minnesota	www.dhs.state.mn.us/Licensing
Mississippi	www.msdh.state.ms.us
Missouri	www.dss.mo.gov/cd/childcare/
Montana	www.dphhs.mt.gov/index.shtml

Nebraska	www.hhs.state.ne.us/crl/childcare/ childcareindex.htm
Nevada	www.dcfs.state.nv.us/
New Hampshire	www.dhhs.state.nh.us/dhhs/bccl
New Jersey	www.state.nj.us/humanservices/ dyfs/licensing.html
New Mexico	www.newmexicokids.org
New York	www.ocfs.state.ny.us/main/becs/

For residents of the five boroughs of New York City: Manhattan, Queens, Brooklyn, Bronx, and Staten Island   www.nyc.gov/html/doh/html/dc/dc.shtml

North Carolina	http://ncchildcare.dhhs.state.nc.us/ providers/pv_sn2_lr.asp
North Dakota	www.ndchildcare.org
Ohio	http://jfs.ohio.gov/cdc/
Oklahoma	www.okdhs.org/childcare/ ProviderInfo/provinfo_licensing.htm
Oregon	http://findit.emp.state.or.us/childcare/
Pennsylvania	www.dpw.state.pa.us/child/ ChildCare/003670452.htm
Rhode Island	www.dcyf.ri.gov/index.htm
South Carolina	www.state.sc.us/dss/cdclrs/
South Dakota	www.state.sd.us/social/CCS/CCShome.htm
Tennessee	http://tennessee.gov/humanserv/childcare.htm
Texas	www.dfps.state.tx.us
Utah	www.health.utah.gov/licensing
Vermont	www.dcf.state.vt.us/cdd/
Virginia	www.dss.state.va.us/division/license/
Washington	www1.dshs.wa.gov/esa/dccel/
West Virginia	www.wvdhhr.org/bcf/
Wisconsin	www.dhfs.state.wi.us/rl_dcfs/index.htm
Wyoming	http://dfsweb.state.wy.us/

This information is drawn from the National Child Care Information Center and is updated regularly. If one of these addresses isn't working for you, try going to the NCCIC site (www.nccic.org/statedata/dirs/regoffic.html) to see if it has changed.

Sample Forms and Worksheets

Following are a variety of sample forms to help you organize your business. These forms were discussed in earlier chapters.

Sample Emergency Telephone Number Chart

FIRE: 911 or _____

POLICE: 911 or _____

MEDICAL EMERGENCY: 911 or _____

POISON CONTROL (800) 222–1222 or _____

My address _____

_____

My phone number _____

Sample Family Benefits-Sacrifices Chart

Family Member	Benefits	Sacrifices
(You)		
Spouse		
Child #1		
Child #2		
Child #3		
Child #4		

Sample Start-Up Expenses Worksheet

Start-Up Expenses	Cost
Fees	
Child-care license	
Business license	
Other necessary permits	
Fingerprinting fee	
Child Abuse Index fee	
Fire inspection	
TB test	
Membership dues	
Other	
Equipment	
Fire extinguishers	
Fencing	
Altering locks	
Outdoor play equipment	
Furniture (small table and chairs)	
Other	
Land Improvements	
Repairs and maintenance	
Supplies	
Toys	
Books and tapes	
Activity supplies (art, science, etc.)	
Other	
Office Expenses	
Equipment (filing cabinet)	
Supplies (copies, file folders)	
Training and Education	
Resource and Referral agency–sponsored classes	
Other	
Total Start-up Costs	

Sample Ongoing Expenses Worksheet

Ongoing Expenses	Cost per Month
Food (your cost after the food program reimburses you)	
Car Expenses	
Gas/mileage	
Additional Insurance	
Liability Insurance	
Office Expenses	
Postage	
Membership dues	
Publications subscriptions	
Bank charges	
Laundry and Cleaning Supplies	
Other Household or Yard Items	
Repairs and Maintenance	
Supplies	
Toys, books, and tapes	
Activity supplies (art, science, etc.)	
Other	
Training and Education	
Other	
Total Monthly Costs	

Sample Profitability Worksheet
Gross income per month:
Expenses per month:
Net income (profit):
Set aside for taxes:
Take-home pay:

Sample Enrollment Record

Name _____

Address _____

Phone _____

Age _____ Date of birth _____

Mother _____ Father _____

Home Address _____ Home Address _____

_____ _____

Phone _____ Phone _____

Workplace _____ Workplace _____

_____ _____

Emergency contact person if parent is unavailable

_____ _____

_____ _____

_____ _____

List of people other than parents who are authorized to pick the child up

_____ _____

_____ _____

Special instructions

_____

_____

_____

Date child entered care _____ Date child left care _____

Sample Addendum to the Parent-Provider Agreement

_____ agrees to accept the following child(ren)
(Provider Name)

Name(s)   At the reduced rate of

_____   _____

_____   _____

_____   _____

• This agreement is for one child only.

• If, at any time, fewer than ____ children attend, the rate will return to the regular, full fee for each child present.

All other standard fee policies, late fees, vacation fees, meal fees, and any other special occasion fees apply, as stated in the Parent-Provider Agreement.

This special rate agreement will be in effect until either party gives two weeks' notice.

_____   _____
Provider   Date

_____   _____
Parent   Date

Sample Meal Attendance Record

Date: Record Daily Attendance:			Monday ATT _____
Amount Ages 1–2	Amount Age 3–6		Food Items
¼ cup ½ slice ¼ cup ½ cup	½ cup ½ slice ⅓ cup ¾ cup	**Breakfast** Vegetable or fruit or juice Bread /equivalent or cereal Milk	 #
See your food-program guide for snack amounts		**A.M. Snack** Choose 1 item from 2 groups: Meat, Bread, Milk, Fruit-Veg	 #
1 oz. ¼ cup Total ½ slice ½ cup	1½ oz. ½ cup Total ½ slice ¾ cup	**Lunch** Meat and/or meat alternative 2 Fruits or 2 Vegetables or 1 of each Bread/equivalent Milk	 #
See your food-program guide for snack amounts		**P.M. Snack** Choose 1 item from 2 groups: Meat, Bread, Milk, Fruit-Veg	 #
1 oz. ¼ cup Total ½ slice ½ cup	1½ oz. ½ cup Total ½ slice ¾ cup	**Dinner** Meat and/or meat alternative 2 Fruits or 2 Vegetables or 1 of each Bread/equivalent Milk	 #
See your food-program guide for snack amounts		**Evening Snack** Choose 1 item from 2 groups: Meat, Bread, Milk, Fruit-Veg	 #

Note: Where you see the symbol #, please enter the number of children claimed at this meal.

Tuesday ATT _____	Wednesday ATT _____	Thursday ATT _____	Friday ATT_____
Food Items	Food Items	Food Items	Food Items
#	#	#	#
#	#	#	#
#	#	#	#
#	#	#	#
#	#	#	#
#	#	#	#

Sample Monthly Payment Record

Child:	Week of:	Week of:	Week of:	Week of:

Sample Invoice

INVOICE

Bill to		Date	Invoice #

Number of Days	Child's Name	Rate	Amount

Sample Parent Complaint Form

Date _____

1. Parent's name _____
2. Child's name _____
3. Description of problem

   _____

   _____

   _____

4. Action taken (or will take)

   _____

   _____

   _____

5. Other notes, observations

   _____

   _____

   _____

   _____

   _____

   _____

Sample Parent Conference Form

Date _____

Child's name _____

Parent's name _____

Description of problem

_____

_____

_____

Other relevant information or circumstances

_____

_____

_____

_____

Ideas for solving the problem (just make a list here—the ideas can be good, bad, or silly)

_____

_____

_____

_____

Plan of action

_____

_____

_____

_____

Date at which parent and provider will evaluate progress

_____

_____

Sample Dismissal Form

Date _____

Child's name _____

Parent's name _____

Termination notice given _____

Last day of care _____

___ Provider's choice

___ Parent's choice

Notes

_____

_____

_____

_____

_____

___ R&R notified (if necessary)

Field Trip Permission Form

Date _____

Activity _____

Child's Name _____ Date of birth _____

Parent's Name _____ Daytime phone # _____

Address _____ Cell phone # _____

City _____ State ___ Zip _____

Child's Physician _____ Phone number _____

Medical Information: Please advise if the child has any of the following:
❑ Special diet ❑ Allergies ❑ Chronic/recurring illness ❑ Recent surgeries/illness
❑ Medication ❑ Physical conditions that limit activity. If yes, explain below.

_____

_____

_____

_____

_____

I give permission for my child to participate in the activity listed above and authorize _____ to administer emergency first aid to my child and to act in my stead, should I not be reachable, approving necessary medical care. This authorization shall cover this activity and travel to and from this activity.

_____   _____
Signature of parent or guardian   Date

[Your Family Child-Care Name]
Mid-Year Evaluation

Name _____ Date _____

Date of birth _____ Child-care provider _____

Self-Help Skills	**Learning**	**Mastered**
Solves problems without adult help	❏	❏
Independent with own needs	❏	❏

Social/Emotional Skills		
Displays self-motivation	❏	❏
Follows child-care rules	❏	❏
Stays on task	❏	❏
Attentive during group time	❏	❏
Respects/interacts well with peers	❏	❏

Play		
Individual play	❏	❏
Parallel play	❏	❏
Cooperative play with 1–2 friends	❏	❏
Cooperative play with a group	❏	❏
Initiates play with others	❏	❏

Preschool Activities	**Does not participate**	**Participates**
Art	❏	❏
Dramatic play	❏	❏
Singing	❏	❏
Story time	❏	❏
Manipulatives (blocks, puzzles, etc.)	❏	❏
Group activities	❏	❏
Cleanup	❏	❏

Physical Development		
Small motor skill development	❏	❏
Large motor skill development	❏	❏

Appendix

Frequently Asked Questions

Do I need a license to care for children in my home?
It depends on where you live. Most states require a license. Some states have voluntary registration. It's your responsibility to check with your state and find out what the requirements are.

How do I get a license?
You can go online to find your state's licensing homepage or go to your phone book and look up your local department of community care licensing.

What will happen if I care for children without a license?
In most places, it is legal to care for children who are related to you or the children of one family (which is considered babysitting). If you care for children for pay and are not licensed in a state that requires licensing, then you will likely be fined and your business will be shut down. Every state is different; check your state's regulations.

Can I care for children for pay while I'm going through the licensing process?
In most cases, no. You must be licensed before you can operate as a family child care. Always check with your licensing department before making assumptions.

How much will I have to invest to start up a family child care?
It varies widely. Some providers I talked to invested as little as $100. Another one invested a very large amount to add a special play room to her house when she upgraded to a large license. Licensing fees are different in each state—for example, in Washington state, where I live, the licensing fee is currently $24; in California it ranges from $60 to $115. It also depends on how equipped your home already is for child care. If you are obliged to fence a yard, the cost will be higher; if all you need to do is install child-safety locks in your kitchen and bathroom, it will cost you less. It's worth attending a licensing orientation meeting in your county (usually free) to find out what your state will require before you start spending money.

How many children can I enroll?
In general, you can care for either six children (a small license) or twelve children (a large license). Your own children will count in your capacity. Individual states can vary slightly in their rules.

How much money can I make?

That depends on how many children you care for, how much you will charge for care, and what kind of expenses you have. The providers I interviewed for this book were largely very pleased with the income they were able to produce. In more populous, urban areas, you can usually charge more money; in more rural areas, less. In the United States, child care ranges from $304 a month to $1,000 a month.* One provider I spoke with here in western Washington services an area filled with Microsoft employees; she charges $800 a month for a baby and $750 for two-year-olds on up. My friend in suburban Denver reports the average rate is $600 per month for a preschooler. Call your local Resource and Referral agency to find out what the going rates are in your area.

How do I get children to enroll?

After you have your license, you can list your child care with your local Resource & Referral agency. You would be wise, however, to use a variety of marketing methods: advertising, posters, word-of-mouth referrals, and referrals from other providers who are already full.

Is there someone I can call for advice as I'm getting started?

You can join the National Association for Family Child Care and contact your local branch; this group will become a nice source of support. The state licensing departments offer orientation programs and other information. Your local R&R agency and food-program provider will also offer you much help and guidance. If you know someone who already does family child care, then her insight obviously will be helpful to you. The Redleaf National Institute (www.redleafinstitute.org) is another source of information and support.

What will the state licensing people be looking for during the home inspection?

A safe environment for children. They will scout for any unsafe conditions. There's a significant portion of this book devoted toward making your home child-safe; it's not that difficult to implement. Pay close attention to your state's requirements and follow them. If an inspector finds a problem, he or she will likely give you a certain amount of time to rectify it before your license is granted.

---

* Statistics from the report *Child Care in America* at www.naccrra.org.

Index

About the Author

Shari Steelsmith and her husband are the parents of three children, ages sixteen, twelve, and nine. Shari is a full-time mother and freelance writer focusing on parenting, educational, and family-related topics. She writes the weekly *Tip & Tool* articles for the Web site, www.parentingpress.com.

Shari is also the author of *Go to Your Room! Consequences that Teach,* the board-book series *Feelings for Little Children, Peekaboo and Other Games to Play with Your Baby,* and two biographies for children about historical women.

Shari and her family live and work near Mt. Rainier in Washington state.